THE CPA PROFESSION
Opportunities, Responsibilities, and Services

Harry T. Magill, MS. Acc., CPA
School of Accountancy
Arizona State University
Tempe, Arizona

Gary John Previts, Ph.D., CPA
The Weatherhead School of Management
Case Western Reserve University
Cleveland, Ohio

Thomas R. Robinson, Ph.D., CPA
School of Business Administration
University of Miami
Coral Gables, Florida

PRENTICE HALL, Upper Saddle River, New Jersey 07458

*This work is dedicated to our families
in appreciation of their support.*

Editor-in-Chief: *P.J. Boardman*
Editorial Assistant: *Jane Avery*
Production Editor: *Lynda Paolucci*
Managing Editor: *Katherine Evancie*
Senior Manufacturing Supervisor: *Paul Smolenski*
Production Coordinator: *Cindy Spreder*
Cover Designer: *Lorraine Castellano*

 © 1998 by Prentice Hall, Inc.
A Simon & Schuster Company
Upper Saddle River, NJ 07458

Library of Congress Cataloging-in-Publication Data
Magill, Harry T.
      The CPA Profession: opportunities, responsibilities, and services
      / Harry T. Magill, Gary John Previts, Thomas R. Robinson.
         p.   cm.
      Includes bibliographical references and index.
      ISBN 0-13-737792-4 (alk. paper)
      1. Accounting--United States. 2. Accountants--Professional
ethics--United States. 3. Accounting--Vocational guidance--United
States. I. Previts, Gary John. II. Robinson, Thomas R.
III. Title.
HF5616.U5M249 1998
657'.0973--dc21   97-40486
                                       CIP

Printed in the United States of America

10 9 8 7 6 5 4 3 2 1

ISBN 0-13-737792-4

Prentice-Hall International (UK) Limited, *London*
Prentice-Hall of Australia Pty. Limited, *Sydney*
Prentice-Hall Canada Inc., *Toronto*
Prentice-Hall Hispanoamericana, S.A., *Mexico*
Prentice-Hall of India Private Limited, *New Delhi*
Prentice-Hall of Japan, Inc., *Tokyo*
Simon & Schuster Asia Pte. Ltd., *Singapore*
Editora Prentice-Hall do Brasil, Ltda., *Rio de Janiero*

CONTENTS

FOREWORD

We usually think that books about accounting deal only with the increasingly complex web of technical principles, rules, and interpretations governing the reporting of financial transactions. Indeed, acquiring knowledge of such matters is a critical part of the education of any aspiring CPA. However, in today's business and social environment, we are increasingly aware of another critical need, for practitioners as well as for students--and that is understanding the ethical, legal, and institutional imperatives underlying the practice of a profession such as ours. Harry Magill, Gary Previts, and Thomas Robinson have addressed this need in a timely and eminently readable fashion.

For students interested in what may lie ahead, this book describes the nature of the CPA profession, the process by which that title is acquired, and information on career paths and compensation. Although the focus of much of the writing inevitably is on the CPA in public practice, the fact is that CPAs in corporate practice, government, and academe now outweigh in sheer numbers those following the more traditional occupations, and the text explores the implications of this change in demographics. For those of us already in practice as well as students, this book reminds us of the historical roots giving rise to the sine qua non of professional behavior, integrity, and objectivity. It supplies information regarding our legal duties and responsibilities, institutional support in the form of self regulation, and personal responsibility for ethical behavior. It offers a perspective on the scope of services to be performed now and in the future, and describes the market forces with which we must cope as we shape the profession and seek to prepare it for the future.

The contents of this book are thought-provoking and serious, but the style and grace of the writing style make reading it a pleasure. The reader must come away with a sense of pride in his or her chosen profession, and a renewed dedication to its principles. We should be grateful for this unique contribution to our literature.

Robert Mednick, CPA

Managing Partner
Professional and Regulatory Matters
Andersen Worldwide

INTRODUCTION

This book is about the profession of accountancy and the duties and responsibilities assumed by its practitioners, specifically by certified public accountants (CPAs). Much attention is being devoted in today's business and professional environment to "ethical behavior," however that term is defined. In outlining the legal, institutional, and personal expectations relating to a CPA's practice, the authors seek to illuminate the problems and challenges these expectations pose for serious aspirants to the status of "accounting professional." The significance of these areas is highlighted by content of the Uniform CPA Examination which includes a section on Business Law and Professional Responsibilities. Professional and Legal Responsibilities comprise 15% of this section of the examination.

The authors also examine the opportunities provided for students in the CPA profession and the evolving scope of CPA services. Although the CPA is most commonly associated with **public** practice, many CPAs are practicing their profession in academe, privately and publicly held companies, and government service. Unless the contents indicates otherwise, references in the text to *accountants, public accountants, the profession*, or similar designation should be understood to mean those holding or seeking the CPA certificate, wherever they may practice.

Accounting education too long has been exclusively addressed to the technical aspects of the discipline of accountancy--how to make debits and credits appropriate to the circumstances and as mandated by pronouncements of authoritative bodies. Such knowledge, of course, is essential to the would-be practitioner; expertise in the skills of a craft is a prerequisite to its successful practice. However, the essential of "professionalism" has so far been largely ignored, with the possible exception of a minimal coverage of ethical codes in an auditing course, an elective "policy" course, or perhaps a course in philosophy, logic, or ethics. Seldom has attention been directed to these matters as they impact specifically on CPAs.

The authors believe this void in the education of an accountant needs to be filled, particularly for aspiring CPAs, but also for all students entering this field where the production of objective, understandable information is so essential to our free private enterprise economy. Accordingly, this book has been prepared for use as a supplement to accounting courses beginning at the intermediate level and as a primary text in an undergraduate or graduate seminar in professional practice. It describes the environment into which the student will be thrust, and the institutions that will be so important to the behavioral and political aspects of professional life, quite apart from a need for technical mastery of the subject matter. It will orient students to the opportunities which are provided by the profession and the responsibilities which naturally come with those opportunities. The text will serve to acquaint students with a wide variety of topics in this area, and will expose them to the ill-structured, ambiguous considerations often faced in practice.

After the introduction, the text is divided into four parts, as follows:

Part I. **Orientation to a Dynamic Profession**. This section serves as an orientation to the profession. It is designed for new or prospective entrants to the profession. The first chapter defines what is meant by a **professional**, and explores how the CPA fits this definition. This chapter introduces several key professional concepts such as integrity and objectivity which will be explored in more detail in later chapters. The second presents information on the process of becoming a CPA and maintaining competence and licensure. This chapter provides information on the opportunities found in practice as a CPA, including career paths and salaries. Chapter 3 provides a historical perspective of the CPA profession. This chapter outlines the history of the public profession, from its roots in the United Kingdom (U.K.) to present day organizations in the United States (U.S.), and the development of concepts such as independence.

Part II. **Legal, Regulatory, and Social Environment**. This section examines the environment in which the CPA practices and the resulting impact on the profession. Chapter 4, covers the CPA's legal liabilities and responsibilities, with particular emphasis on the professional in public practice. This chapter includes recent legislative initiatives such as Tort reform and the appearance of Limited Liability Companies, as well as recent court cases involving the profession. Chapter 5 discusses the various institutions such as state boards of accountancy, the American Institute of Certified Public Accountants (AICPA), the Financial Accounting Standards Board (FASB), and the Securities and Exchange Commission (SEC), that are important to the regulation, social direction, and political control of the profession. Chapter 6 outlines the personal responsibility of professionals for their own behavior, and suggests ways in which this attribute may be developed. The chapter includes a discussion of the AICPA Code of Professional Conduct and the resolution of ethical dilemmas.

Part III. **The Marketplace for CPA Services.** This section focuses on the Services provided by CPAs, including those which are mandated and market driven. Chapter 7 discusses the economic and business environment in which the CPA operates and the impact of the market on CPA practice. Chapter 8 describes the evolving scope of CPA services in public and corporate practice which has moved far beyond the traditional audit driven model. It also identifies a number of high profile cases which have drawn a great deal of media attention to CPAs.

Part IV. **The Next Horizons.** The final chapter examines the continuing evolution of the CPA profession in the global capital marketplace where knowledge is the ultimate resource. A variety of horizons are viewed. Current and proposed initiatives which will drive the profession into the future are discussed.

Appendices. The book includes a number of important appendices, including the AICPA Code of Professional Conduct, a table of state CPA regulations, contact information for state boards of accountancy and state CPA societies, and a listing of relevant Internet World Wide Web sites.

Each chapter is followed by questions suggested for study and discussion. These should be used by the students to test their comprehension of the factual material presented, and may be used by the instructor as a basis for classroom analysis. The authors believe strongly that discussion of the concepts and ideas presented in the book is an important part of the learning process in a topic such as is herein presented, and urge instructors to use the questions (presented in the book or their own) in this way. The profession of accountancy is a vital, changing institution, and cannot be studied successfully absent the exchange of views that can only come from guided discussion.

If this book is used in a seminar on professional practice, the instructor might consider allocating time to the various topical areas covered herein somewhat as follows: Part 1, 3 weeks; Part II, 5 weeks; Part III, 5 weeks; and Part IV, 2 weeks. This provides time to focus the discussion on chapters of Parts II and III. Alternatively, the authors suggest a general discussion of the chapter in the first week followed by student presentations the following week. Students can be formed into groups to examine and report on issues addressed in the chapters. For example, following the Chapter 4 discussion students could present a discussion of the recent *Ibanez* or *American Express* cases. These times are based on a semester and can be easily related to a quarter schedule with one week per chapter. The timing varies of course depending also upon the composition of the class and the background of the students. The authors believe it is important that the students be exposed to as much other historical and contemporary literature as practicable, and therefore that the various chapters in the book be used as a "core" reading and to introduce topics. Extensive endnotes accompany each chapter. Therein can be found periodical and journal citations which will provide more extensive detail material.

We also encourage having the students become familiar with the AICPA Code of Professional Conduct, not for purposes of rote recognition, but to acquaint them with a fundamental document in the discussions of the course. Use of internet web sites, including the AICPA site [www.aicpa.org] are encouraged.

Supplementary readings might include, for example, legal reports on significant cases affecting the profession. Current publications of the American Institute of CPAs and other professional groups, particularly the recent committee reports on business reporting, assurance services, and the Independence Standards Board, can be used to supplement studies of the structure, scope of service, and future activities of the profession.

This book would be useful in several accounting courses beginning at the Intermediate level. Part I would be relevant for prospective CPAs in that it provides a great deal of information of the profession and careers in accounting. Parts II and III would provide an introduction to the regulation of accountancy and the current state of practice. In an auditing course, the instructor may wish to use the chapters in Part I to assist in the introduction of the concepts of CPA professionalism, and the influences from the United Kingdom and elsewhere driving their development. Part II would be particularly relevant when considering the legal responsibilities of auditors, and the ethical aspects of practice. Part III addresses the scope of services including the expansion of assurance services. If time permits, of course, the student may be encouraged to read or report on the entire book for general background information, when preparing reports, or undertaking research projects relating to particular topics covered here. Selective coverage of even a limited number of chapters will serve to expand the understanding of the student regarding practice and the scope of CPA services.

We wish to acknowledge the technical and editing assistance received from Jenny Byron, Kevin Carduff, Nancy Morgan, and Matt Previts. As is customary in such an eclectic endeavor such as attempting to paint a portrait of a dynamic profession, errors and inconsistencies will no doubt be found by our readers. We invite you to bring them to our attention through the website (www.prenhall.com/magill) which will support this book. The website will contain an index of subject matter and a glossary of acronyms related to professional course topics. That site will be linked to the Rutgers Accounting Web [RAW].

Harry T. Magill	**Gary John Previts**	**Thomas R. Robinson**
Scottsdale, Arizona	**Cleveland, Ohio**	**Coral Gables, Florida**

Orientation to a Dynamic Profession

CHAPTER 1

The CPA Profession

*The rise to professional status
is one of the most familiar and cherished
parts of the American achievement ideal.*
James Fallows[1]

*If we seize the opportunity presented by
the information explosion sweeping through
our society, I visualize broad new uses of the
data-gathering, analyzing, and evaluating skills
of every CPA to guide managers and others through
the bewildering array of available data to
find what they need.*
Robert Mednick[2]

Introduction

This book is about the Certified Public Accountant (CPA) profession. This profession has evolved over the past century and continues to evolve as we move into the next century. The CPA, once perceived primarily in the role of auditor, now provides a variety of services in areas such as accounting, auditing, taxation, financial planning, litigation support, and consulting. The CPA is currently envisioned as "the premier information professional in a world of electronic commerce and virtual global trade."[3] This book is intended to provide an orientation to this dynamic profession and the opportunities, responsibilities and services associated with this profession.

A **profession** is a discipline practiced by an individual; it is at the same time a vital, continuing social organization that survives the individual. The individual **represents** a profession, and a significant measure of prestige derives from that fact alone. By the same token, a profession is judged by the performance of its practitioners, and a failure on the part of one to meet expectations diminishes the whole. A delicate and tenuous relationship prevails between a profession and the society that reveres, tolerates, or condemns it as circumstances seem to dictate.

Accountancy is believed by its practitioners to be a profession, not a commercial venture. The distinctions are not always clear, and many of the characteristics claimed by professionals also may be exhibited by highly principled, ethical business people. Still, we may intuitively recognize that a transaction between a buyer and seller of a commodity involves different characteristics and interpersonal relationships than the delivery by a professional of a service to a client. This chapter explores these differences. It includes a discussion of the characteristics of public accountancy, the licensing, regulatory and educational aspects of its development and guidance, and the attributes of its practitioners.

Who Is a Professional?

The word **professional** may have a number of meanings, but two of them are mentioned here to highlight the sense in which the present discussion is carried out. A professional may be defined by contrast with an **amateur**; the distinction between one who is paid for some endeavor (often in sports) and one who engages in it purely for enjoyment, not gain. Competition and the advancement of one's own condition, however, are critical elements in either category.

On the other hand, a professional in the context of this book is one who possesses a "... degree of responsibility, wisdom and concern for the public welfare, neither necessary nor commonly found in occupations not meriting the description 'profession.' "[4] It is expected that this attribute will override the desire for personal gain if there is a conflict. Some have identified other essential characteristics in the objective of professional practice and the training necessary for its fulfillment: "The key words ... are 'a distinct practical purpose'... for which 'special training is required.' "[5] This implies the necessity for an educational grounding in a specialized field as a basis for the delivery of a service deemed essential to society.

The traditional, so-called learned, professions are medicine, law, and religious leadership (e.g., that furnished by clerics). All of them share an equal level of educational achievement, usually at the graduate level, but two of them, medicine and law, also are market-based. For the former two, at least in western cultures where there is some recognized separation between religious and secular matters, a distinguishing characteristic is governmental licensure. Today, however, many groups and occupations seek the mantle of **professionalism**. The number of organized, learned (graduate-degree based) and licensed (regulated in the public interest) occupations has increased to the point where sociologists note that "Many occupations engage in the heroic struggle for professional identification; few make the grade."[6]

There is, of course, likely to be a debate about those that have made the grade, but some often included in a short list of market-based professions in today's world are: accounting, architecture, dentistry, engineering, law, and medicine. Criteria identified for this categorization include:[7]

1. professional education (usually at the graduate level);

2. a system of self regulation based in a Code of Professional Ethics (conduct); and

3. governmental review and/or licensure.

The application of each of these criteria to the profession of accountancy is considered in the following section.

Who Is a CPA?

Who is a Certified Public Accountant (CPA) and how does a CPA fit into the criteria presented above for a professional? A Certified Public Accountant (CPA) is an individual who has been licensed by the state as having met a series of requirements which demonstrate competence to provide public accounting services. These requirements include education, examination, experience, continuing education, and demonstration of ethical behavior. According to the American Institute of Certified Public Accountants (AICPA) and the National Association of State Boards of Accountancy (NASBA):[8]

> State legislators and the courts have determined that it is in the public interest to license and regulate those individuals who have met prescribed requirements and who hold themselves out to the public as qualified to practice public accounting. Accountancy laws governing the licensing of professional accountants have been enacted in all fifty (50) states, the District of Columbia,

Guam, Puerto Rico, and the U.S. Virgin Islands. These laws set forth education, examination, experience, and other requirements for licensure and establish a state board of accountancy (or an equivalent public authority) to administer and enforce the law.

Certified Public Accountants (CPAs) are licensed in all 54 jurisdictions. The accountancy law in each of these jurisdictions restricts the use of the title "certified public accountant" to individuals who are registered as such with the state regulatory authority.

Regulatory laws in all but three states prohibit nonlicensees (i.e., persons not registered with the state regulatory authority) from expressing opinions or issuing prohibited forms of reports on financial statements. In other words, the laws restrict the performance of specific professional accounting services to licensees.

Each jurisdiction has its own definition as to what services constitute "public accounting." In general, public accounting involves the preparation of reports on financial statements of organizations. These reports might constitute a compilation, review or audit of the underlying financial information and are intended to provide comfort that financial data presented fairly reflects the underlying financial condition and performance of the organization. As we shall see in later chapters, the practice of public accounting includes a wide array of services, not limited to those specified above. Additionally, many CPAs do not practice as "public accountants," but rather work for businesses, educational institutions, and not-for-profit entities. These CPAs are still professional accountants and are bound by the same rules regarding competence and ethical behavior. As we can see, the CPA profession meets the third criteria (governmental review and/or licensure) presented above. Let's look at the remaining two criteria.

Professional Accountancy Education

Education provides to the professional aspirant the technical knowledge, skills, and abilities with which to competently practice. Education also provides an introduction to the "culture" of the profession, which may be described as an appreciation of the qualities or ideals that comprise a practitioner's mind-set and the habits followed in addressing a distinctive role in society. For instance, a medical school should assist would-be physicians in developing a sense of obligation and concern for the physical and mental well-being of the patient. The failure to focus on this imperative sometimes manifests itself in the doctor who refers to symptoms rather than to the patient (e.g., "the appendix in bed 3", rather than "Mr. Jones"). Similarly, the "culture" imparted by law schools, as distinguished from other professional programs, is one of advocacy on behalf of the rights of the client; beyond that, of course, is the idea that the purpose of the practice of law is to seek the truth. Thus, an overriding social concern, properly upon occasion, may influence or intrude on the lawyer/client relationship.

The "culture" of the public accountancy profession may be described as concern with competently providing objective (unbiased) information and advice to facilitate decision making in a market-based economy. This information is used by investors, creditors, employees, government agencies and others in making important decisions and ensuring that those responsible for such decisions can achieve an efficient allocation of society's limited resources—truly a lofty ideal. Critical to this definition is the concept of "objective" information—factual, unbiased, not slanted to present a point of view. By whatever words described, the effectiveness of the process nevertheless rests fundamentally on whether users of information believe the provider seeks to be unbiased, has integrity and, therefore, is trustworthy. No one in our present international information age can be expected to make appropriate judgments without credible facts on which to rely. To provide them is the CPA's role within a capital market system.

Four personal attributes are necessary to the participation by a CPA in fulfilling this social role: **a commitment to serve, integrity, objectivity, and competence**. These attributes, of course, are shared by all professionals and are not unique to accountancy.

Individuals with a specialized technical expertise who place the interest of the customer, client, or patient above their own self interest are acting in accordance with that most important precept of professionalism: a commitment to serve. "The essence of being a professional is a sense of moral authority which places the well being of those we are asked or expected to serve above our own well being." [9] And, "the word 'commitment' shifts the axis away from the self (either self-denial or self-fulfillment) toward connectedness with the world. The commitment may be to people, institutions, objects, beliefs, ideas . . . [or] callings." [10] On the other hand, feigning such commitment in order to achieve the endorsement of others to benefit oneself in the long run—a form of motivation sometimes called "enlightened self interest"—does not represent the sense of commitment. [11]

The characteristic of integrity means that one expresses one's views and recommendations genuinely, and not falsely or under the artificial influence of another. Without integrity, the other attributes mean little or nothing. Objectivity is a state of mind, which establishes an expectation of intellectual honesty and freedom from conflicts of interest. The attribute of competence speaks for itself. The knowledge, training, and motivation to perform with skill and economy are so fundamental an expectation that one cannot rightly be referred to as "professional" without them.

Whether the current educational process deals with these attributes in a proper way is highly questionable. Robert K. Mautz puts it this way:

> *My experience has been that accounting education tends to emphasize technical skill and understanding with little attention to social responsibility... Accounting has nothing even faintly resembling the 'officer of the court' tradition that influences the graduate of a good law school.*[12]

Although Mautz speaks specifically of social responsibility (commitment), his observations are applicable as well to the other necessary personal characteristics of any professional. Even if attention is given to this aspect of practice, however, others question whether the educational process can make a difference anyway, a person's ethical views being fixed early on by other factors such as family and religious beliefs. In an article regarding ethical training in college, David Vogel offered a plea: "If anyone has evidence that being taught ethics in school affects people's subsequent professional behavior, I wish he would share it with us."[13]

The authors' view is that continuing and stepped-up efforts to affect professional behavior can make a difference and, in any event, should not be abandoned prematurely by the educational establishment. Major public accounting firms agree. In a recent publication, the managing partners of the then so-called Big Eight firms,[14] pledging a five-year commitment of up to $4 million in support of educational programs in accountancy, outlined the joint responsibility of practitioners and academics thus:

> *We recognize that the role of the profession is to specify and communicate the skills and knowledge needed to be an accomplished practitioner. Responsibility for curriculum development and appropriate teaching methods rests primarily with the academic community.*[15]

And:

> *Practitioners must also be able to identify ethical issues and apply a value-based reasoning system to ethical questions.*[16]

Self Regulation and a Code of Professional Conduct

The American Institute of Certified Public Accountants' (AICPA) Mission Statement provides the basis for establishing professional ideals, and thus a code of conduct. It also forms the basis for the AICPA's authority for the self regulation of members who voluntarily ascribe to the precepts and standards of the organization. This mission statement reads as follows: [17]

> *The American Institute of Certified Public Accountants is the national, professional organization for all Certified Public Accountants. Its mission is to provide members with the resources, information, and leadership that enable them to provide valuable services in the highest professional manner to benefit the public as well as employers and clients.*
>
> *In fulfilling its mission, the AICPA works with state CPA organizations and gives priority to those areas where public reliance on CPA skills is most significant.*
>
> *To achieve its mission, the Institute:*
>
> *Advocacy*
>
> *Serves as the national representative of CPAs before governments, regulatory bodies, and other organizations in protecting and promoting members' interests.*
>
> *Certification and Licensing*
>
> *Seeks the highest possible level of uniform certification and licensing standards and promotes and protects the CPA designation.*
>
> *Communications*
>
> *Promotes public awareness and confidence in the integrity, objectivity, competence, and professionalism of CPAs and monitors the needs and views of CPAs.*
>
> *Recruiting and Education*
>
> *Encourages highly qualified individuals to become CPAs and supports the development of outstanding academic programs.*
>
> *Standards and Performance*
>
> *Establishes professional standards; assists members in continually improving their professional conduct, performance, and expertise; and monitors such performance to enforce current standards and requirements.*

Initially a national code of ethics was officially sanctioned by CPAs in 1917.[18] The Code of Professional Conduct was adopted in 1988 by a vote of the membership of the AICPA. The most recent revision of the code, amended January 14, 1992, is reproduced in Appendix A. Of some significance is the focus on professional conduct in the new code, rather than upon ethics. This code recognizes the unique responsibilities of CPAs in public practice, corporate practice, government, and education, all of whom play a vital role in providing a broad range of information, consulting and "knowledge" services to decision makers. The code sets out Principles and Rules which apply to all members of the AICPA. The Principles state:[19]

Responsibilities

In carrying out their responsibilities as professionals, members should exercise sensitive professional and moral judgments in all their activities.

The Public Interest

Members should accept the obligation to act in a way that will serve the public interest, honor the public trust, and demonstrate commitment to professionalism.

Integrity

To maintain and broaden public confidence, members should perform all professional responsibilities with the highest sense of integrity.

Objectivity and Independence

A member should maintain objectivity and be free of conflicts of interest in discharging professional responsibilities. A member in public practice should be independent in fact and appearance when providing auditing and other attestation services.

Due Care

A member should observe the profession's technical and ethical standards, strive continually to improve competence and the quality of services, and discharge professional responsibility to the best of the member's ability.

Scope and Nature of Services

A member in public practice should observe the Principles of the Code of Professional Conduct in determining the scope and nature of services to be provided.

Proper CPA conduct, ethical behavior if you will, rests on the disposition or habit of conducting oneself in accordance with these standards. Collectively, these rules and ideals comprise codes of ethics. The present code also relates the rules of conduct to technical standards as a measure of competence. In fact, the AICPA's ethical rules specifically require compliance with relevant technical standards, the breach of which is deemed by definition to be an ethical violation.

Additionally, it is expected that the CPA will exercise the highest level of moral and ethical standards in all aspects of professional life. The AICPA recently issued a statement of their policy on Discrimination and Sexual and Other Forms of Harassment in the Workplace. In this statement, the AICPA condemns discrimination and harassment and encourages all members to adopt policies in their organizations to prevent such behavior.

There is a danger in ethical codes in that, without recognition of the need to be "committed to serve others", the professional may come to regard rules, in themselves, as proper measures of behavior, rather than as minimums which, ideally, should be exceeded. Many believe that professionalism suffers in a practice oriented and guided by rules. Professor Zeff observed:

> *Also compatible with a possible dilution in professionalism is rule-dominated practice. Professional judgment frequently gives way to an increasing dependence on arbitrary rules.*[20]

Nevertheless, a code of ethics is evidence of the self regulation so necessary to a profession. Society grants professions a monopoly to practice their crafts because of their necessary expertise in a field of specialized knowledge—and in return accepts a pledge of ethical behavior. An interesting aspect of this notion is that self regulation provides economies as well as ethical benefits to society.

Perfection Is Unattainable

But even considered, well-formed judgments later may be found imperfect, incomplete, or just plain wrong. Striving for perfection does not guarantee its attainment. To belabor the obvious, CPAs are human. Humanity has its limitations and our society, including our professions, is the product of these limitations. Without perfect people, perfect results are impossible.

One of the episodes in the long-running TV show, "Dragnet," may illustrate the point. Sergeant Joe Friday arrested the leader of a group of self-styled intellectuals who decided to disavow allegiance to any authority and migrate to an offshore island to establish a "perfect society." Their plans were foiled when they were arrested while attempting to steal camping supplies from a store. The leader castigated Friday for the failures of "his generation," and stated that the group would have been able to do better if they had not been stopped by the cops.

"We were going to build a perfect society," exclaimed the leader, *"and now you have ruined it!"*

"No, you wouldn't have, son," said Friday.

"And why not?" challenged the youth.

"Because," Friday responded, *"you wouldn't have perfect people."*

Summary

This chapter has explored factors that distinguish a profession from other forms of employment. Principal among these are the dedication of the professional to the well-being of clients and a concern for the public well-being, both in preference to self-interest. Professionalism is manifested and nourished by education in a specialized field of knowledge, guided by a code of ethical behavior, and overseen by governmental licensure. CPAs provide a service critical to society—the competent delivery of objective, unbiased information for the use of decision makers.

Important personal characteristics of an accounting professional include commitment to service, integrity, objectivity, and competence in the technical practice of the discipline. Because moral/ethical considerations in the practice of public accountancy are important, the development of proper habits of conscience and behavior, likewise, is important. The process of ethical decision making, in a complex and dynamic profession, may not be perfect—but we should have high expectations of ourselves and our peers.

The expectations of the public and its elected representatives, a CPA's mission to serve the public, the recognition of the role of ideals in establishing our ethical code, and knowledge of the appropriate technical standards, together provide the CPA with guidance to choose among alternatives in determining proper conduct. In each set of circumstances, this can most effectively be accomplished by education and experience within the culture of the profession, as aided by instruction and guidance by mature professionals in actual practice.

The CPA profession provides a variety of opportunities to those entering the profession. CPAs are essential to the proper functioning of capital markets and decision making in all types of organizations. While a required level of education and competence is necessary to enter the profession, there is no large capital requirement. A CPA can start a practice with a pencil and a calculator (although computers and other accouterments would be useful). Many CPA firms offer flex time, enabling CPAs who are parents to be professionally productive and maintain an active family life. Some CPAs work out of their homes, while others prefer positions which permit travel. Many firms offer formal diversity programs designed to provide opportunities for all entrants to the profession.

The CPA profession is dynamic. Opportunities and services are continuously being expanded. The AICPA recently formed a Special Committee on Assurance Services which examined current and potential services provided by CPAs. The Committee identified a number of new assurance services, such as Health Care Performance Measurement, Electronic Commerce, and ElderCare Plus. The latter involves monitoring the care of the elderly to ensure that care givers are providing the necessary level and quality of services. The following chapters will explore the opportunities, responsibilities, and services of the CPA profession in greater depth.

Discussion Questions

1. Define a professional, and indicate in what respects accountancy may or may not fit that definition.

2. What is the principal objective and concern of the CPA in today's society?

3. Name and describe the principal personal attributes necessary to the practitioner in fulfilling this objective.

4. What part can formal education play in training the aspiring professional to meet ethical demands?

5. Is a written code of ethics a necessary part of the culture of a profession, or does it tend to reduce the practitioner's behavior to one of just "reading the rules"?

6. What is the AICPA? What is its mission? How does the AICPA achieve its mission?

7. Define the following: integrity, objectivity, independence, and due care.

8. What types of services do CPAs perform for clients?

9. Discuss an example of a CPA's ethical/unethical behavior taken from a recent news report. Do you agree or disagree with the reported behavior? Why?

Endnotes

[1] Fallows, James, "The Case Against Credentialism," *The Atlantic Monthly* (December, 1985): 50.

[2] Mednick, Robert, as quoted in "AICPA Chair Envisions Expanded Role for CPAs as Premier Information Professionals," News & Views, *The CPA Journal* (December, 1996): 13.

[3] "AICPA Chair Envisions Expanded Role for CPAs as Premier Information Professionals," News & Views, *The CPA Journal* (December, 1996): 13.

[4] Mautz, Robert K., "Public Accounting: Which Kind of Professionalism?," *Accounting Horizons* (September, 1988).

[5] Barzun, Jacques, "The Professions Under Siege," *Harper's Magazine* (October, 1978): 62.

[6] Wilensky, Harold L., "The Professionalization of Everyone," *The American Journal of Sociology* (September, 1964): 137.

[7] Wilensky, Harold L., op. cit., 143.

[8] American Institute of Certified Public Accountants and National Association of State Boards of Accountancy, *Digest of State Accountancy Laws and State Board Regulations* (1996): vi.

[9] Previts, Gary John, "A Culture for Accountancy Education: Lessons from Medicine, Law and Management," (Proceedings of the Tenth Annual Meeting, Federation of Schools of Accountancy, 1986): 135.

[10] Yankelovich, Daniel, "Toward an Ethic of Commitment," *Industry Week* (June 15, 1981).

[11] Lowe, Herman J., "Ethics in Our 100-year History," *Journal of Accountancy* (May, 1987).

[12] Mautz, Robert K., Expanded Role for CPAs: 124.

[13] Vogel, David, "Could an Ethics Course Have Kept Ivan From Going Bad?," *The Wall Street Journal* (27 April 1987).

[14] This term has been used in the past to identify certain CPA firms which, by their very size and client base, could conveniently be so grouped. In alphabetical order these were: Arthur Andersen & Co., Arthur Young, Coopers & Lybrand, Deloitte Haskins & Sells, Ernst & Whinney, Peat Marwick Main & Co., Price Waterhouse, and Touche Ross. Mergers of several of the firms in the late 1980s, however, have reduced the numbers of individual entities, as well as changed and combined the names.

[15] Arthur Andersen & Co. et al., *Perspectives on Education: Capabilities for Success in the Accounting Profession* (New York: April, 1989), foreword.

[16] Ibid, 6.

[17] *Mission Statement of the AICPA* (New York: AICPA, November 1995).

[18] Lambert, Joyce, and Lambert, S. J., "The Evolution of Ethical Codes in Accounting," (Working Paper No. 23, The Academy of Accounting Historians Working Paper Series, Volume 2,1979. School of Accounting, James Madison University).

[19] *Code of Professional Conduct*, as amended January 14, 1992, AICPA, New York, 1992.
[20] Zeff, Stephen A., "Does the CPA Belong to a Profession?," *Accounting Horizons* (June, 1987): 67.

CHAPTER 2

A Career as a CPA

CPAs are professionals, distinguished from other accountants by stringent licensing requirements. . . .CPAs provide audit, review and compilation services for businesses. They also provide tax assistance, management advisory services and estate and personal financial planning. CPAs act as advisors to individuals, businesses, financial institutions, nonprofit organizations and government agencies on a wide range of finance-related matters. CPAs also work as financial managers in industry, education, and various levels of government.[1]

American Institute of CPAs

Introduction

This chapter focuses on the process of entering the CPA profession, the profession's structure, and membership. It is meaningful to assert at this point that, just as physicians and attorneys retain their identity as doctors or lawyers irrespective of whether they work in public practice or in corporate practice (i.e., whether they work directly for a patient or client or whether they are a part of corporate management), a doctor is still a doctor and a lawyer is still a lawyer. So also the CPA possesses a "monolithic identity." A CPA is a CPA whether in public practice or corporate practice. The AICPA membership and ethical requirements place the corporate practicing CPA under the same expectations as the public practice CPA.[2]

Popular perceptions of accountants as "number crunchers, tax figure heads, or management's bean counters" do not necessarily transfer to CPAs. The CPA is distinguished from an accountant, per se, by virtue of the education, testing, experience, and continuing education requirements which must be met. It is likely that the differential nature of CPA practice in public accounting and in corporate accounting will continue as the scope of professional services in each of these areas responds to even greater demand for increasingly specialized knowledge.[3] One manifestation of this change is the formation by the AICPA of programs which accredit specialized practitioners in the fields of personal financial planning and business valuation. As early as 1974 the leaders of the AICPA noted that:

> . . .the profession has been under mounting pressure to supplement its basic accounting skills with varied disciplines in providing a wide range of advisory services. These pressures are a natural outgrowth of an economy which involves intricate business transactions, highly developed capital-raising techniques, elaborate entity structures, and extensive intervention by government in the private sector.[4]

Requirements for Certification

As noted in Chapter 1, a CPA is governed by the regulations of the state in which he or she practices. There is a great deal of uniformity in these regulations. Essentially the states have requirements concerning an individual's initial education for entry into the profession, passing the comprehensive Uniform CPA Examination, obtaining sufficient relevant work experience, maintaining continuing education and supplemental requirements such as demonstrating ethical behavior. In this section we will explore the requirements in each of these areas.

Education

The substance of accountancy education has been the subject of intense study and debate.[5] The report of a major select Committee of the American Accounting Association (AAA), and the findings of several follow-up committees have established the need to transform the educational process into one that provides a graduate professional entry-level degree for CPAs. Several recommendations of the AAA select group, known as the Bedford Committee, are included in Table 2.1.

The evolution of accountancy into a graduate entry-level profession, along with the recent changes to place more emphasis on the CPA examination as an objective-question-based licensure test, is consistent with the manner in which other learned professions have come to establish themselves.[6] When one thinks of a physician the first expectation is that the person has an MD, an academic degree.

The fact that a state medical practice license examination is involved is considered more as a matter that is legally necessary but of itself not sufficient to establish the person as being a "doctor." The status of doctor-physician is equated not with the passage of the state licensing test but with the attainment of a graduate professional degree in medicine. The same is also true in other learned professions, for example, law. The future of accountancy will be affected by similar developments in graduate professional education and licensure.

Table 2.1   The American Accounting Association Committee on the
Future Structure, Content and Scope of Accounting Education
The Bedford Committee, 1986

Selected Recommendations*

- Accounting should be viewed as a broad economic information development and distribution process, based on the design, implementation, and operation of multiple types of information systems.

- University accounting education should emphasize the skills and capacities needed for lifelong learning.

- Specialized accounting education should be offered only at the graduate level. Thus a complete curriculum covering all three levels of education (General Education, General Professional Accounting Education, and Specialized Professional Accounting Education) will normally take a minimum of five years.

- Faculties should design educational experiences for students that require them to be active, independent learners and problem solvers rather than passive recipients of information.

- Greater interaction should be encouraged among faculty members in accounting and the liberal arts.

- In preparing students for the future, accounting faculty should rely on accounting practice and research, and on multidisciplinary research in establishing curriculum content rather than merely preparing students to qualify for current practice.

*The Bedford Report contains twenty-eight recommendations relating to the scope, content, and structure of programs, faculty and administration, accreditation, professional examinations, and institutional information regarding accounting education.[7]

Since the CPA certificate is awarded by the state, candidates for the certificate must meet the educational requirements of their state of practice (or states if they desire to be certified in more than one jurisdiction). In a later chapter, we will discuss recent movements toward a national licensing environment. Appendix B provides a summary of educational and other requirements for each state. Appendices C and D provide contact information for State Boards of Accountancy and State CPA Societies. You should contact these organizations for additional information regarding requirements for your jurisdiction.

The direction of the states in educational requirements has been evolving towards graduate education. Most states have moved towards a requirement that students have 150 semester hours of education in order to obtain a CPA certificate. This is equivalent to four years of full time study at the undergraduate level and one year of post-graduate study. A graduate degree is not necessarily required. Most states, however, require at least a baccalaureate degree. A handful of states do not require a degree and may permit the candidate to obtain a CPA license provided that a higher level of work experience than normal is obtained. For example, in North Dakota a candidate is currently required to have either a baccalaureate degree with thirty credits in accounting and law or four years of qualifying experience. Many states specify a number of required accounting courses. For example, Florida which requires the equivalent of 150 semester hours of education specifies that a minimum number of hours must be in upper division accounting courses. Of these, there are also minimum hours required in some areas (e.g. auditing) and maximum hours in others (e.g. internship programs). Table 2.2 presents those states that have adopted the 150-hour education requirement.

Examination

Once an individual has completed the educational requirement and any other general qualifications as required by their state (e.g., age or citizenship), they generally become eligible to take the Uniform CPA Examination. The examination is a comprehensive examination offered twice per year. It consists of four sections:

> Business Law & Professional Responsibilities
> Auditing
> Accounting & Reporting - Taxation, Managerial and Governmental and Not-
>   for-Profit Organizations
> Financial Accounting & Reporting - Business Enterprises

Table 2.2   States/Jurisdictions with a 150-Hour Education Requirement

State/Juridiction	Effective Date
Alabama	January 1, 1995
Alaska	September 1, 1997
Arkansas	January 1, 1998
Connecticut	January 1, 2000
District of Columbia	January 2, 2000
Florida	August 1, 1983
Georgia	January 1, 1998
Guam	June 1, 2000
Hawaii	December 31, 1978
Idaho	July 1, 2000
Illinois	January 1, 2001
Indiana	January 1, 2000
Iowa	January 1, 2001
Kansas	June 30, 1997
Kentucky	January 1, 2000
Louisiana	December 31, 1996
Maryland	July 1, 1999
Mississippi	February 1, 1995
Missouri	June 30, 1999
Montana	July 1, 1997
Nebraska	January 1, 1998
Nevada	January 1, 2001
New Jersey	July 2, 2000
North Dakota	January 1, 2000
Ohio	January 1, 2000
Puerto Rico	January 1, 2000
Rhode Island	July 1, 1999
South Carolina	July 1, 1997
South Dakota	January 1, 1998
Tennessee	April 14, 1993
Texas	August 31, 1997
Utah	July 1, 1994
Washington	July 1, 2000
West Virginia	July 1, 2000
Wisconsin	January 1, 2001
Wyoming	January 1, 2000

Source: AICPA Website 1997 at www.aicpa.org

A candidate must pass all four parts of the examination with a score of 75 or higher. According to the National Association of State Boards of Accountancy (NASBA), 59,970 candidates sat for the May 1995 exam and 66,463 candidates sat for the November 1995 exam.[8] For those candidates sitting for the first time, 17.0% passed all of the parts taken. Another 31.2% passed some parts, while the remainder passed no parts. If a candidate does not pass all four parts on the first attempt, they may be able to retain credit for those sections passed. In most states, if a candidate passes at least two parts and receives at least a 50% in the parts not passed, they need only take the remaining parts on subsequent exams. If the state's criteria is not met the candidate must retake all parts. For repeat candidates, 28.3% passed all remaining subjects taken on the November 1995 examination.

As you can see, completion of the educational requirement is no guarantee of success on the Uniform CPA Examination. The examination is comprehensive and rigorous. It requires a great deal of preparation. Many candidates take review courses specifically designed to prepare them for the examination.

Experience

After completing the educational and examination requirements, a candidate becomes eligible to obtain a CPA certificate and a license or permit to practice from the state. Many states require (see Appendix B) that the candidate also obtain one or more years of experience prior to receiving the certificate and license. The number of years of required experience can vary based upon the level of education and the nature of the experience. For example, Ohio currently requires two years of experience in public accounting. For candidates with a masters degree in accounting or business administration, the requirement is reduced to one year. If a candidate's experience is not in public accounting the Ohio Board of Accountancy determines how many equivalent years are needed based upon the nature of the candidate's specific experience.

Other Requirements

Each jurisdiction has its own individual requirements other than education, examination, and experience. Most jurisdictions require that the candidate complete a special examination or course in Professional Ethics. Once these requirements are met the candidate receives a certificate. In order to practice a candidate must also have a current license or permit to practice. The license is typically valid for one to three years before it must be renewed. In order to maintain the license the jurisdictions generally mandate that a holder obtains sufficient continuing professional education. In general, approximately 40 hours per year are required. Some jurisdictions require a certain number of hours of continuing education in specific areas such as accounting and auditing, while other permit the hours to be in the individual's primary area of practice. Education never ends for a CPA. In order to maintain one's competence to practice accounting, an individual must keep up to date on laws, standards, and regulations in their area of practice.

Career Opportunities

While obtaining a CPA certificate entitles an individual to practice "public accounting," there are a wide variety of opportunities for CPAs and CPA candidates within public accounting, corporate practice, government, not-for-profit entities, and education. The American Institute of CPAs with more than 331,000 members [1997] is a proxy for a census of CPAs.[9] However, the actual number of CPAs is higher since not all CPAs are members of the AICPA. Of this number about 42% are in corporate practice, 40% in public practice, 4.0% in government, 2.0% in education, and the remainder (12%) are in a variety of practices or retired. Less than half of the AICPA members actually practice public accounting. Many CPAs start their career with public accounting firms, and later move to corporate practice, government, or education. Recently, as specialization has become more important, public accounting firms have been hiring individuals who began their careers outside of public accounting in order to take advantage of their specific industry knowledge and experience. Just as there are a variety of career paths from which to choose, the CPA profession provides opportunities a varied career where an individual may work in some or all of these areas.

By the start of the twenty-first century increasing numbers of CPAs will attain a graduate degree or its equivalent as preparation for a career as a CPA. An increasing number of these degrees will be from professional graduate programs, which emphasize not only the technical competency that the market place expects, but also the cultural and social values that differentiate CPAs in today's information society. As will be seen in the next chapter, the origin of the CPA profession was related to the development of corporations and capital markets. Now information technology is affecting the role of CPAs as auditors, tax preparers, and consultants, requiring individual CPAs to exhibit broader skills and to provide new information products for an information age. CPAs are becoming independent information professionals, whose commitment to serve reflects the ideals of integrity, objectivity, and competence and provides a basis for confidence in the system of information dependent international capital markets.

In short, CPAs are a strategic resource necessary to insure future economic prosperity in a global economy that is interdependent for its decision making and resource allocation information.[10] For as technological dependencies in the information area expand, the need for reliable, impartial, cost-effective, timely information will expand. The individuals who can best serve this market will be economically successful and socially recognized.

CPAs in Public Practice

CPAs in public practice provide services to corporations, not-for-profit organizations, individuals, and governmental units, to name just a few. They fulfill a need for independent, objective review or advice and provide a source of specialized knowledge and experience. CPA firms are typically organized as partnerships, sole proprietorships, professional corporations, or limited liability companies, depending upon the state of organization. The firms can range in size from a sole practitioner in a single office to thousands of partners in hundreds of offices worldwide. Table 2.3 presents a summary of the 20 largest firms providing public accounting and tax services as determined by *Accounting Today*.[11]

Table 2.3 provides a breakdown of fees into accounting and auditing (A&A), tax and consulting (MAS) services. These are the three broad categories of services generally associated with public accounting firms. Accounting and auditing services primarily involve the **compilation**, **review,** or **audit** of an enterprise's financial statements. In a compilation the CPA prepares a set of financial statements, while in a review or an audit the CPA attest to the fairness of presentation of financial statements prepared by management of the enterprise. In the tax area, a CPA may assist clients in preparing required tax filings, perform research on tax rules and advise clients on how best to structure transactions from a tax perspective. The consulting area involves a variety of areas where the CPA can provide services based upon specialized knowledge and experience. Examples include computer systems consulting, personnel management, and activity-based costing. Some CPA firms offer a wide array of services while others specialize in particular areas of practice. *Accounting Today* reports a wide array of "niche" services provided by the top 100 firms. These services include business valuations, computer systems, litigation support, employee benefits, and personal financial planning, among others.[12]

The AICPA now offers specialty designations in two of these areas; personal financial planning and business valuation. These specialty designations indicate that an individual has obtained both knowledge and experience in the specialty area beyond that required for the CPA examination and certification. The **Personal Financial Specialist** program accredits CPAs who specialize in personal financial planning. Personal financial planning involves assisting individuals in defining their financial goals and designing a plan to meet those goals. For example, assisting clients in planning for a child's college education or for the client's retirement. This area requires knowledge of income taxes, estate taxes, insurance, retirement plans, and investments. The Personal Financial Planning Division of the AICPA provides educational and other resources for CPAs who practice in this area. The **Accredited in Business Valuation** designation was recently approved by the AICPA. Business valuation involves determining an estimate of the value of a business enterprise. This is frequently done, for example, in the process of buying or selling a business, for estate tax purposes, or for Employee Stock Ownership Plans. Both of these specialties require that the individual pass a rigorous examination and demonstrate substantial experience in the area. The AICPA offers courses to assist individuals in acquiring competence in these areas through its Certificate in Educational Achievement Program.

Table 2.3   Top 20 Tax and Accounting Firms

Firm	Revenue (millions)	Offices	Partners	Professionals	Total Employees	Fee Split % (A&A/ Tax/ MAS)
Andersen Worldwide	4,511.0	94	1,575	27,000	38,924	31/15/54
Ernst & Young	3,571.0	89	1,933	14,969	23,072	39/22/39
Deloitte & Touche	2,925.0	106	1,556	14,031	19,764	40/19/41
KPMG Peat Marwick	2,530.0	121	1,515	10,020	16,065	40/19/41
Coopers & Lybrand	2,115.0	115	1,241	11,785	16,826	43/21/36
Price Waterhouse	2,020.0	94	963	10,512	15,203	37/23/40
H&R Block Tax Services	750.4	8,400	8,232	0	84,000	0/100/0
Grant Thornton	266.0	48	285	1,798	2,697	45/30/25
McGladrey & Pullen	251.1	66	388	1,793	2,816	47/32/21
BDO Seidman	211.0	40	223	1,103	1,633	53/27/20
Crowe, Chizek and Co.	86.0	9	87	682	949	34/18/48
Baird Kurtz & Dobson	81.9	20	117	525	801	49/28/23
Plante & Moran	74.7	14	107	513	818	58/23/19
Clifton Gunderson & Co.	68.6	43	110	547	938	54/33/13
Jackson Hewitt	66.8	1,342	695	1,624	2,319	0/100/0
Moss Adams	63.0	16	87	392	557	45/39/16
Richard A. Eisner & Co.	55.0	4	61	269	407	41/23/36
Geo. S. Olive & Co.	52.2	11	68	339	533	44/40/16
American Express Tax and Business Services	49.2	41	60	382	543	49/35/16
Altschuler, Melvoin & Glasser	49.1	6	45	300	470	50/22/28
Data represents U.S. operations only Adapted from The 1997 Accounting Today Top 100 Tax and Accounting Firms, Accounting Today, March 17-April 6, 1997 Reprinted with permission of Faulkner & Gray						

Specific CPA firm career paths can differ from firm to firm and from department to department within firms. In general the professional positions can be categorized as follows: staff accountant, senior accountant, manager or supervisor, and partner or shareholder. A **staff accountant** represents the entry-level position. A staff accountant is typically assigned to a team and is under the direct supervision of a senior accountant. Once a staff accountant has obtained sufficient experience, promotion to senior accountant occurs. This can take several years depending upon the education and experience of the staff member. The **senior accountant** assists in planning the work to be performed as well as supervising the work of staff accountants. The next level, manager, entails more managerial responsibly. The **manager** is not only responsible for supervising senior and staff accountants, but is expected to develop new clients and service existing clients. The most senior level of responsibility rests with the **partner**. Depending upon the organizational form, this individual may be a shareholder. Some firms also have designations such as principle which represents an equivalent level of responsibility without ownership.

While there are many rewards to being a professional accountant, a concern to many individuals is the financial reward. Salaries in public accounting vary among firms, regions, and specialization. Table 2.4 provides aggregate salary information from Robert Half International.[13] For entry-level positions, candidates earn from $24,750 to $34,250 depending upon the size of the firm. As you can see the financial rewards increase to the Manager/Director level with salaries ranging from $54,750 to $87,000. Partner compensation varies based upon profitability of the firm, individual offices and units within an office.

As the CPA profession adjusts to market demands and expands its scope and range of professional service offerings, the number and types of arrangements involved in providing public practice services will change too. The public practice units of CPAs may come to resemble in operating form what in health care is known as an HMO (Health Maintenance Organization). HMO is a term used to describe an association of health care facilities within a defined geographic service area which includes not only hospitals and clinics, but specialty health care establishments of other types such as rehabilitative facilities, etc. In the future, a public practice CPA firm may become a form of Information Maintenance Organization (IMO), managing and providing a broad range of specialized information services to assist clients whose need for such specialized skills warrants engaging a professional. And just as physicians direct health care and patient well-being for the HMO, CPAs will direct the information and client services in these expanded practice units. IMOs will provide a variety of specialized services to meet the internal and external decision making, information, tax, and reporting needs of corporations, investors, government, and the public. Some firms may be limited to the skills of one or two CPAs with specialties that are "leveraged" by a larger group of support staff and paraprofessionals. At the other extreme, a CPA firm may employ thousands of CPAs, paraprofessionals, staff, and hundreds of partners at locations throughout the world.

Table 2.4   1997 Accounting Salaries
Public Accounting: Audit, Tax, Management Services

Large Firms (Over $150 million in sales)

Experience/Title	1997 Salary Range
To 1 year	$29,000-34,250
1-3 years	$31,000-37,250
Senior	$35,500-46,000
Manager	$45,000-65,000
Mgr/Director	$57,250-87,000

Medium Firms ($15 to $150 million in sales)

Experience/Title	1997 Salary Range
To 1 year	$26,500-30,000
1-3 years	$28,500-36,000
Senior	$34,750-45,000
Manager	$45,500-64,000
Mgr/Director	$57,000-83,000

Small Firms (up to $15 million in sales)

Experience/Title	1997 Salary Range
To 1 year	$24,750-28,000
1-3 years	$28,000-34,000
Senior	$32,000-44,000
Manager	$44,000-58,750
Mgr/Director	$54,750-76,000

1997 Robert Half and Accountemps Salary Guide
Reprinted with permission

The economics of such a form of practice recognizes the value of comparative advantage. A large or small information organization develops a particular expertise. Clients seek the expert service as needed. Service is provided at a price more reasonable than would be incurred overall if the client hired the staff internally on a full time basis. The information organization exists because it supplies a specialized service which clients choose to rent rather than buy. Just as a homeowner engages an electrician on occasion rather than hire one full time, both parties find the economics of a structured specialty marketplace conducive to their needs.

CPAs in Corporate Practice

CPAs practicing outside of public accounting are alternatively said to be in corporate practice, industry, or private accounting. We will use the term corporate practice here to include all areas of business outside of public accounting, both incorporated and unincorporated enterprises. As noted above, this is the largest area of CPA practice. The rising profile of corporate practice membership in the AICPA societies continues, and with it comes a new facet to the identity of the CPA in the United States. Just as the public practitioner's identity is no longer limited to audit or tax activities, but reflects the implications of specialization and consulting work, so too the CPA in corporate practice expands the realm of opportunity for career choices among CPAs. This development further challenges the leadership, the educational processes, and the forces in the capital markets and corporate sectors to make best use of the talent found in the CPA profession. Career path differences within the AICPA membership can be expected to be less noticed in the future, given the experience of other professions such as medicine and law, which suggests that the public does not make sharp distinctions between practitioners in public or corporate practice. For example, Meinert writes:

> The October 1986 survey Louis Harris and Associates, on the views of the ethics and morality of 12 key leadership and professional groups, states that "CPAs emerged at the top or close to it among all the key groups." The survey further reported that CPAs employed by companies also ranked very high, only "slightly lower" than independent auditors, while "accountants who are not CPAs but are employed as accountants for corporations received a much lower rating." The report clearly states that "all of the groups surveyed make a critical distinction between an accountant who is a CPA and one who is not" and that "CPAs who work directly in corporations are highly regarded."[14]

CPAs are found in a wide variety of positions in corporate practice, including Chief Financial Officer and Chief Executive Officer. These companies range from small closely-held organizations to large publicly traded corporations. Within these organizations CPAs work in a variety of areas such as general accounting, financial reporting, cost accounting, internal auditing, electronic data processing (EDP) auditing, tax accounting, controllership, and treasury operations. The career path is somewhat similar to that in public accounting, although each firm has it own unique terminology for each position. Table 2.5 provides Robert Half International salary data for the corporate practice environment.

The importance of this area of practice to the CPA profession is highlighted by the recent formation of the **Center for Excellence in Financial Management (CEFM)** by the AICPA. The CEFM is an alliance of activities of the AICPA geared towards members in corporate practice. The CEFM provides resources in the areas of professional education, education, research, benchmarking, information, and publications. It serves as an area where members in corporate practice can obtain new skills, improve existing skills, and compare their company's performance and operations to the best practices of other companies.

CPAs in Government Practice and Not-for-Profit Organizations

CPAs whose career occupation are in government or not-for-profit organizations (e.g., United Way) constitute a small but increasingly significant element of the profession. Government accountability legislation suggests that CPAs will become increasingly involved in government practice. Examples of important legislation include the Inspector General Act of 1978, which created the office of Inspector General in each major cabinet level agency; the Federal Manager's Financial Integrity Act of 1982, which requires involvement of the highest department official in the review of financial accountability and performance of an agency; and the Single Audit Act of 1984, which mandates an annual audit for state and local government programs receiving directly or indirectly $100,000 or more a year in federal financial assistance. Recently enacted accounting standards promulgated by the Financial Accounting Standards Board (FASB) require not-for-profit organizations to follow many of the same standards as publicly held corporations.

Government practice also includes the important function of policy setting and oversight. CPAs have held important positions such as Comptroller General of the United States, Chairman of the Federal Deposit Insurance Corporation (FDIC), Chief Accountant of the Securities and Exchange Commission, and the Inspectors General of cabinet level agencies. CPAs also serve in a variety of state and local positions; most noted among these is as the principal fiscal and/or budgetary officer for municipal, county, and state government. CPAs also serve as governmental auditors in the GAO, in Defense Department agencies, in the Internal Revenue Service (IRS), and the Defense Contract Audit Agency (DCAA). The Federal Bureau of Investigation also seeks special agents with the training and qualifications of CPAs to assist in investigations related to criminal enforcement. With the Government Accounting Standards Board (GASB) as a private sector agency to set governmental accounting standards, and the Cost Accounting Standards Board (CASB), there is greater likelihood that there will be an increase in the demand by public sector agencies for qualified CPAs to meet the expectation among taxpayers and holders of government financial instruments for more accountability.

Table 2.5   1997 Accounting Salaries

Corporate Practice

General, Audit and Cost Accountants
Large Companies (Over $150 million in sales)

1997 Salary Range	
To 1 year	$28,500-31,500
1 to 3 years	$30,000-37,250
Senior	$37,500-46,250
Manager	$45,000-65,500

Corporate Controller

Company Volume in millions

250+	$85,000-138,000
50-250	$69,000-91,250
10-50	$54,000-71,250
To 10	$47,000-61,750

Tax Manager

Company Volume in millions

250+	$69,000-110,000
50-250	$58,000-75,000

CFO, Treasurers

Company Volume in millions

500+	$238,000-307,000
250-500	$145,000-244,500
100-250	$95,000-148,000
50-100	$75,000-96,500
To 50	$62,000-88,000

1997 Robert Half and Accountemps Salary Guide
Reprinted with permission

CPAs in Education

During the early years of this century when the CPA profession was forming its collegiate educational base, it was common for practitioners to teach and to staff the accountancy faculty of universities. Most major universities relied on practitioner-teachers through the World War II era. Thereafter collegiate education became, as with other CPA activities, an increasingly specialized vocation. Gradually, full time accountancy faculty who planned careers in education began to seek the doctorate.[15] This provided an improved resource for teaching and participation in professional service and committees. Further, advanced degrees were deemed desirable as a base to undertake the specialized basic and applied research that is customarily the province of the academic branch of a discipline.

However, during the post World War II era until the late 1960s, doctorates were not a credential required by the principal body accrediting business programs. The master's degree and CPA certificate were accepted as the terminal equivalent of a formal doctoral degree. In 1967 the American Assembly of Collegiate Schools of Business, the principal accreditation agency for business programs, established that the doctorate was to be the terminal of degree requirement for accountancy faculty. During the past two decades increasing numbers of doctoral programs in accountancy have been initiated. With the advent of the initial accreditation of accountancy programs in 1982, it seems evident that individuals seeking to establish themselves in full academic careers at four year colleges and universities and professional schools of accountancy, once having become CPAs, are well-advised to explore the program of study leading to a doctorate.

The role of education in preparing the future CPA professional will be a specialized and demanding task, requiring not only competence in areas related to practice, but also the ability to conduct basic and/or applied research into matters of import to the discipline. The most significant task facing university programs relates to providing a high degree of knowledge transfer in the classroom while exploring the applications of new technology and developing research programs conducive to providing a base of intellectual capital as found in other learned professions.

Equality of Opportunity

Because qualified accountants and CPAs are continually in demand, the opportunity for individuals of both genders and all backgrounds to succeed continues to make accounting careers in general attractive to all candidates. Entry-level positions in accounting, as in medicine and law, require increasing periods of education. The AICPA and state societies have established educational development programs, with the AICPA in particular, devoting substantial sums, now totaling in the millions, to support minority education at the collegiate level. Minorities and women members serve in the highest offices of the profession: as presidents of state societies, on the board of directors of the Institute, and as deans and professors of accounting and business schools.

Much remains to be accomplished, however, if the profession is to continue to warrant its reputation as the "opportunity" profession--a reputation it has earned by virtue of the fact that it has been the economic vehicle for thousands of its members to effectively utilize their skills and education while contributing to the needs of society and improving their own standards of living and position. The future of women in the profession, for instance, is dictated by their relatively recent and increasing presence. In a survey reported in a recent issue of the *Journal of Accountancy*, more than 70% of the women who responded as being active in the profession were under age 40.[16]   Additionally AICPA data shows that while women make up less than 25% of total membership, they comprise about 50% of new entrants. This suggests that as women continue to rise toward managerial and partnership levels their representation in those ranks will likely increase.

Summary

The CPA profession is a dynamic one offering entrants a wide variety of opportunities. Most evident is the recent shift in the majority basis of AICPA membership to non-public practicing CPAs from a century-long profile of public practice CPAs being the majority. The growing influence of corporate practice CPAs and the rise of women and minorities in the profession also has begun what will likely become a more prominent profile of these groups among all CPA occupations.

The changing demands upon CPAs will in turn bring about changes in the form of practice and the economies of scale in providing new information products and services. As the scope of services develops it is likely in turn to place greater demands upon the educational process that society and the profession at large charge with the responsibility of preparing qualified professionals. The future will likely see greater comparability between preparation for accountancy and the preparation found in other graduate entry level professions such as medicine and law.

Discussion Questions

1. What are the general requirement which must be met to earn a CPA certificate?

2. What is the 150-hour requirement?   How many jurisdictions have such a requirement?

3. What types of information is tested on the CPA examination? How would you characterize the rigor of this examination?

4. What must someone who has passed the CPA examination do in order to obtain a license or permit to practice?

5. What are the most common CPA occupations and what type of specializations exist in each?

6. What is the most common structure for CPA firms?

7. What firms comprise the Big Six?

8. How do you think the careers of a public CPA versus a corporate CPA differ?

9. In what economic manner can the CPA profession be described as a national strategic resource?

10. How might recent technological advances, such as the growth of the Internet, impact CPA practice?

Endnotes

[1] *A Guide to Understanding and Using CPA Services* (New York: AICPA,1984).
[2] Chenok, P. B. "The New Ethics Code," *Journal of Accountancy* (June 1989): 4.
[3] Mednick, R., and Previts, G. J., "The Scope of CPA Services: A View of the Future," *Journal of Accountancy* (May 1987): 220-238.
[4] *Final Report of the Committee on Scope and Structure* (New York: AICPA, 1974).
[5] Arthur Andersen & Co. et al., *Perspectives on Education: Capabilities for Success in the Accounting Profession* (New York: April 1989).
[6] Young, David, "The Economic Theory of Regulation: Evidence from the Uniform CPA Examination," *The Accounting Review* (April 1988: 283-291).
[7] "Future Accounting Education: Preparing for the Expanding Profession," Report of the Committee on the Future Structure, Content, and Scope of Accounting Education, *Issues in Accounting Education* (Spring 1986: 168-195).
[8] "CPA Candidate Performance on the Uniform CPA Examination," National Association of State Boards of Accountancy (1996 Edition): 5.
[9] "Frequently Asked Questions about the AICPA," AICPA Website, www.aicpa.org (June 6, 1997).
[10] Mednick R., "Our Profession in the Year 2000: A Blueprint of the Future," *Journal of Accountancy* (August 1988): 54-58.
[11] "The 1997 Accounting Today Top 100 Tax and Accounting Firms," *Accounting Today* (March 17-April 6, 1997): 28.

[12]Ibid., 26.

[13]1997 Salary Guide, Robert Half International (1997).

[14] Meinart, John, "The CPA in Business--A Look at Our Past, Present and Future," *Journal of Accountancy* (May 1987): 262, 274-5.

[15] Schultz, J. J., editor, "Reorienting Accounting Education: Studies on the Professoriate, the Curriculum and the Environment of Accounting" (Education Monograph No.10, American Accounting Association, 1989).

[16] Ried, G. E., Acken, B. T., and Jancura, E. G., "An Historical Perspective on Women in Accounting," *Journal of Accountancy* (May 1987: 346).

CHAPTER 3

A Historical Perspective

*Throughout the last hundred years, the profession
has made a significant contribution not only to the
operations of the capital markets but also to society as a whole.
The certified public accountant has long held a position
of great responsibility and trust, serving the public by
assuring that the highest standards are maintained
in the preparation of financial statements.*[1]

William S. Kanaga, J. Michael Cook, and Philip B. Chenok, 1987

Introduction

To provide a background affording a better understanding of our complex
contemporary regulatory structure as we consider it throughout the text, this chapter
gives a perspective on the origin, development, and ethical concepts of the CPA
profession. The personal responsibility of today's accounting professionals to their
peers, clients, and the public are part of an interlocking system of oversight by
governmental and self-regulatory institutions which have developed over the past
century. Writing in 1904, Arthur Lowes Dickinson, one of the profession's early
leaders, noted:

> *The Profession of Public Accountant, in the modern sense of the term, is a
> product of the Nineteenth Century, and owes its existence and progress to the
> great expansion of industry and commerce for which that period is remarkable,*

and in particular to the rapid growth of....the joint stock company or industrial corporation.[2]

Similarly, the services offered by CPAs are a product of the development of the industrial enterprise and the capital markets in the United States over this period.

Roots of a Profession

The CPA profession was born in the United States (U.S.); however, its genealogical roots lie in the United Kingdom (U.K.). Individuals holding themselves out as public accountants were noted to exist in the early 1700s in both the United States and United Kingdom; however, the organization of individuals into professional groups began at a later date.[3] One impetus for an organized profession has been attributed to a U.S. visit in 1886 by Edwin Guthrie, a U.K. Chartered Accountant.[4] In the United Kingdom, several societies of chartered accountants were in place by 1880. Formed under royal grants or "charters" that constituted public recognition of their professional status, these societies operated privately, without the form of legislative licensure to become known in the United States. Societies developed the Chartered Accountant (CA) or an Incorporated Accountant designation. The societies assumed responsibility for evaluating and regulating entry-level competence for professionals. They were also responsible for the ongoing regulation of the U.K. accountancy professional in these early times, and continue to maintain the emphasis on professional self-regulation today. The British government has never attempted to regulate conditions for entry to the accountancy profession. These conditions have remained firmly under the control of the accountancy bodies.[5]

The role of legislation in the United Kingdom, however, did assist the profession's development, since legislative initiatives created the market for the CA's services by mandating, in 1948, that audits of public companies be conducted by chartered, incorporated, or certified accountants.[6]

In the United States, private sector activity during the post Civil War period included groups such as the Institute of Accounts (New York). The Institute was originally formed as the Institute of Accountants and Bookkeepers in 1882 to provide accounting education and literature, and it remained in operation until 1908.[7] Private sector activity in the organized public accountancy profession continued with the formation in 1887 of the American Association of Public Accountants (AAPA).

Rivalry existed between these two organizations. The Institute of Accounts promoted a CPA law in New York which required, among other things, that a CPA be a U.S. citizen. This was disadvantageous to the many British members of the AAPA. Agreement was reached between the two groups, however, and the final legislation required that New York CPAs either be U.S. citizens or have duly declared to become a citizen. Unlike the United Kingdom, the U.S. professional designation of CPA was a result of legislative authority rather than professional associations.

Development of Certification Requirements

Initially, the Institute of Accounts and American Association of Public Accountants provided certificates of proficiency to their members based on examination or experience.[8] Possession of such a certificate might indicate proficiency in the subject; however, it did not enable the accountant to perform duties beyond those of "noncertified" accountants.

The first state law establishing the Certified Public Accountant was approved in New York on April 17, 1896. Legislation provided that individuals practicing public accounting since January 1, 1890 could waive the CPA examination. In 1896 and 1897, 108 individuals obtained the certificate under this provision. Another four individuals received certificates upon completing the first CPA examination offered in December 1896.[9]

After passage of the New York legislation, similar provisions were enacted in the remaining states. By 1967, with passage in Guam, 54 states and jurisdictions (e.g. Puerto Rico, Virgin Islands) had CPA legislation.[10]

Siegel and Rigsby studied the development of education and experience requirements for CPAs from 1915 through 1985. In 1915, 26 out of 38 states required at least a high school education for the CPA certificate. At that time, college was not required. By 1985, 47 out of 54 states and jurisdictions required some college education, while the remaining seven required a high school education. Experience requirements also existed during this period. Seigel and Rigsby report that, on average, 1.79 years of experience were required for the CPA in 1915. This number has varied over time and in 1985 was 2.39 years on average. Prior to 1969 continuing education was not required. By 1985, 45 out of 54 states or jurisdictions had legislated continuing education requirements.[11]

The passage of legislation restricted the use of the CPA designation to those who met the regulations of a particular state or jurisdiction. Additionally, it restricted certain activities, particular attest services, to those who held a CPA certificate. Legislation, therefore, provided the CPA with a "franchise" to perform services which could not be legally performed by others.

The formation of state CPA societies followed CPA legislation. The New York State Society of Certified Public Accountants (NYSSCPA) was formed in 1897 by five individuals, four of whom were members of the Institute of Accounts.[12] One of the principal functions of the NYSSCPA was to promote the CPA designation as the "sole badge of professional competence."[13] Similar societies appeared in other states and jurisdictions as CPA legislation was adopted throughout the country. Over time, these societies have promoted the CPA and provided a source of support and education for practicing CPAs. For example, today state societies provide extensive continuing education courses to update the accounting, audit, tax, and consulting skills of CPAs.

Development of Professional Services

Professional accountants were providing a wide variety of services prior to receipt of the legislative franchise discussed above. As early as 1718, individual accountants advertised their services in such activities as keeping merchant and shopkeeper books.[14] In the early 1800s, other professional services included serving as a trustee for estates, creditors, bankruptcies, and partnership dissolutions. The conclusion of the Civil War in 1865 led to an increase in the scope of CPA services, as noted by Mednick and Previts:

> The industrialization following the Civil War set the stage for expanded accounting services in an economy that had previously been characterized substantially by trading and agricultural activities. As railroads, steel mills and fabricating and manufacturing companies emerged, complex cost and other calculations became necessary. At the same time, providers of business capital, including the banking community and investors, began to concern themselves with measuring the results of operations of major corporate enterprises in which large debt and equity positions were held. The need for consistent, impartial and accurate financial reports, which could be used to evaluate these investments, created steady demand for the services of public accountants who were both competent and free of undue influence - having no axe to grind.[15]

An analysis of services provided in 1880 by a large U.K. accounting firm shows that 72% of fees resulted from insolvency work, while 10% came from auditing services.[16] Over the ensuing 25 years the proportion of auditing work grew substantially to about 58% of services. An advertisement by Selden R. Hopkins in 1880 reflects the type of services provided at that time by a sole practitioner:

> Will render assistance to lawyers in the examination of accounts in litigation; aid agents and administrators of estates in adjusting accounts. Will give counsel upon improved methods of keeping the accounts of corporated companies. Assists book-keepers and business men in straightening out intricate and improperly kept books. Adjusts complicated partnership accounts. Examines books for stockholders and creditors.[17]

The appearance and growth of audit services in this period was independent of any legal requirements for an audit. The need for audit service increased with the passage of the Securities Acts of 1933 and 1934. The Securities Acts followed the 1929 stock market crash and the failure of a pyramid scheme created by Ivan Kreuger using stock in a publicly-traded company.

The Securities Acts required that financial statements of public companies be certified by independent public or certified public accountants. The passage of these acts gave public accountants an expanded franchise and emphasized the importance of the concept of independence. The formation of the Securities and Exchange Commission (SEC) to oversee these acts provided additional regulatory structure and responsibilities to the profession. CPAs are subject to the authority of the SEC as it relates to the SEC's oversight of capital markets. Additionally, while the SEC has the legal authority to establish accounting principles for publicly-traded entities, the SEC has relegated that responsibility to the accounting profession.

Other legislation enacted throughout the years created new opportunities for CPAs to use their skills in providing additional services to clients. The passage of tax legislation is one of the main sources of opportunity. Beginning in 1861 a variety of tax acts were passed. Initially taxes were of a temporary nature or applied only to businesses. With the passage of the Sixteenth Amendment to the Constitution, taxation of individuals became common. The importance of taxes to both individuals and corporations has grown over time:

> *In 1939 fewer than 6% of all individuals in the United States were legally required to pay any federal income tax. By the end of World War II, over 74% of a larger population had to pay it. During these six years, the top marginal rate on taxable corporate income doubled, from 19% to 38%, while the top marginal rate on individual incomes increased from 79% to 94%. This rapid expansion in the taxpaying population, along with the exceedingly high marginal rates for individuals, soon made the federal income tax dominate the U.S. tax system... .*

> *The rapidly increasing complexity of the income tax rules between 1945 and 1986 therefore made the services of the CPA and other tax practitioners indispensable for many taxpayers. Sophisticated investors as well as general business managers soon discovered that it is unwise to engage in even routine business or personal transactions without first consulting tax advisers to determine the most advantageous ways of arranging them.*[18]

Through the years, CPAs have offered a variety of services other than audit and tax. Today these services are generally classified in the broad category term, "consulting." While, for a time, audit and tax services dominated CPA services, consulting began to play a major role during the 1950s and 1960s.[19] This growth caused concern since a CPA often provided attest (audit) and consulting services to the same client, which created the appearance of a potential conflict. On the other hand, the provision of such services improved the CPA's ability to understand the client's business and, therefore, provide a more effective audit. Recently the Independence Standards Board was formed which will operate within the AICPA and be under the oversight of the SEC to deal with these types of issues. Today, consulting services provide a major percentage of revenue for CPA firms.

The types of services within each area (attest, tax, and consulting) has evolved and continues to evolve. While the focus of an audit was initially on financial statements, complex business transactions and the need by capital markets for information (other than items such as profit and loss or total assets) have led to greater disclosures of both financial and nonfinancial information.

Increased disclosure has provided additional responsibilities as well as opportunities for CPAs. Recent professional committees, such as the AICPA Special Committee on Financial Reporting and the AICPA Special Committee on Assurance Services, are evidence of the further expansion of CPA services. The Special Committee on Financial Reporting (also known as the Jenkins Committee) demonstrates a need to move from financial reporting to business reporting, incorporating the need for more nonfinancial types of information. The Special Committee on Assurance Services (also known as the Elliott Committee) proposes broadening the scope of attest services to areas outside the traditional financial statement audit.

Development of CPA Ideals

Ethical rules are a way to express a CPA's duties and responsibilities to others. The codification of ethical rules for CPAs was, of course, not an accomplished fact when the first CPA examination was given in December, 1896. Yet the first question in the auditing section of the first CPA examination was: "Give a brief outline of the duties of an auditor and his responsibilities." The recommended answer provided what we might call the traditional altruistic view:

> *In the absence of any legal or specific definement, the duties as well as the responsibilities of an auditor must be regarded from purely ideal and moral stand points ....*[20]

The emphasis on personal responsibility, based on purely ideal and moral standpoints, should be appreciated for what it represented; namely, a belief in the role of the individual and the values that educated and professional persons were expected to uphold. These values were similar to those which were the basis of audit practice in the more established British profession.

The accountancy profession in Britain, formed in the Victorian era, demonstrated an orientation to the reputed high virtue of that period. Professor Dicksee was a British author of a series of texts on auditing which were also widely read in the United States. He listed the desirable qualities of an auditor as follows: "Tact, caution, firmness, fairness, good temper, courage, integrity, discretion, industry, judgment, patience, clear-headedness and reliability." And, he said, ". . . in accountancy . . . it is only he who aims at absolute perfection who can expect to attain even to a decent mediocrity."[21]

Considering the times, this form of rhetoric was not uncommon, and reflected the serious commitment made by early practitioners and professors to the ideals of client and public service in the practice of auditing that comprised the principal economic and statutory activity of CPAs.

Robert Montgomery edited Dicksee's American version through a collaboration arranged by Arthur Lowes Dickinson. Montgomery, a native-born American, and Dickinson, an Englishman, worked together in early professional organizations which later established ethics committees and self-regulatory processes.

Professional Organization Activity

Lowe, writing in 1987 about the first CPA ethics committee, observed the following:

> *In 1906 the AAPA established a formal committee on ethics to develop standards to which members should adhere. It wasn't until 10 years later, though, that this committee was officially empowered to consider and evaluate a member's conduct in terms of compliance with those standards.*[22]

The yearbook for the 1907 AAPA meeting contains a substantial section dealing with professional ethics. The major paper was presented by Joseph E. Sterrett, who relied heavily on the experiences of what he termed "older professions" and gave examples from ethical canons, codes and drafts of bar associations, medical associations, and the Institute of Electrical Engineers. He further developed his commentary into three categories of conduct:

1. Duties and Responsibilities of a Public Accountant in Relation to His Clients

2. The Accountant's Relation to the Public

3. The Accountant's Relation to his Professional Brethren

The five rules of professional ethics adopted by the AAPA in 1907 were prohibitions, each beginning "No member shall . . . ." The rules prohibited:

1.   AAPA identity from being used by anyone but members;

2.   sharing professional fees with the laity;

3.   incompatible occupations;

4.   certifying of accountancy work without proper involvement or supervision of an AAPA member;

5.   members from using CPA or similar (CA) designations in business advertisements or recognizing any organization using same unless said designation is authorized by law in the State.[23]

The fact that the recently-established CPA profession emphasized prohibitory, self-regulatory rules to control use of the CPA identity (while pioneering its own code of ethics) is understandable given that, as of 1912, Montgomery noted:

American courts have never laid down specific rules regulating the duties or obligations of public accountants....[24]

Montgomery argued that it was desirable to weed out poor work because "a few irresponsible men can offset the good work of ten times their number."[25] This argument for self-regulation is indicative of similar arguments based on enlightened self-interest; namely, it is proper given our duty to others, but also helps us as persons conducting a business to weed out incompetency, and as professionals to do more for clients than the law requires.

Early Cooperation Between National and State Societies

At the 1908 AAPA annual meeting, a report from the ethics committee noted that state societies had been requested to provide their views on issues to be addressed, including "whether or not it is desirable that recognized bodies of accountants throughout the United States should adopt a code of ethical rules suitable to the profession of public accounting."[26]

Responding to the request, the Illinois Society indicated its support for a code, and also noted concerns about the use of the corporate form by audit firms--particularly when such corporate forms used boards of directors as principals to solicit business.

Such early efforts at coordination between the national and state professional groups in matters of ethics established the pattern for the present system of joint enforcement.

By 1916, when the American Institute of Accountants (AIA) had succeeded the AAPA, the ethics committee was officially empowered to consider and evaluate a member's conduct, and the AIA governing council served as a form of trial board to provide a panel of peers in the event of a hearing.[27]

Setting a Structure in Place

Following this foundation period, the next three decades of professional ethics development reflect the combined effects of works written by Thornton, Richardson, and Carey, and the leadership of Sterrett and Cooper at the AIA. The former provided literature for the area; the latter the leadership. These same individuals also contributed to both the leadership and literature of self-regulation.

As the number of individuals in the CPA profession grew from a few hundred to thousands, the courts, congress, and state and federal governmental agencies became more involved in specifying the role of CPAs. This was first done with regard to attest functions, and eventually in broader areas of service, particularly tax and consulting. During both World War I and World War II, government work by CPAs involved with overseeing cost allocation, contract termination, and arbitration increased the professional exposure of these professionals to oversight of the technical standards and rules of conduct.

CPA public practice units first became regional, and then national and international in the extent of practice. As matters involving duties, responsibilities and establishing patterns for self-discipline evolved, quality control over practice units became increasingly complex. Practice management of such concerns became a prominent component of the economics of practice.

The public's image of the duties of a CPA during this growth period were still rudimentary. A CPA was often viewed as a well-paid person who performed accounting or tax work--and perhaps also as one who was dedicated and trustworthy, but not necessarily a broad-thinking or creative individual. This stereotype, to the extent it exists today, limits the ability of the CPA profession to impress upon the public its true value and ability (because of the perception of the limitations on creativity), and yet also reinforces that the public has an expectation of trustworthiness of those who are CPAs--a high mark indeed.[28]

Major Works on CPA Ethics

During the period 1930 through 1952 the CPA profession, as evidenced by Institute membership, grew at increasing annual rates from thousands to tens of thousands. This rapid change was accompanied by an expansion of the scope of services and the need for materials to identify practitioner standards. By 1960, several important publications on accounting ethics had been printed, and a chapter in the *CPA Handbook*, issued in 1952, also addressed the subject.[29]

The first known work written in this country and dedicated solely to CPA Ethics was written in 1931 by A. P. Richardson, an Englishman who served as the Institute's first permanent secretary or principal staff person. Entitled *The Ethics of a Profession* and published by the Institute, it contained 159 pages on topics including solicitation, advertising, fees, contingent fees, secrecy and bidding. In the Foreword, Richardson observes:

> *In accountancy, which is the newest of the professions, it has been rather easier to adopt high ethical standards than in any other profession, but that does not imply that those standards have been invariably observed. There are men and women calling themselves accountants who deride the argument that accountancy is a profession at all. They say, with a fair amount of apparent justification, that the accountant is merely engaged in a business service very much like that of an appraisal company or a statistical venture; that be should perform his work honestly, of course, and to the best of his ability, but that to consider himself on a plane with the lawyer, the physician or surgeon is preposterous. The greater number of accountants, however, are firmly convinced that the practice of accountancy is professional purely, and they are supported by statute and judgement.[30]*

By 1946, when Carey wrote his first work on ethics, the post-war expansion of the profession's members and activities had begun. During this era, the foundation of professional ethics was the personal commitment and character of the individual practitioner. The existing code of ethics consisted of enforceable rules and focused on ethical concerns in the fashion devised by Sterret, i.e., (a) those related to the public; (b) those related to the client; and (c) those related to peers.

A cornerstone ethical concept of the post-war period was **independence**, which evidenced the view of the public that auditing is the franchise of public practice.[31] Many individuals have wrestled with the issues surrounding independence and the concept has a literature of its own. It is safe to argue that historical evidence suggests that the meaning of independence has evolved over time and, in turn, it is likely that the term's meaning will continue to evolve as the scope of CPA services changes in concert with the needs of society.

Carey, who served many years as the AICPA's chief staff officer, wrote the following about the meaning of independence:

> *Independence is an abstract concept, and it is difficult to define either generally or in its peculiar application to the certified public accountant. Essentially it is a state of mind. It is partly synonymous with honesty, integrity, courage, character. It means in simplest terms, that the certified public accountant will tell the truth as he sees it. And will permit no influence, financial or sentimental, to turn him from that course.*[32]

Writing nearly a generation later (in 1985) on the subject of independence Carey observed:

> *This is a word with at least 15 different meanings. The word independent was first used in conjunction with "accountant" (i. e. independent accountant) in the same sense as in the phrase independent contractor--as the dictionary says, "not subject to another's authority." But the noun form, "independence" also denotes the admirable quality of being "not influenced or controlled by others in matters of opinion or conduct." It was not difficult, by subtle thought transmission, for independent accountants, perhaps with some self-satisfaction, to invest themselves with the admirable quality of independence.*

Carey continues:

> *However, in the absolute and literal sense, tt is obviously impossible for any human being except a hermit to avoid being influenced by others to some extent--not necessarily for evil.*

> *. . . . In the **Tentative Statement of Auditing Standards**, issued in 1947, independence was equated with complete intellectual honesty, honest disinterestedness, unbiased judgment, objective consideration of facts, judicial impartiality.*

> *. . . .We can say with confidence that audit independence means integrity and objectivity.*

> *. . . . But alas, the discussion cannot end here.*[33]

Nor should it be expected to--for to seek a **solution** to an individual case is one matter, but to expect a **conclusion** to the cornerstone issue of the CPA profession would suggest stagnation of practice and of the profession.

The definition of independence may be expected to acquire added meanings as the relationships of practitioners encounter new circumstances.[34]

Carey further notes that the federal Securities Acts' administrative regulations introduced the distinction between independence in fact (a state of mind) and the **appearance of independence**. In these 1985 writings, he warned of the ethical, legal, and semantic morass which results from this distinction between reality and perception.

Early court cases decided during the period, along with statutory requirements, expanded the responsibility of the CPA as auditor. As a result, the CPA-auditor became more exposed to lawsuits from a broader element within the investment community. While the Securities Acts increased the demand for audit services, a corresponding increase occurred in expectations for, and oversight of, the professional conduct and competence of CPAs providing professional services to public companies. One of the principal architects of CPA ethics, John L. Carey, depicted the ethical view of the post World War II era as follows:

A professional attitude must be learned. It is not a natural gift. It is natural to be selfish and greedy—to place personal gain ahead of service.... The rules of ethics are guides to right action that will develop the professional attitude, and thus win public confidence.[35]

In the 1970s, the base of Institute ethical rules which members were required to observe was expanded so that violations of generally accepted accounting principles and auditing standards by members were considered a breach of ethics.

Beginning with a salvo of accusations in a congressional staff study entitled *The Accounting Establishment*, issued in October, 1976, and continuing through the 1980s, which included a study by The Treadway Commission, a private sector group, the activities of CPAs in public accounting and corporate practice were subjected to extensive review in hearings and studies. The aftermath of these reviews resulted in a series of unprecedented self-regulatory initiatives by professional organizations, principally the AICPA and state societies. These initiatives included the establishment of a Division for Firms within the AICPA. This Division enrolled practice units as members based upon the client base, that is, a Private Companies Practice Section and an SEC Practice Section.

Public practice specialization reflecting the changing scope of services also led the Institute to formally establish practice divisions for taxation, advisory services, and financial planning.

In October, 1983, the AICPA established a Special Committee on Standards of Professional Conduct for CPAs, chaired by former AICPA chairman George Anderson, to evaluate the need for a major revision of the code of ethics because of the changing scope of public practice and the increasing number of CPAs in corporate practice. Membership data indicated that, as the profession entered the 1980s, the AICPA, if representative of the organized profession was identified with careers not only in public practice, but also in corporate practice as financial managers, corporate reporting executives and chief financial officers.

In late 1987 and early 1988, the AICPA membership overwhelmingly approved six changes to the code of ethics and membership requirements, based upon recommendations by the Anderson Committee. The recommendations:

1. updated the rules of conduct and emphasized positive goal oriented statements including integrity, objectivity, and competence as the basis for all CPA services;

2. established a practice monitoring program for members in public practice;

3. restructured the joint Trial Board and reduced duplication of enforcement procedures;

4. established minimum continuing professional education (CPE) requirements for members in public practice;

5. established minimum CPE requirements for members not in public practice;

6. adopted a membership admission requirement that, after the year 2000, applicants must have at least 150 collegiate-level semester hours, including a bachelor's degree or its equivalent.

A large number of state CPA societies subsequently voted to conform their state society requirements to those adopted by the AICPA membership referendum.

A seventh Anderson recommendation, that a member practicing with a firm with one or more SEC clients may retain that membership only if the firm is a member of the SEC Practice Section, was approved as part of a separate ballot in late 1989. The Anderson initiatives focused on the need for recognition of several fundamental ideals such as integrity, objectivity, and competence as a basis for professional qualification and proper conduct.[36] The CPA acculturation to these ideals has grown from the same social contract for medicine (e.g., patient well being above self-interest of the physician) and law (e.g., advocacy at law above self-interest of the lawyer). There can be no capital market activity on a large scale if the information profession is not functioning with integrity and objectivity.

The Treadway Commissioners released their final report of October, 1987. Their recommendations for improvements in the financial reporting system and to reduce fraudulent financial reports encompassed four areas: (a) the public company itself; (b) independent public accountants; (c) the SEC and others involved in establishing the regulatory environment; and (d) the education community.[37]

Summary

Past events in the development of the CPA profession remain an important part of the prologue to the contemporary practice environment and serve to explain how things came to be as they are. These past events in the financial and investment community suggest that the need for the positive influence of the CPA professional and the need for the integrity and objectivity set forth in the code of conduct have not diminished.

Certainly we can expect that the current code of ethics will change to provide assurances as to the integrity and objectivity of professional accountants as long as it is required by society. The tradition of our profession does provide a strong basis from which to meet the difficult challenges of the marketplace. That tradition, as recently reported in a 1989 survey by The Pinnacle Group, a consortium of public relations firms, continues to be highly valued by the public. The Pinnacle survey, using honesty and integrity as determinants, ranked accountants, doctors, and dentists at the top of the list of a variety of professions.[38]

Discussion Questions

1. How do Chartered Accountants in the United Kingdom differ from Certified Public Accountants in the United States?

2. What role did legislation play in the formation of the organized independent public accounting profession in the United States? In the United Kingdom? What is the significance of the differences, if any?

3. List two early professional accounting organizations. Do these organizations exist today?

4. How do the professional services of today's CPA differ from those of early CPAs?

5. What has been the impact of federal legislation on the accounting profession?

6. How do the ethics rules adopted by the AAPA in 1907 differ from today's Code of Professional Conduct?

7. Why is independence a cornerstone ethical concept of the CPA profession?

8. The Anderson Committee of the AICPA was formed in 1983. What are the major recommendations which resulted from its final report?

9. What was the general subject of the Treadway Commission's hearings and studies? What are the constituencies affected by the recommendations of the Treadway Commission?

Endnotes

[1] Kanaga, William S., Cook, J. Michael, and Chenok, Philip B., "Letter to the Membership," *Journal of Accountancy* (May 1987): 9.

[2] Dickinson, Arthur L., *The Duties and Responsibilities of the Public Accountant* (Price Waterhouse & Co., 1904).

[3] Previts, Gary J., and Merino, Barbara D., *A History of Accounting in America* (John Wiley & Sons, Inc., 1979): 9.

[4] Edwards, James D., and Miranti, Jr., Paul J., "The AICPA: A Professional Institution in a Dynamic Society," *Journal of Accountancy* (May 1987): 22.

[5] Parker, R. H., "The Development of the Accountancy Profession in Britain to the Early Twentieth Century Monograph Five;" (The Academy of Accounting Historians, 1986, School of Accountancy James Madison University): 46.

[6] Ibid., 39.

[7] Previts and Merino, *A History of Accounting in America*: 93.

[8] Flesher, Dale L., Miranti, Paul J., and Previts, Gary J., "The First Century of the CPA," *Journal of Accountancy* (October 1996): 51.

[9] Previts and Merino, *A History of Accounting in America*: 98.

[10] Seigel, Philip H., and Rigsby, John R., "An Analysis of the Development of Education and Experience Requirements for CPAs," *Research in Accounting Regulation* (Volume 3, 1989): 45-68.

[11] Ibid.

[12] Kyj, Larissa S., and Romeo, George C., "Paving the Way for the NYSSCPA: The Institute of Accounts," *The CPA Journal* (June 1997): 11.

[13] Miranti, Paul J., *Accountancy Comes of Age: The Development of an American Profession, 1886-1940* (The University of North Carolina Press, 1990): 58.

[14] Previts and Merino, *A History of Accounting in America*: 9.

[15] Mednick, Robert and Previts, Gary J., "The Scope of CPA Services: A View of the Future From the Perspective of a Century of Progress," *Journal of Accountancy* (May 1987): 222.

[16]Ibid.

[17]Advertisement by Selden R. Hopkins in *The Book-keeper*, November 23, 1880, as cited in Mednick and Previts, "The Scope of CPA Services," (May 1987): 222.

[18]Sommerfeld, Ray M., and Easton, John E., "The CPA's Tax Practice Today - and How It Got That Way," *Journal of Accountancy* (May 1987): 166.

[19]Mednick, Robert and Previts, Gary J., "The Scope of CPA Services" (May 1987): 226-7.

[20] Broaker, F., and Chapman, R., *The American Accountants Manual, Vol. 1.* (New York: 1897): 45.

[21]Lawrence R. Dicksee, *Auditing: A Practical Manual for Auditors*, ed. R. H. Montgomery, Authorized American Edition (New York, 1905): 260.

[22]Lowe, H. J., "Ethics in Our 100-Year History," *Journal of Accountancy* (May, 1987).

[23]Lambert, Joyce, and Lambert, S. J., "The Evolution of Ethical Codes in Accounting," Working Paper 23, (The Academy of Accounting Historians Working Paper Series. Volume 2., 1979, School of Accounting, James Madison University).

[24]Montgomery, R. H., *Auditing Theory and Practice* (New York: Ronald Press, 1912), 571 ff.

[25]Ibid.

[26]Report of the Committee on Ethical Rules, *Twenty-First Anniversary Year Book*, (The American Association of Public Accountants, 1908), 98-100.

[27]Lowe, H. J., op. cit.

[28]Report from Louis Harris and Associates, American Institute of Certified Public Accountants, Council, Minutes of Meeting (October 18,1986): 6-8.

[29]*The Ethical Problems of Modern Accountancy* (Lectures delivered in 1932), (New York: Ronald Press, 1933) (Reprint 1980 New York: Arno Press Co.), Carey, J. L., *Professional Ethics of Public Accounting* (New York: American Institute of [Certified Public] Accountants, 1946), Carey, J. L., *Professional Ethics of Certified Public Accountants*, (New York: American Institute of Certified Public Accountants, 1956).

[30]Richardson, A. P., *The Ethics of a Profession* (New York: The Century Co., 1931).

[31]Committee, Bruce Edward, "Independence of Accountants and Legislative Intent", Administrative Law Review (Winter 1989): 33-57.

[32]Carey, John L., *Professional Ethics of Public Accounting*, (New York: American Institute of Accountants 1946): 7.

[33]Carey, John L., "The Independence Concept Revisited," *The Ohio CPA Journal* (Spring, 1985): 5-8.

[34]Committee, Bruce E., "Independence of Accountants and Legislative Intent," *Administrative Law Review* (Winter, 1989): 33-59. Writing in 1944, Maurice Peloubet, a practitioner, commented as follows: It is not really independence, which some glib and uninformed writers discuss so freely, it is rather integrity, which is so necessary to the practice of the profession. "Independence - A Blessed Word," *The Journal of Accountancy* (January, 1944): 69.

[35]Carey, J. L., "Practical Applications of Professional Ethics," Chapter 5, *CPA Handbook* (American Institute of [Certified Public] Accountants, 1952): 2.

[36]"Restructuring Professional Standards to Achieve Professional Excellence in a Changing Environment," Report of the Special Committee on Standards of Professional Conduct for Certified Public Accountants, AICPA, New York, 1986. See also The CPA Letter of the AICPA dated May 29,1987 for detailed results of the balloting.

[37]Report of the National Commission on Fraudulent Financial Reporting, October 1987, National Commission on Fraudulent Financial Reporting, 1701 Pennsylvania Avenue N. W., Washington D.C. 20006.

[38]"Ethics Survey Compares Various Professions," *PR Reporter* (August 14,1989).

Legal, Regulatory, and Social Environment

CHAPTER 4

Legal Aspects
of Practice

*Today effective practitioners of public accounting not
only must be aware of the possibility of legal
involvement, but also must be able to deal effectively
with the litigious environment in which they operate.
Practitioners who ignore the possibility of legal
involvement, or who fail to understand the legal duties
that they owe to the users of their work product, will
soon find themselves unable to conduct their
professional practices in a profitable manner.*[1]
Jonathan J. Davies

Introduction

This chapter discusses legal responsibilities and potential liabilities that are of
particular concern to CPAs. Most statutory enactments affecting accountants in
public practice deal with their reporting responsibilities as auditors (e.g., the various
federal securities acts) and most cases alleging violations of those statutes or relevant
common law duties are similarly focused. Accordingly, the emphasis herein is on
the auditing and accounting aspects of the profession's services. Nevertheless,
litigation has been brought in connection with tax and other services offered by
public accountants, and can be expected to increase in the future. Parallel concepts
of legal responsibilities and potential liabilities are developing in those areas as well.

CPAs in government agencies or privately employed in corporate practice or academe also have legal responsibilities and potential liabilities, but these are shared with others similarly situated or bear generally on the conduct of any citizen. They do not necessarily arise because of public practice or professional designation, but may arise from financial reporting responsibilities imposed by the federal securities acts or otherwise.

The diversity of views regarding CPAs' duties and responsibilities, particularly those regarding reporting on the financial statements of client companies, seems to create conflicts of expectations that lead inevitably to conflicts over related legal duties and responsibilities. Some possible causes of this diversity are covered in this chapter. Legal liabilities of public accountants are discussed in the context of contracts (between a CPA and a client), common law, and statutory law. The development and expansion of common law concepts as they affect the profession is of continuing concern, and this also is discussed, together with some consideration of the social and ethical changes over time that may be driving forces in this respect. The federal securities acts, including the important 1995 amendments thereto, and other legislation affecting accountants' duties are discussed, as well as aspects of criminal law that have been applied to CPAs. Finally included is a description of current efforts to mitigate the effects of the litigation that some feel so unduly burdens the profession today, including recent changes in forms of organization under which CPAs are permitted to practice.

As will become evident in the discussion to follow, the developments in this field are rapid and appear, with some exceptions, generally over time to broaden the legal exposure of the CPA in public practice, rather than to limit it. This chapter is a survey of the important factors affecting the public practitioner in this field, and some of the considerations affecting those CPAs not in public practice. It does not purport to be exhaustive or to cover all aspects of the topic. Most important, the authors are not engaged in offering legal services, and readers should not attempt themselves to apply the principles outlined herein to particular factual circumstances, but should seek competent legal counsel.

What's the Problem?

It is difficult for many in public practice to view current concepts of a CPA's legal responsibilities and potential liabilities dispassionately. No serious student of these matters would suggest that practitioners be insulated from responsibility for their actions. Yet there has been, seemingly from the beginning, a disparity between what CPAs have seen as their duty and what others have seen. This is being tested and reconciled by the courts, as it must be in an orderly society, but the results have expanded the audience for the CPA's work far beyond early contemplation, with the imposition of allegedly unreasonable monetary damages for failure to meet unforeseen expectations.

An early and often quoted expression of the feared ultimate consequences of this trend can be found in Judge Cardozo's reasoning in the *Ultramares* case,[2] rejecting the imposition of an auditor's liability to third parties (not in privity) for ordinary negligence:

> *If liability for negligence exists, a thoughtless slip or blunder, the failure to detect a theft or forgery beneath the cover of deceptive entries, may expose accountants to a liability in an indeterminate amount for an indeterminate time to an indeterminate class. The hazards of a business conducted on these terms are so extreme as to enkindle doubt whether a flaw may not exist in the implication of a duty that exposes to these consequences.*

What now is being explored is a contemporary definition of that duty -- and, indeed, the development of tools (procedures) to meet it -- which it is hoped will satisfy the reasonable expectations of those who use professional accounting services. This can only be an open-ended task, since definitions and expectations are ever changing.

The Causes of It All

Public accounting and its practitioners until mid-century seem not to have been a highly visible part of the commercial scene. As late as 1960, T. A. Wise was able to grab the attention of the business community by an in-depth study of the profession entitled "The Auditors Have Arrived."[3] Since that time, economic and societal changes have affected the CPA in a manner often disturbing to the profession, even though the effects probably have been consistent with those regarding other professions and occupations.

Henry R. Jaenicke attributed these developments to (a) the rise of consumerism, (b) the implementation of new concepts of insurance, and (c) the increasing presence of auditors in all aspects of commercial transactions.[4] The first can be seen as an attempt to redress what may have been viewed as an imbalance between the rights of consumers and commercial interests. The second involves, among other things, the so-called "deep pocket" theory (sue anyone who appears to have economic resources regardless of the degree of culpability), the increasing view of auditors as guarantors rather than as objective observers and reporters, and the "socialization of risk" (the placing of liability on those who are perceived to be in a position either to prevent loss or to shift its costs through higher charges to all users). And finally, the third cause is viewed as a reflection of the growing importance of accounting information in the investment process and the attendant publicity given in the press and elsewhere to alleged abuses such as so-called "creative" accounting practices condoned by CPAs.

Underlying and facilitating all these changes seems to be a continuing evolution in the concepts of a tort. A tort is ". . . a private or civil wrong or injury independent of contract, resulting from a breach of duty. . . . The essential elements of a tort are the existence of a legal duty owed by the defendant to the plaintiff, breach of that duty, and a causal relationship between defendant's conduct and the resulting damages to plaintiff."[5] The broadening of the legal duties of public accountants and the classes of persons to whom such duties extend, and the erosion of the notion that fault (causal relationship between conduct and damage) on the part of the defendant is a necessary condition to monetary recovery, have been pointed to as prime reasons for the so-called "litigation explosion." Those concerned with halting or reversing the trend are calling for nothing less than reform of the tort system. Victor M. Earle III asserts that:

> *We must restore fault as the principal basis for tort liability and adopt reforms consistent with that objective. More specifically, both the state and federal courts should return to common law concepts of fault and contributory fault.*[6]

Because so many of the suits filed against accountants arise in cases involving business bankruptcies or other failures where investors have lost money, it is evident that confusion exists regarding the distinction between a *business* failure and an *audit* failure. It is not an entirely unreasonable conclusion that this distinction, intentionally or innocently, is blurred by plaintiffs' bar. The fact that an auditor's client encounters business difficulties and is unable to overcome them without loss is entirely unrelated to the question of whether the auditor carried out attest responsibilities in a professional manner and in conformity with professional standards. An auditor examines and reports on a client's financial statements; he bears no responsibility for the client's decisions or acumen in handling business affairs. Indeed, he has no authority in this area. Nevertheless, as a result of fuzzy concepts of an auditor's duties and responsibilities, the stigma of client failure seems to carry over and become, in the minds of others, audit failure.

This stigma is exacerbated where there is undetected management fraud, and where this fraud comes to light because of a business failure or otherwise. Auditors have long contended that they had no responsibility to find fraud, indeed, that the very nature of auditing based upon tests and samples of accounting data made detection of fraud unlikely -- although such detection could occur and would be dealt with as necessary.

Because of a continuing belief on the part of the public that the purpose of an audit is to catch evildoers, the AICPA's Auditing Standards Board (ASB) in 1988 attempted to clarify this situation by saying that an auditor indeed had the responsibility to "design the audit to provide reasonable assurance of detecting errors [unintentional mistakes] and irregularities [intentional misstatements, including fraud] that are material to the financial statements."[7] This is quite a logical step, since the audit opinion deals with the "fair presentation" of financial information; if this fairness is materially distorted by undetected irregularities, the opinion is as much at fault as in the case of undetected errors. The fact that irregularities can be more difficult to detect because of the possibility of collusion and the like is rather beside the point. In 1997, the ASB issued further guidance to the auditors in fulfilling this responsibility.[8]

The Litigation Storm

A major concern of the profession with the legal aspects of its environment is the number of suits (principally by or on behalf of nonclient third parties) against CPA firms and individuals, alleging professional malpractice. Another is the amount of damages awarded to plaintiffs in such actions. Measures of these factors are only broadly useful since they do not take into account out-of-court settlements reached by litigants or potential litigants. Further, there is no clearinghouse for such information, and defendants are understandably reluctant to furnish details regarding their own troubles. Nevertheless, available data do point to trends and trends clearly indicate that both measures are on the increase, perhaps drastically, in recent years.

T.J. Fiflis asserted that "[i]n 1967, the statement was made correctly that 'suits against accountants by persons other than their clients have been almost uniformly unsuccessful.' "[9] Then, after citing several subsequent seminal cases to the contrary in the late 1960s, he further stated that "[t]his trickle of cases has swollen to hundreds of pending suits against accountants."[10] In its annual report for 1973, Arthur Andersen & Co. estimated then pending suits or claims in process against accountants to number 500. Shortly thereafter, in 1974, Carl D. Liggio estimated 500 to 1,000 cases.[11] Over 20 years later, in the 1996 report of the Arthur Andersen Public Review board, it was stated that:

> The costs of ... lawsuits have exploded in recent years. Just five years ago, in 1991, the direct costs of litigation for the Big Six firms in the United States were $367 million, or approximately 7 percent of accounting and auditing revenues; three years later, in 1994 (the last year for which statistics are available), the direct costs of litigation for these firms had tripled to more than $1 billion dollars, or about 20 percent of such revenues. Perhaps most ominously litigation against Big Six firms as been occurring increasingly in countries other than the United States.[12]

The chair of the AICPA Board of Directors, Robert Mednick, gloomily assessed the situation in a recent speech:

> This may represent the highest cost of litigation ever sustained by any industry or profession in the United States, except for small aircraft manufacturers who

*eventually went out of business as a result....and [worse] there remained over
$30 billion in damage claims facing the Big Six [accounting firms] as a whole
in this country at the end of ...[1995], which represented more than 20 times
the aggregate capital of the six firms.*[13]

Nor is this just a Big Six problem. Smaller and medium size firms increasingly
also are considering the risks of providing attest services, especially to public
corporations. The consequences to our free private enterprise system of the resulting
risk aversion activities of all firms may be severe if significant numbers of them
withdraw or limit their attest services, and in effect deny corporations the ability to
raise capital by denying them audits.[14] At least two "second tier" firms, Laventhol &
Horwath and Pannell Kerr & Forster, were forced into bankruptcy in the early 1990s,
in part because of legal troubles.

The *Handbook of Accounting and Auditing* described the situation over ten
years ago in dramatic language:

*Regrettably [because of recent legal events], it is not an overstatement to
describe the recent past as the most traumatic in the profession's history. It
remains to be seen how long this season of adverse developments will endure,
but as of July 1985 there is no basis for confidence that this has been a
completed or short-term phenomenon.*[15]

The words now seem prophetic in the light of current and continuing developments.

Some attempts have been made to equate increases and decreases in such
activity with the business cycle and/or the incidence of business failures, but with
results that perhaps are as much intuitive as quantified or quantifiable. Many believe
that the predicament of the CPA reflects some fundamental changes in public
attitudes which are affecting accountants along with every other element of society.
One author states that "The liability crisis results from the adolescent desire to blame
someone else for everything that goes wrong."[16] This comment must have some
meaning to anyone who picks up the daily newspaper to read of the many suits
against doctors, accountants, and other professionals, as well as against
commercial and industrial concerns -- and, in some cases against governmental
bodies, law enforcement agencies, and the like.

Governments, as well as private litigants, increasingly are seeking redress in
court, alleging accounting malpractice. Both the Federal Deposit Insurance
Corporation (FDIC) and the U.S. Department of Justice have filed suits against
auditors in connection with the failure of a major U. S. banking institution, and the
government of the United Kingdom filed suit in the United States seeking to recoup
losses incurred in financing a now-defunct automobile manufacturing concern.

Nor is the litigation confined to the United States. In a recent speech, the president of a large international insurance broker reported that claims against accountants had arisen in at least 70 countries, and that the then largest pending such suit anywhere in the world was not in the United States, but in the United Kingdom. Further, out of the suits seeking damages in excess of $1 billion, three out of five were in non-U.S. jurisdictions.[17]

The Insurance Crisis

An important by-product of this trend is the radical increase in the cost of professional malpractice insurance — or in some cases, its unavailability at any cost. Changing concepts of tort liability have had their effect; increased insurance payouts inevitably result in higher insurance premiums. Opinions differ whether losses reported by insurance companies are the fault of such payouts, or somehow are a result of bad business and investment practices of the insurers, but there is no question of the impact.

A related factor may be the perceived tendency of jurors in a malpractice trial to assess damages in large amounts on the basis that the costs will be paid by an insurer and not by the defendant. Victor M. Earle III asserts that ". . . [jurors] typically justify their largess by assuming the defendant was insured. Jurors apparently also assume that the premiums are paid by the tooth fairy."[18] Not everyone agrees, and there is some research to the effect that jury awards are less generous than those arising from settlement agreements or arbitration awards. Nevertheless, these alternative considerations add another perspective to the issue.

The more obvious consequences of increased awards in cases involving tort law ultimately may not be as important as the indirect consequences. Ronald C. Horn sees the real crisis as involving serious and largely unrecognized (or at least unaddressed) public policy problems. These include (a) "legal-flation" (staggering increases in the cost of goods and services to cover insurance premiums), (b) "defensive medicine" (the application of procedures and tests merely to protect against possible future malpractice claims), (c) "public health" (withdrawal of doctors from certain areas of practice such as obstetrics; limitation of production of vaccines), (d) "corporate insolvencies" (bankruptcies which have serious consequences for employees and stockholders), and (e) other effects such as the closing down of child care centers, amusement parks, and other facilities where insurance costs cannot reasonably be passed on to customers or the risks even with insurance are deemed unacceptable.[19] Although not so dramatic in terms of their effect on human life, these problems have their direct counterpart in the accounting profession.

Legal Responsibilities

The legal responsibilities and potential liabilities arising from the practice of public accountancy may be imposed by contract, by common law (accumulated judicial precedent), by statutory law, or by a combination. They may involve a breach of contract, a tort (a private wrong against a person, resulting from breach of a legal duty), or a crime (any act contrary to the public good; a wrong that the government has determined is injurious to the public). They are different with respect to clients and nonclients. Where contractual relationships are involved the question of privity arises, since persons who are not parties to a contract (nonclients) may be precluded from asserting rights under that contract.

Legal liability usually involves some failure by the CPA to exercise due care in carrying out professional activities, which failure causes damage to others. Due care is the exercise of at least that degree of skill and competence possessed by members of the profession and required by professional standards. Failure to exercise that due care constitutes negligence. The nature of liability, and the parties to whom it extends, depends upon the degree of that negligence, which exists along a continuum from ordinary negligence through gross negligence and recklessness to fraud. Ordinary negligence connotes an intention to exercise due care, but a shortcoming in fulfilling that intention. Fraud connotes a conscious knowledge of a falsity and action with intent to deceive.

Contracts for Professional Services

The principles of law relating to contracts in general also apply to contracts between a CPA in public practice and a client, and to contracts negotiated by and between CPAs in industry or academe on their own or an employer's behalf -- principles such as the necessity for offer and acceptance, and for consideration, in order for an enforceable agreement to be in place. Failure to perform under or to complete a contract, say for an annual audit, without good cause may give rise to damage claims. Practitioners, therefore, should be cautious in withdrawing from an engagement once contracted for, and consultation with counsel before making such a decision is wise. Apart from these commonalities, however, there are several factors affecting the profession in this area that are of particular interest to practitioners.

Traditional common law principles do not permit third parties to sue for breach of contract. However, as discussed later in this chapter, in some states such third parties now may develop a cause of action based upon charges of negligence. The barrier of privity once thought to shield accountants from third party actions alleging ordinary negligence have been relaxed from the strict standards established in the *Ultramares* case.

A contract may be either written or oral. This is not unique in its application to CPAs, whether or not in public practice. However, the difference is of critical importance if it becomes necessary to establish the parameters of any arrangement with some particularity -- which is bound to be required in any dispute.[20] Therefore, it behooves the careful practitioner always to reduce the understanding with a client to writing (an engagement letter), regardless of whether the services to be furnished relate to auditing, accounting, tax, or other services.

Common Law Responsibilities and Potential Liabilities

Legal actions alleging common law violations are based in tort, and the plaintiffs must allege some misrepresentation (or withholding) of a material fact relied upon to their detriment. Regarding auditing or accounting services, this misrepresentation generally arises in connection with financial statements and notes, and reports thereon. Whether the accountant's actions constitute negligence, gross negligence, or fraud depends upon the circumstances of the case. Even where the accountant is an innocent participant in a misrepresentation, liability may exist because of a duty to know the truth which, in the event, was breached.

The auditor's common law liability to clients can be differentiated from liability to third parties not in privity under a contract for professional services. A public accountant may be liable to clients for ordinary negligence as well as for breach of contract. Negligence itself may represent also a breach of a contract for professional services, which implies the exercise of due care in its fulfillment. Liability for gross negligence or fraud, however, may arise as to noncontracting third parties as well as to clients. On the other hand, the CPA's liability to third parties for ordinary negligence has expanded over time with the erosion of the privity barrier, and can be traced in terms of the persons or classes of persons now included as potential litigants.

Until well into this century, accountants were liable at common law for ordinary negligence in the performance of their professional engagements only to their clients. Although much of common law in the United States derives from English precedents, the rule in this country regarding public accounting for over 30 years was based on the *Ultramares* case. Here the court made an essentially economic argument for limiting an auditor's responsibility to the client because of the hazards of a business conducted under the burden of possible liability to third parties for negligence.

The court in *Ultramares* also stated that liability to third parties for negligence should not be imposed if the audit report was "primarily for the benefit of the [client]." This so-called "primary benefit" rule recognized that financial statements are prepared for many purposes, not all of which should justify breaking the barrier of privity. In so doing, however, the court opened up the notion of some liability to third parties if the financial statements were prepared and audited for the primary benefit of such third parties. This rule in practice subsequently was applied strictly to insulate accountants from third-party liability for ordinary negligence even where the auditor knew the audit report was to be furnished to a third party who might be expected to rely upon it in making an investment or lending decision.[21] Third parties, under *Ultramares*, therefore apparently were having difficulty in placing themselves as primary beneficiaries.

Despite the subsequent actions in other jurisdictions expanding auditors' liability to ever-widening classes of financial statement users, a recent case in the same court as *Ultramares* seems to reaffirm in modified form the privity barrier thereby established.[22] Under this case, three prerequisites must be satisfied before liability for negligence will be imposed on behalf of noncontracting third parties:

1. The accountants must have been aware that the financial reports were to be used for a particular purpose or purposes,

2. A known party or parties intended to rely on the reports, for such purpose (primary beneficiaries?), and

3. Some conduct on the part of the auditors linking them to the parties and evidencing an understanding of the proposed reliance.

It is uncertain what effect, if any, this decision will have on the general trend of cases involving CPAs' common law liability for negligence.

In 1965, the American Law Institute (ALI), in its *Restatement (Second) of Torts*, adopted language aimed at limiting liability for negligently given information not to a particular plaintiff identified in advance, but to the comparatively small group whom the defendant expects and intends to influence.[23] This was intended to eliminate liability to the very large class of persons who may foreseeably be influenced, thus drawing a distinction between "foreseen" and "foreseeable." The *Restatement*, however, specifically includes as potential beneficiaries certain parties clearly not in privity as well as those who otherwise might not be considered primary beneficiaries.

A 1968 case, *Rusch Factors* v. *Levin*,[24] affirmed the logic in the ALI's *Restatement*, and advanced two arguments for extending an auditor's liability for negligence to a party not in privity. First, the court believed the public accountant was best able to bear the burden of loss because of the ability to pass the cost of malpractice along to clients, thus enabling society ultimately to judge the value of the services rendered, including the risk of negligence therein. Second, the court reasoned that the expansion of the accountant's liability would force action by CPAs to avoid costly mistakes.[25] The first arguably is an evidence of the tendency to socialize accounting malpractice risks; although perhaps not driven by this case, the promise of the second has been affirmed in the profession's (and individual firms') actions subsequently taken to improve professional quality control.

Whether the logic of *Rusch Factors* will persist or whether accountants' liabilities will be extended from foreseen parties to foreseeable parties remains to be seen. A 1976 case in Minnesota[26] came very close to doing the latter by extending the class entitled to recompense for negligence to include local insurance agents, who relied upon the state insurance commissioner, who reviewed (and relied upon) some workpapers shown to the commissioner's representatives by the accountant. If local agents in this case, why not also policyholders? Why not public shareholders purchasing shares from an underwriter known to the accountant to be relying on an audit report? (Liability to such shareholders, of course, already may arise in connection with a filing under one of the federal securities acts.)

R. James Gormley sees pressure toward "foreseeability" as a criterion of the class entitled to claim protection against negligence. He speculates that the foreseen class test really protects only the sophisticated who make certain that their participation indeed is foreseen by the accountant, whereas the less sophisticated cannot or do not take such precautions but may plead successfully for protection nonetheless.[27]

Statutory Responsibilities and Potential Liabilities

Although the common law affects many areas of a public accountant's practice, statutes (legislative enactments) are equally or more important. Such statutes include federal mail fraud laws and state blue sky laws. More recently, the *Racketeer Influenced and Corrupt Organizations Act* (RICO) appeared on the scene, although claims under this statute evidently will be sharply curtailed by 1995 amendments to the federal securities acts. The principal focus of this section is on two of the most important initial (federal) statutes affecting the practice of public accounting, the *Securities Act of 1933* and the *Securities Exchange Act of 1934*, on *RICO*, and on the newcomer, the *Private Securities Reform Act of 1995*.

Both of the securities acts deal with transactions in interstate commerce involving securities. The interpretation of the meaning of each of the key phrases here (interstate commerce and securities) is beyond the scope of this chapter; suffice it to say both have been drawn quite broadly. For example, a security may include any investment in which a person turns his money or property over to another to manage for profit[28] and not just stocks or bonds. It behooves the prudent public accountant to realize the diversity of circumstances in which potential liability under the securities acts may arise.

The Securities Act of 1933

The 1933 Act sometimes is characterized as a disclosure law; that is, its provisions basically are intended to supply information to potential purchasers of new issues of securities so they can make an informed decision.   It does not forbid selling worthless securities, although purchasers of those that turn out to be so often seek redress under other guises (e.g., claims of inadequate or inaccurate disclosures in a registration statement). With certain exceptions (such as for intrastate transactions) the sale of securities requires the prior existence of an effective registration statement filed with the SEC. Section 11 of the Act gives purchasers of securities so registered a right of recovery for resulting losses against various persons -- including independent public accountants who consent to the use of their report therein -- if the registration statement contains any misstatement of a material fact (tell nothing but the truth) or omits to state a material fact necessary to make the statements made not misleading (tell the whole truth).

A purchaser of securities registered under the 1933 Act who sustains a loss need prove only a material misstatement or omission in the audited financial statements in order to proceed against the auditor.[29] Proof is not required of auditor negligence, the holder's reliance on the audit report (unless the securities were acquired after the registrant had issued an earnings statement for a period of at least twelve months beginning after the effective date of the registration statement), or a causal relationship between the omission or misstatement and any loss sustained. At this point the burden shifts to the auditor, who may in defense prove due care was exercised (i.e., no negligence) in the work, there was no causal relationship between any misstatement or omission and the plaintiff's loss, or the plaintiff knew of the misstatement or omission when acquiring the security.

These burdens may be heavy. Because of the total import of the 1933 Act, George O. May, a leader of the profession at the time, was moved to say, with some passion:

> *I cannot believe that a law is just or can long be maintained in effect which deliberately contemplated the possibility that a purchaser may recover from a person from whom he has not bought, in respect of a statement which at the time of his purchase he had not read, contained in a document which he did not then know to exist, a sum which is not to be measured by injury resulting from falsity in such statement.*[30]

In the usual audit engagement, the date of the auditor's report signals the end of all significant audit field work, including inquiry into events after the balance sheet date (subsequent events) which may affect or should be disclosed in the financial statements under examination.[31] Section 11(b) of the 1933 Act extends the time of responsibility for knowledge regarding such events and therefore the auditor must make a specific review for this purpose up to the effective date[32] of the registration statement. The content and extent of this review (sometimes called an S-1 review, after the name of the principal form used for the filing) is specified in professional literature[33] and its appropriate completion is a necessary part of the auditor's proof that the examination was carried out in a nonnegligent manner (with the exercise of due care).

The Securities Exchange Act of 1934

The 1934 Act may be explained most expeditiously by pointing out its differences from the 1933 Act described above. First, the 1934 Act applies both to purchasers and sellers of securities already issued; the 1933 Act applies only to purchasers of new issues. Second, Section 18(a) of the 1934 Act requires more in the way of proof by plaintiffs than Section 11 of the 1933 Act. For example, defendant's liability is limited to errors or omissions in reports filed with the SEC, plaintiffs must prove reliance on false representations (or improper omissions) in those filings, and further must prove that damages were caused by that reliance.

An auditor's defense against a complaint under Section 18(a) lies in proving that the auditor acted in good faith and had no knowledge that the statements were false or misleading. Negligence is not a factor; scienter (knowledge of a falsity and its use with intent to deceive) is. This would appear a lighter burden than the proof of due care necessary under Section 11 of the 1933 Act.

A more active cause of action under the 1934 Act is Section 10(b), and SEC Rule 10b-5 thereunder. These provide that in connection with the purchase or sale of any security it is unlawful:

1. to employ any device, scheme, or artifice to defraud;

2. to make any untrue statement of a material fact or to omit to state a material fact necessary in order to make the statements made, in the light of the circumstances under which they were made, not misleading; or

3. to engage in any act, practice, or course of business which operates or would operate as a fraud or deceit upon any person.

Although the words "in connection with" have been broadly construed, and the definition of fraud or deceit is not entirely clear, the application of this Section and Rule to public accountants has been at least partly defined in the *Hochfelder* case.[34] Here the U.S. Supreme Court held that negligence will not suffice to impose liability, but left unresolved exactly what level of culpability will result in such liability.[35] In saying that the statute clearly uses words implying intentional or willful conduct, there is evidence that the court intended to impose a scienter test for liability, but left open the possibility of a lesser standard by observing that under the case presented (an action in damages only for negligence) the court need not consider whether, in some circumstances, reckless behavior is sufficient for civil liability.[36]

Since *Hochfelder*, courts have recognized that scienter is not a rigid concept explicitly requiring intent, and often have substituted recklessness as a standard, thus inferring culpability without a finding of motive.[37] "The amount of litigation based on Section 10(b) does not seem to be decreasing since the *Hochfelder* decision. Courts have been applying varying degrees of recklessness as a substitute for scienter with recklessness being defined as everything from 'inaction' to 'knowledge of the falsity.' "[38]

A recent decision by the U.S. Supreme Court may serve to limit some actions brought under Section 10(b), although only time will tell whether potential plaintiffs can find alternative theories for asserting claims. In *Central Bank of Denver*, the court held that parties alleged to have aided and abetted a securities fraud cannot be held liable for civil damages in a private action under Section 10(b)[39]. This has been the basis for much of what the accounting profession has regarded as "strike suits," seeking damage awards from those perceived to have financial resources, without regard to the degree of culpability, if any.

Private Securities Litigation Reform Act of 1995

In December, 1995, Congress passed this Act over the veto of President Clinton. This represented the culmination of intensive efforts by business and professional groups over a number of years to rein in what had become perceived to be abusive use of the legal system by the plaintiffs' bar. Some of the more important provisions of this Act are as follows:

1. Joint and several liability (under which any one defendant can be forced to bear the entire brunt of any damages) is replaced with a modified form of proportional liability (under which each defendant is responsible only for that portion of the damages corresponding to its own culpability).

2. Certain provisions impose stricter pleading standards on plaintiff's counsel, eliminate abusive discovery practices, and control the use of "professional plaintiffs," among other things.

3. "Safe Harbor" provisions are included that exempt forward-looking statements made in good faith from serving as a basis for liability under the federal securities laws.

4. Securities fraud is eliminated as a "predicate act" under the Racketeering and Corrupt Organizations Act (RICO), thus eliminating the ability of plaintiffs to claim treble damages in securities suits.

There are some indications that the early effects of this legislation include driving more cases to state courts, where the protections of the new federal legislation are not available. A study by two Stanford University law professors found that in the year following the passage of the *Reform Act* there was no significant variation in the number of companies sued for securities fraud in class action cases from previous years, but a decline in federal court filings was offset by a comparable rise in those filed in state courts.[40]

Racketeer Influenced and Corrupt Organizations Act (RICO)

The RICO act was passed by Congress in 1970, ostensibly to provide a weapon against organized crime. In it were specified certain activities deemed to constitute racketeering, including mail fraud and fraud in the sale of securities, as well as murder, arson, bribery, and the like. It was declared unlawful for a person to engage in a "pattern of racketeering," which was defined as the commission of two or more of the proscribed activities in a ten year period. Three provisions of the act are particularly important to accountants and others charged as defendants: civil suits by private citizens are permitted, plaintiffs need prove their case only by a preponderance of the evidence (rather than by the standard required in a criminal case of "beyond a reasonable doubt"), and RICO provides for the award of triple damages to successful plaintiffs.

There is substantial disagreement whether, in fact, the use of RICO in private commercial litigation exceeds the intent of Congress. Numerous efforts to amend RICO on this point failed, until Congress passed the *Private Securities Litigation Reform Act of 1995* in December of that year. Among other things, this legislation removes securities fraud as a predicate offense for a RICO claim, thus eliminating plaintiffs' ability to claim treble damages in securities suits.

Other Matters

Other developments in connection with a CPA's legal responsibilities and liabilities include a significant case finding criminal, rather than civil, misbehavior by three public accountants, the assertion by the United States Supreme Court that an accountant's duties to the public on occasion may override duties to clients, and changes made in permissible forms of public practice by CPAs that provide some protection against unlimited liability for negligence of professional associates in the same firm.

Criminal Guilt

Although cases involving alleged criminal behavior on the part of accountants while carrying out their professional duties have not been numerous, CPAs nevertheless should be aware of their potential liability in this regard. Conviction in a civil case may result in monetary fines, but conviction in a criminal case carries with it the additional possibility of imprisonment and/or loss of certain rights of citizenship such as the right to vote. In either case, of course, subsequent actions by professional societies and state boards of accountancy also could result in loss of membership in the former instance and loss of the right to practice in the latter.

General mail fraud statutes, laws prohibiting false statements to government personnel or departments, and behavior constituting aiding and abetting others who commit crimes, may give rise to such liability. Both the Securities Act of 1933 and the Securities Exchange Act of 1934 include provisions imposing criminal liability under certain circumstances. State statutes vary, but usually contain prohibitions against making false or misleading statements to state authorities. A common element in all of the statutes is the concept of **willful** and **knowing** behavior.

A significant, but still perhaps not widely appreciated result of a leading criminal case against a CPA is the proposition that compliance with generally accepted accounting principles, while important, will not necessarily insulate an accountant against liability (civil or criminal). This issue turns on whether the language in the auditor's report that the financial statements ". . . present fairly [financial position, results of operations, etc.] . . . in conformity with generally accepted accounting principles" means that fairness is attained by conformity alone, or whether another, more subjective, meaning of fairness is the appropriate standard. The judge and jury in the *Continental Vending* case[41] settled for the latter concept, leaving the auditor perhaps with a more slender reed to lean upon (conformity with generally accepted accounting principles) in issuing opinions on financial statements than was previously believed to be the case. Two partners and an audit manager of the accounting firm were convicted in this case, and the conviction was upheld on appeal.

CPAs' Responsibility to the Public

A Supreme Court decision in 1984 in the case of *United States* v. *Arthur Young & Co.*, although limited to the question whether tax accrual working papers prepared by an accountant for the purpose of issuing an audit report may be subpoenaed by the IRS (yes, they may), will undoubtedly continue to influence the development of the law.[42] Of particular importance, Justice Burger's dictum regarding a public accountant's duties was troubling to the accounting profession because of its seemingly open-ended reach:

> *In certifying the public reports that depict a corporation's financial status, the accountant performs a **public** responsibility transcending any employment relationship with the client, and owes allegiance to the corporation's creditors and stockholders, as well as to the investing public. [emphasis in original]*[43]

Critics of the opinion believed it to be an unnecessary simplification of the auditor's role that might indicate that the accountant was "liable to the world."[44] On the other hand, leaders of the profession for years have emphasized the public responsibilities of the CPA, and the independent and objective evaluation made of financial statements under audit. It may have been somewhat disconcerting, however, to see that self-asserted duty so clearly affirmed by the highest court in the land.

Limited Liability Partnerships (LLPs)

While seeking legislative solutions to the general question of the liability of CPAs, accountants also have made changes in the forms of organizations under which they may practice their profession. Once ethical rules allowed CPAs to practice only as sole practitioners or in partnership with other CPAs. Now Rule 505 of the AICPA's Code of Professional Conduct provides, in part, that "[a] member may practice public accounting only in a form permitted by state law or regulation whose characteristics conform to resolutions of council." As of September, 1996, 48 jurisdictions (out of 50 states, the District of Columbia, Guam, Puerto Rico, and the Virgin Islands) had passed legislation allowing professionals (including accountants) to form LLPs,[45] a form acceptable to council.

Although the particulars in each state differ, the most significant feature of LLPs is that their members (partners) have some form of limited liability. "...[M]ost LLP statutes provide that LLP partners are not individually liable for the negligence or other misconduct of other partners or employees unless the partner participated in or supervised the wrongdoing....Under most statutes LLP partners *are* liable for several categories of conduct, particularly including conduct that is no more than a breach of contract. Under other statutes LLP partners have limited liability for all categories of claims."[46]

Another form of organization, Limited Liability Companies (LLCs), also is available to accountants and other professionals, and many states have enacted statutes regarding them. For some rather technical reasons, however, it is easier for CPAs to form LLPs, and many have done so. In either case, the effect is to move from the partnership form of organization, with its unlimited liability for all partners, to a form providing some shield for personal assets from damage and other claims. In this respect, LLPs and LLCs provide some of the same benefits of the corporate form of organization, while being treated generally for tax and other purposes as a partnership.

Proposals For Change

The accounting profession now is engaged in the difficult task of seeking changes in state securities laws to incorporate provisions similar to those in the *Private Securities Litigation Reform Act of 1995* at the federal level. Some states have adopted forms of proportionate liability (replacing joint and several liability), and others have passed so-called "privity" statutes, limiting the parties that can sue for negligence to those having a contractual relationships. A major attempt to turn away such reforms was made in California in 1996 with a ballot initiative, Proposition 211. This was soundly rejected by the voters. Had it been adopted, Proposition 211 would have effectively nullified the changes in the federal statutes, among other things allowing California courts to hear securities fraud class action suits involving even non-California companies so long as a single investor was resident in the state.

Other changes being sought at both the state and federal levels include increasing the ability of the courts to assess costs against unsuccessful plaintiffs, thus discouraging nuisance suits, and using "masters" appointed by the courts in cases involving complex professional matters. Some efforts at so-called "tort reform" legislation focus on the possibility of placing dollar limits on punitive and/or noneconomic (pain and suffering) damages. These changes have been enacted in some states but whether the move will spread or whether suggested changes indeed will be effective remains to the future to determine. There is substantial opposition to any modification of current concepts and the issue is not likely to be resolved expeditiously.

Summary

In this chapter we have considered the various sources from which a CPA's legal duties and responsibilities flow, and the social trends from which increases in those duties and responsibilities seem to be coming. Contracts with clients, common law, and statutory law, together create the legal environment in which the CPA must operate. We have discussed those matters and have considered particular laws, such as the federal securities acts, having specific professional practice implications, particularly for those accountants who are employed by companies issuing securities to the public or who have them as clients. Efforts of CPAs and other professionals to effect changes in their statutory responsibilities and potential liabilities have been discussed, along with changes made in forms of practice for CPAs in public practice. Some continuing proposals for further changes in this area were outlined, but movement in this area is likely to be slow and of uncertain direction.

Discussion Questions

1. What are some of the social and economic factors that have led to an expansion of the CPA's legal responsibilities and liabilities?

2. Does a business failure indicate an audit failure? Could an audit failure lead to a business failure?

3. Discuss an auditor's responsibility to detect fraud, and ability to do so.

4. What are the implications to the practice of public accountancy of increasing legal exposure and high damage awards? Direct consequences? Indirect consequences?

5. What is "due care," and what legal implications arise from the failure of the CPA to exercise it in providing professional services?

6. Differentiate a CPA's liability under common law to clients and to third parties not in privity. How has this evolved over time?

7. State in your own words the present status of the common law liability of CPAs.

8. Differentiate the liability of CPAs under the Securities Act of 1933 and the Securities Exchange Act of 1934. What are the standards of proof required of plaintiffs and the standards of defense required of defendants under the respective acts?

9. Why is the case of *United States* v. *Arthur Young & Co.*, after all a case limited to the access to audit working papers granted the IRS, so important in defining the function and responsibilities of CPAs?

10. Would you make any changes to the legal responsibilities and duties of the CPA as they presently are understood? If so, why and in what respect?

11. How and in what respect should CPAs in industry, government, and academe be concerned with the legal responsibilities and potential liabilities of CPAs in public practice?

12. Discuss some of the reasons for the apparent increase over time in cases against CPAs in public practice. Is this a good or bad thing for the profession? For society at large?

13. What important changes were made in the application of the federal securities acts by the *Private Securities Litigation Reform Act of 1995?*

14. What are LLPs? What is the significance of this new form of organization for CPAs?

15. What additional steps are being taken by CPAs to modify their statutory and common law responsibilities and potential liabilities?

Endnotes

[1] Davies, Jonathan J., *CPA Liability: A Manual for Practitioners* (New York: John Wiley & Sons, 1983), v.

[2] *Ultramares Corp.* v. *Touche*, 255 N.Y. 170, 174 N.E. 441 (1931).

[3] Wise, T.A., "The Auditors Have Arrived," *Fortune,* November and December, 1960.

[4] Jaenicke, Henry R., "The Effect of Litigation on Independent Auditors," *Research Study No. 1*, Commission on Auditors' Responsibilities, New York, 1977, 3-5.

[5] Gifis, Steven H., *Law Dictionary* (New York: Barron's Educational Series, Inc., 1975).

[6] Earle III, Victor M., "The Fantasy of Life Without Risk," *Fortune* (February 16, 1987): 116.

[7] Section 316.05, *AICPA Professional Standards,* Commerce Clearing House, Inc., Chicago, June 1, 1988.

[8] *Statement on Auditing Standards No. 82*, "Consideration of Fraud in a Financial Statement Audit," AICPA, 1997.

[9] Fiflis, T. J., "Current Problems of Accountants' Responsibilities to Third Parties," *Vanderbilt Law Review,* January, 1975, 32.

[10] Ibid., 33.

[11] Liggio, Carl D., "Expanding Concepts of Accountants' Liability," *California CPA Quarterly* (September, 1974): 18-19.

[12] *Report of the Public Review Board,* Andersen Worldwide, 1996, 4.

[13] Mednick, Robert, in address to The Sixth Jerusalem Conference on Accountancy, November 12, 1996.

[14] From 1994 through April, 1997, the Big Six accounting firms dropped a total of 275 publicly traded audit clients because of perceived unacceptable legal risks. *The Wall Street Journal,* April 26, 1997.

[15] Burton, John C., Palmer, Russell E., and Kay, Robert S., *Handbook of Accounting and Auditing*, 1986 Update, (Boston: Warren, Gorham & Lamont, 1985), 44-1.

[16] Earle, Victor M. III, op. cit., 113.

[17] Robert Mednick, "Chair's Corner" commentary, *The CPA Letter,* AICPA, January/February, 1997.

[18] Earle, Victor M. III, op. cit., 113.

[19] Horn, Ronald C., "America's Lawsuits and Liability Insurance Headaches," *Baylor Business Review,* Winter, 1987.

[20] See, for example, *1136 Tenants' Corp.* v. *Max Rothenberg & Co.,* 36 AD 2nd 804, 319 NYS 2nd 1007 (1971). Here the accountants suffered the consequences of (among other things) the failure to document their understanding of the nature and scope of an engagement as being limited to "write-up" work (rather than auditing) and were held responsible for failure to detect irregularities (defalcations).

[21] *C.I.T. Financial Corp.* v. *Glover,* 224 F. 2d 44 (2d Cir. 1955)

[22] *Credit Alliance Corp.* v. *Arthur Andersen & Co.,* 65 N.Y., 2d 536 (1985)

[23] Gormley, R. James, *The Law of Accountants and Auditors,* (Boston: Warren, Gorham & Lamont, 1981), 6-6, quoting from the ALI reporter's memorandum for discussion regarding the *Restatement.*

[24] *Rusch Factors, Inc.* v. *Levin,* 284 F Supp 85 (D.R.I. 1968).

[25] Davies, Jonathan J., op. cit., 86-87.

[26] *Bonhiver* v. *Graff,* 311 Minn 111, 248 NW 2d 291 (1976).

[27] Gormley, R. James, op. cit., 6-17.

[28] Windal, Floyd W., & Corley, Robert N., *The Accounting Professional* (Englewood Cliffs, New Jersey: Prentice-Hall, Inc., 1980), 259.

[29] This seems to be the common understanding of the basis for the auditor's potential liability. However, Gormley correctly asserts that the proper basis should be misstatements or omissions in the auditor's opinion, not the financial statements (Gormley, R. James, op. cit., 7-12). In most cases, the result likely would be the same.

[30] May, George O., *Twenty-Five Years of Accounting Responsibility,* Vol. 2 (New York: American Institute Publishing Co., 1936), 69.

[31] Sections AU 530 and AU 560, AICPA *Professional Standards,* CCH Incorporated, Chicago, June 1, 1995.

[32] The date following review of the filing by the SEC and any changes by the registrant, when offers to sell securities legally may be made and purchase orders accepted.

[33] Section AU 711, AICPA *Professional Standards,* CCH Incorporated, Chicago, June 1, 1995.

[34] *Ernst & Ernst* v. *Hochfelder,* 425 U.S. 185 (1976).

[35] Gormley, R. James, op. cit., 9-24.

[36] Ibid., 9-27.

[37] Barnett, Andrew H., and Galer, F. Fulton, "Scienter Since Hochfelder," *The CPA Journal,* November, 1982.

[38] Ibid.

[39] *Central Bank of Denver, N.A.* v. *First Interstate Bank of Denver, N.A.,* 114 S Ct 1439 (1994).

[40] As reported in *The Arizona Republic,* April 4, 1997.

[41] *United States* v. *Simon*, 425 F2nd 796 (2d Cir. 1969), *cert. denied* 397 U.S. 1006 (1970).

[42] Burton, John C., Palmer, Russell E., and Kay, Robert S., op. cit., 1985 edition, 44-2.

[43] As reported in *Taxation and Accounting* (Washington: The Bureau of National Affairs, March 22, 1984).

[44] Burton, John C., Palmer, Russell E., and Kay, Robert S. op. cit., 1985 edition, 44-3.

[45] AICPA *Journal of Accountancy,* September, 1996, 58.

[46] Bromberg, Alan R., and Ribstein, Larry E., *Limited Liability Partnerships and the Revised Uniform Partnership Act,* (Boston: Little, Brown and Company, 1995 edition), 15.

CHAPTER 5

Regulatory and Professional Organizations

The attention presently focused on the accounting profession does not appear to be a fleeting phenomenon. This statement is one of the few that produces consensus among experts in accounting. The issue of regulation is simply not going to disappear, say, because the profession has initiated some reforms.[1]

Buckley and Weston

Introduction

The term "regulation" connotes control of an activity by a governing or superior body charged with that responsibility. This usually means the development and enforcement of various rules to direct behavior and to assure clients and employers of an individual's qualifications, holding him or her to a high standard of performance. In the case of the accounting profession (and indeed of any profession), this simple model is complicated by the very nature of the activity itself. Professionals deliver services in a field where they have particular expertise and knowledge, and therefore quality is likely to be more elusive, harder to measure and control by those lacking such expertise and knowledge. Regulation comes from the public sector in the form of state licensing and the oversight of various administrative agencies, and from the private sector in the form of the ethical rules of employers and various voluntary professional organizations.

Society, having recognized a profession's expertise and therefore dependence upon it, nonetheless seeks assurance that professionals are qualified and are acting responsibly in what is perceived to be the best public interest. Thus, the several state governments grant (and revoke) licenses to practice, establish regulatory boards, and generally monitor the results of that dependence. Such licenses usually are based upon criteria established by members of the profession, who also largely may comprise any regulatory board. A question often arises, therefore, whether the social control thereby provided is effective or is circumvented by the intervention of those sought to be controlled. The public in a sense is frustrated by its dependence at every turn on the knowledge, and indeed the good faith, of professionals. This frustration often evidences itself in collective attempts at control through restrictive legislation, and by the mandatory inclusion of lay persons on professional regulatory boards.

In the case of CPAs in corporate practice, the web of regulatory constraints is more complex. They may be relieved of any responsibility to maintain independence from their employer, in the sense that CPAs performing the attest function must do, but still are subject to the requirements of accounting standards as articulated by the Financial Accounting Standards Board, the rules of the several state boards of accountancy, the Securities and Exchange Commission, and now the AICPA's Code of Professional Conduct. They may also be subject to the ethical codes of employers and of such organizations as the Institute of Internal Auditors or the Institute of Management Accountants.

As the headnote above implies, much of the recent history of the accounting profession has been characterized by reactive behavior -- reforms, if you will. Charges of unprofessional performance, malpractice, and other failures have been met by organizational changes in professional societies, by the issuance of professional guidelines to meet challenges to expand duties and responsibilities, and by shifting the focus of standard setting away from wholly professional bodies to others presumably more responsive to broader concerns. Many actions of the profession, it is true, have been impelled by outside events and pressures; still, this can be regarded as a positive (responsive to changing circumstances) rather than a negative. Seeking a balance between public and private (self) regulation will continue to provide a dynamic tension, the achieved equilibrium of which will determine the future of the profession and its practitioners. The basic need for this activity is the profession's perception of its ultimate responsibility to serve the public need, and to be assured that its practitioners are qualified for that task. The Massachusetts Medical Society, in 1781, justified it thus: "...[A] just discrimination should be made between such as are duly educated, and properly qualified for the duties of their profession, and those who may ignorantly and wickedly administer medicine."[2]

The profession itself is ambivalent about just where to establish this balance between public and self-regulation. Indeed, accountants and other professionals (and many occupations not falling into that category) actively seek governmental participation and assistance in their affairs. State licensing, for example, is sought because it carries at least the implication of official quality control and sanction for an activity. The title "certified" public accountant certainly has that connotation. Indeed, one of the earliest initiatives of the first professional accounting organization in the United States (The American Association of Public Accountants, AAPA) was to seek legislative recognition from the state of New York, which in 1896 passed a bill "To Regulate the Profession of Public Accountants," the first such statute in this country.[3]

This chapter includes a discussion of regulation of the accounting profession by society. Such regulation involves the establishment of certain controls over professional behavior -- through state licensing, for example. The relationship of the accounting profession to the Securities and Exchange Commission is outlined, and the importance of the several state boards of accountancy to regulation is described. The intervention of legislative bodies through hearings and investigations of the profession, and the influence of litigation on professional behavior, is discussed.

Also included is a description of the principal professional accounting institutions in the United States, such as the AICPA, the various state CPA societies, and their ethical and quality controls. The AICPA's Division for CPA Firms is particularly important in this respect, since it provides for the evaluation of individual and firm public practice through peer reviews and the public release of information coming out of such reviews. Although CPAs not in public practice are not subject to the peer review process, the 1988 adoption of the AICPA's Code of Conduct extended that body's disciplinary reach over them in a way never before possible. The functions of the Public Oversight Board (POB) and the Quality Control Inquiry Committee (QCIC), both important to the functioning of the SEC Section of the Division, are described. Finally, the chapter includes a section covering the development of accounting standards, and the ongoing consideration of whether such standards should be established in the public or the private sector.

Social Control

The requirements society places upon the accounting profession are, of course, expressed through its (society's) institutions. Certain state and federal agencies are most important here, and in the final analysis determinations made in the court system are dispositive. However, some background regarding the concepts leading theorists to suggest or enforce governmental regulation is necessary for an understanding of the dynamics of this process. These concepts include the perceived necessity to exert at least some minimal control over the otherwise unrestrained exercise by professionals of professional practices and discipline, leading to such previously described safeguards as placing lay persons on professional licensing boards. Licensing laws in themselves provide the groundwork for this control.

Three often conflicting ideas have been suggested as driving regulatory agencies in their specific actions.[4] First, the notion that protecting the public interest, however imperfectly conceived, is necessary, particularly in situations of real or potential monopoly where competitive factors cannot be relied upon to serve this function. Second, and antithetical to the first, regulatory agencies may be "captured" by those they seek to regulate, and are seen to operate instead to preserve the interests of a particular industry or group. Finally, political scientists often go beyond either of these motivations and say that regulatory bodies as institutions have ". . . seldom followed paths that would diminish their own importance, but instead promoted policies that would insure their institutional survival and growth."[5] Any or all of these motivations together or in tandem may be present in a particular situation.

Administrative Agencies

The Securities and Exchange Commission. The SEC was created by Congress in 1934 as an independent regulatory agency to administer the federal securities laws; the most important of these laws for the accounting profession are the *Securities Act of 1933* and the *Securities Exchange Act of 1934*. In these acts, the term "independent public accountant" is used to describe the individual (or firm) who is to perform the audit function in connection with the issuance and trading of securities in interstate commerce. Either certified public accountants or public accountants[6] may perform this function, the critical qualifications being only the possession of a current and valid state license, and independence in fact from the client/registrant.

The SEC is headed by a five-member commission, the members of which are appointed for five-year staggered terms by the President of the United States with the approval of the U.S. Senate. One member is designated by the President to be the Chairman. The Commission's staff includes accountants, lawyers, securities analysts, engineers, and other experts who review filings by companies issuing or wishing to issue securities to the public. Of most importance to CPAs, both those in public practice and those employed by companies whose financial statements are registered with the Commission, is the Office of Chief Accountant. The chief accountant is the principal expert advisor to the Commission on accounting and auditing matters. The Enforcement Division of the SEC, of course, also is important to the accounting profession, since the outcome of enforcement actions often is dispositive of appropriate auditing procedures and independence questions. Nevertheless, the day-to-day exchange of views on such matters with the Office of the Chief Accountant is of primary concern to the development of professional ethical and technical guidelines.

The SEC and the accounting profession have had an informal and somewhat symbiotic relationship ever since the Commission was formed in 1934. From the first, the SEC chose to leave standard setting with the private sector,[7] although it had the statutory authority to establish accounting principles and to prescribe the form of reports to be made under the securities acts. However, the SEC has concentrated upon disclosure requirements (rather than upon matters of accounting measurement) and frequently has moved into new ground (e.g., segment reporting) ahead of the profession. The principal SEC publication affecting accountants is Regulation S-X, which prescribes the general form and content of financial statements to be filed with the Commission, the necessary qualifications of accountants, and the technical requirements for the auditor's report.

Although, technically, the SEC has jurisdiction over only the financial and reporting practices of registrants, in practice its influence is felt by smaller, nonpublic entities as well. The accounting practices of public companies become the de facto standards applied by all companies, and the benchmark for judicial and professional judgments made by auditors and CPA employees.

In the very early years, the SEC's role was relatively passive, but became more active beginning in 1972, when John Burton took office as chief accountant. Dr. Burton's view of the Commission vis-à-vis the accounting profession was as a "creative irritant," prodding, pushing, and punishing where necessary. He did not believe that movement from the status quo otherwise would result. He stated that ". . . the accounting world has tended to exhibit comfortable conservative commitment to the status quo in the absence of external stimulus for change," and ". . . if there is to be innovation, the Securities and Exchange Commission must be the principal source. . . . "[8] It is fair to say that his philosophy prevailed during his tenure as the Commission's chief accountant.

The statutory basis for action by the SEC in the development of auditing standards and procedures is less clear than for accounting standards. SEC activities have been correspondingly less definitive, being limited largely to influencing the general content of the auditor's report on financial statements and to matters of auditor independence. While the Commission's input is less direct regarding auditing matters, its influence often is strong, particularly as exerted in connection with disciplinary proceedings under its Rule 2(e), which allows the SEC to suspend or disbar certain persons practicing before it. Strictly speaking, few if any of the major findings in such situations are the result of a Rule 2(e) *proceeding* (investigation followed by formal hearing before the full Commission leading to a judgment in a matter); rather, the auditor-respondent usually consents to the issuance of a document detailing the facts and the Commission's conclusions without admitting or denying any culpability in the case. This information at one time was issued in the form of an "Accounting Series Release" (ASR); now disciplinary publications are called "Accounting and Auditing Enforcement Releases" (AAERs).

Observations made by the SEC as a result of investigations and reports thereon generally are critical of audit performance in areas of concern, and thus caution auditors against potential deficiencies in similar circumstances in the future. In an early case, this led directly to the profession's subsequent adoption of the so-called "extended" auditing procedures of direct confirmation of customer accounts receivable and observation of physical inventories.[9]

State Boards of Accountancy -- Organization. All 50 states (plus Puerto Rico, Guam, the Virgin Islands, and the District of Columbia) have accountancy statutes, administered by the respective boards of accountancy.   Within their statutory authority, these boards set rules for entry into the profession, for appropriate (ethical) behavior during practice, and for disciplining miscreants -- including taking away the right to practice.   Collective action and coordination of the policies of the various state boards is facilitated by the National Association of State Boards of Accountancy (NASBA), a private nonprofit organization to which all belong.

Boards of accountancy are administrative agencies of state governments, and members generally are appointed by the governor.   The membership composition varies from state to state, but usually includes at least a majority who are CPAs, plus a representative of licensed public accountants, if any, and, more and more frequently, so-called public members, or nonlicensees to look after the public interest.

Generally, obtaining a CPA license requires a candidate (a) to have a college degree with a concentration in accounting and related subjects, (b) to pass the uniform CPA examination designed and graded by the AICPA, and (c) to fulfill certain experience (practice) requirements under the direction of a current licensee. Specific requirements vary from state to state.   However, there is a current trend in licensing looking to increasing the educational requirements for CPA candidates.   In particular, the AICPA has adopted a rule requiring 150 semester hours of college credit, including at least a baccalaureate degree, for membership after the year 2000. States likewise are beginning to establish this criterion for granting the CPA license; as of July 31, 1996, 36 jurisdictions have done so.[10] This requirement has profound implications for those colleges and universities with accountancy schools or departments. They must now arrange an appropriate curriculum to meet the new educational objectives.

The vigor with which discipline is exercised varies from state to state as attitudes (and budgetary resources) vary, but seems to be on the increase. More and more boards are adopting positive and aggressive enforcement programs, actively seeking out evidence of substandard performance rather than passively waiting for complaints to be filed. It does seem that the state accountancy boards take their public responsibilities seriously, and NASBA has in recent years been a strong force in the regulation of the profession.   NASBA and the AICPA have cooperated in developing a bill, the Uniform Accountancy Act, and all state boards are urged to work toward the adoption of its provisions as individual statutes are amended over time. Under a contract with the AICPA, NASBA's Examination Review Board annually investigates and evaluates the preparation, administration, and grading practices regarding the uniform CPA examination in order to provide assurances to the several state boards that the examination may be relied upon as part of the licensing process. Further, NASBA's CPA Examination Services arm (CPAES), under contracts with state boards, provides administration services at examination sites, thus relieving the boards of that responsibility. As of January, 1997, CPAES has such agreements with 24 jurisdictions, covering nearly one-half of all candidates in the U.S.[11]

Although the movement toward the adoption of the Uniform Accountancy Act is understandably slow, one proposal receiving considerable attention is that providing for more cross-jurisdictional mobility for CPAs. The various state accountancy statutes contain differing provisions for the circumstances enabling a candidate to sit for the CPA examination and take or retake portions thereof, and for educational and experience requirements. Thus a CPA fully qualified in one state may have considerable difficulty obtaining reciprocity and the right to practice in another. Given the expanding geographical scope of business and technological advances in communications and other fields, this is more and more seen to be an artificial barrier preventing the profession from following business enterprises across state (and international) lines. In February, 1997, a joint committee of NASBA and the AICPA (Joint Committee on Regulation of the Profession) agreed to promote the goal of portability of the CPA certificate through the concept of "substantial equivalency." Under this concept, "....a CPA's ability to practice temporarily in another state or to obtain reciprocity would be permitted if the CPA has a license from a state that utilizes CPA certification criteria that are essentially, or nearly equal to, those outlined in the AICPA/NASBA Uniform Accountancy Act."[12] At its January, 1997, meeting, the NASBA Board of Directors adopted the following definition of "substantial equivalence:"

> *Substantial equivalence is a determination by a Board of Accountancy that the education, examination and experience requirements contained in the Uniform Accountancy Act are comparable to, or exceed, the education, examination and experience requirements contained in their own jurisdiction's statutes and administrative rules.*

> *This determination supports the conclusion that for purposes of reciprocity, an applicant who has an active certificate as a certified public accountant from any jurisdiction and who has obtained from NASBA verification of compliance with the Uniform Accountancy Act's CPA certificate requirements shall be presumed to have qualifications substantially equivalent to his or her own jurisdiction's.[13]*

In the international field, the joint NASBA/AICPA International Qualifications Appraisal Board (IQAB) has been actively reviewing the qualifications of other countries' public accounting practitioners, and, in turn, the other countries have been doing the same with ours. This has resulted so far in signing reciprocal agreements with Australian and Canadian Chartered Accountants. Under the General

Agreement on Trade in Services (GATS), participating countries are encouraged to break down barriers to reciprocity and the free flow of professional services across international borders. One of the principal impediments to CPA reciprocity is the requirement in most non-U.S. jurisdictions that professionals should have practical experience under the supervision of a licensee for periods of time greater than most of our states require for U.S. CPAs. The latter must obtain such experience before being granted reciprocal practice rights abroad.[14]

State Boards of Accountancy -- Challenges. Challenges to the effectiveness of boards of accountancy have come either from public perceptions that they serve mainly to restrict entry into the profession (rather than to protect an unsuspecting and uninformed public from malpractice) or that they are inefficient as a mechanism to carry out legislative intent. The former charge has resulted in placing more and more boards under an umbrella state agency such as a Department of Consumer Affairs and in including nonaccountant public members on the board itself. The latter charge has resulted in so-called "sunset laws" in a number of states, under which all (or selected) state agencies expire under a predetermined schedule unless a pre-expiration review on behalf of the legislature determines that their operations are necessary and are being carried out efficiently.   Whether the expected benefits of either of these actions have been realized is problematical, and the evaluation of the results often depends on whether the evaluator was in favor of the change in the first place. There have been no reports of an accountancy board's being terminated as a result of sunset reviews or otherwise.

More fundamental to the future of the public accounting profession are challenges to the authority of the boards of accountancy to shape the very character of public practice. This has come in the form of attacks in some states on board rules such as those requiring CPAs who practice public accounting to do so in an entity registered with (and therefore regulated by) the board. In such cases, board rules usually also require that a registered entity must be owned in whole or in substantial part by licensees. Issues raised here include the right of free speech. Can a CPA holding a valid certificate be prevented from so informing others for whom he or she provides services ordinarily furnished by public accountants if the employer is not registered with the board of accountancy? Some would argue that this is improper because it incorrectly implies that the employer is registered with the board of accountancy and therefore is subject to board rules regarding qualifications to practice. Further, is the presence of nonlicensee ownership likely to interfere in critical ways with the objectivity and professional behavior of a licensee-employee?

The free speech question was considered by the U.S. Supreme Court in a case involving a Florida CPA who also is a lawyer, and who included both designations in telephone directory yellow pages and on business cards and law office stationery. The board of accountancy reprimanded the licensee for violation of the rule forbidding dual designations of this nature. Since neither designation was false or misleading, and the board of accountancy was unable to demonstrate that its restriction of commercial speech advanced a substantial state interest, the reprimand was overturned.[15] In similar cases in Florida and Texas, CPAs employed by American Express Tax and Business Services, Inc. (AETBS) were permitted to hold themselves out as such and to offer nonattest services, notwithstanding that their employer is not and cannot become registered with the boards of accountancy.

The cases dwelt in part on the free speech issue, because it was AETBS' contention that board regulations denied customers the ability to obtain truthful, nonmisleading and relevant information. The boards' response was that their regulations were proper ethical rules directed toward the protection of the public, and not a matter concerning restriction of speech. The *Ibanez* decision was dispositive in answering this question. More important, it was argued that the use of the CPA designation in offering services constituted "holding out" as a public accountant, and this was intended to trigger heightened regulatory attention, which, in the event, could not be applied in the case of a nonregistered entity. In Florida, the court made clear that its decision was narrowly crafted, saying that "...it was not holding that states cannot lawfully restrict unlicensed firms from using professional designations or performing the attest function."[16] In Texas, the decision raised another interesting question not presently resolved. The Texas court ruled that CPAs may prepare reports for customers of AETBS, but that in doing so they could not refer to AICPA standards. Since Texas Board rules require this reference under such circumstances, the rules and the court finding are again in conflict.[17]

The Courts and the Legislature

Litigation. A very important, but sometimes overlooked, element of regulation is the judicial system where final determinations are made regarding a public accountant's legal obligations and duties. Also, the U.S. Department of Justice and the Federal Trade Commission (FTC), both concerned with allegedly anticompetitive professional activities and rules, have directly and powerfully influenced the "commercial" behavior of CPAs. In 1990, the AICPA entered into a consent agreement with the FTC, providing, among other things, that the AICPA could not interfere with its members if they wished to accept contingent fees from nonattest clients, engage in advertising and solicitation, or to do a number of other things related to commercial (as opposed to ethical) behavior.

Regulation by court enforcement (or, in some cases, development of concepts) of the duties and responsibilities of independent public accountants has had a profound effect. Some pronouncements of the senior technical committees of the AICPA have been the direct result of particular cases. For example, Statement on Auditing Procedure No. 41 was written to address the issues in the Yale Express case,[18] in which the auditors were alleged improperly to have failed to timely disclose information making prior audited financial statements substantially false and misleading. Other topics, such as an auditor's responsibility to search for fraud, also have been dealt with directly in order to spell out in authoritative literature the expectations of those with expertise in a particular matter.[19]

Although conformity with standards adopted by professional bodies is not necessarily a bar to legal liability, particularly in a criminal case, it does provide a prima facie benchmark of appropriate performance. The desire to avoid litigation, with its potential for monetary and other penalties -- including adverse publicity -- has caused individual firms and the profession at large to devote enormous amounts of time and money to improving the quality of practice.

Legislative Intervention. The federal securities acts and state accountancy laws always carry with them the possibility of further legislative attention to their scope and coverage if they are not perceived as appropriately comprehensive to control the activities of independent public accountants. Oversight committees of the U.S. Congress from time to time have inquired into the administration of the securities acts for this purpose. The first such investigations of particular importance were made in the late 1970s by the so-called Metcalf and Moss Committees.[20]

These investigations resulted in some sharp criticisms of the SEC (for "failure to exercise its authority on accounting matters") and of the accounting profession for a number of alleged performance deficiencies. For example, the report of the Metcalf Committee stated (p. 2):

> *The subcommittee began its inquiry into accounting during the fall of 1975. The inquiry was initiated because of general concern over unexpected failures and wrongdoing by publicly owned corporations which were either undetected or not disclosed by the accounting firms acting as independent auditors for those corporations. The subcommittee also received complaints from academics and representatives of small accounting firms that the Nation's eight largest accounting firms--the "Big Eight" firms--were dominating the profession's private standard-setting organizations, and that such dominance was detrimental to the interests of both the general public and the accounting profession as a whole.*

Thus the inquiry encompassed both alleged professional deficiencies and alleged anticompetitive activities — the latter at least on the part of the largest firms.

A number of recommendations were made regarding steps to be taken to mitigate or eliminate such deficiencies. These legislative activities led directly to the establishment of the AICPA's Division for CPA Firms and other reforms that convinced Congress and the SEC that private actions were sufficient, at least for the time being, to offer some hope of addressing the problems perceived at the federal level. Even prior to this time, in 1972, the AICPA had sponsored the formation of the Financial Accounting Foundation (FAF), which, in turn, formed the Financial

Accounting Standards Board (FASB) to be the private sector's independent agency for the articulation of accounting principles (standards).

Congressman Moss actually introduced a bill (HR 13175) to establish a quasi-governmental agency, the National Organization of Securities and Exchange Commission Accountancy, for the purpose of controlling and disciplining public accountants auditing the financial statements of companies whose securities are registered with the SEC. The bill never was acted upon, but is an indication of possible action now or in the future if public accountants fail to meet the expectations of the legislature. Some prominent accountants, including Dr. Burton, former chief accountant for the SEC, have expressed approval of such an organization.

Inquiries into the accounting profession and reporting by publicly held companies have continued. Representative John Dingell, ranking minority member of the House Committee on Commerce, recently released a two-volume report on the accounting profession, prepared by the U.S. General Accounting Office in response to an earlier request from the Committee. Mr. Dingell commented on the report as follows:

> *Public confidence in the fairness and accuracy of financial reporting is critical to the effective functioning of our securities markets. I call upon the profession and the SEC to take prompt action on the issues raised by this excellent report. I would also urge timely and vigorous Congressional oversight hearings at the earliest possible time to assess the amount of progress made and the need for Congressional action to ensure the continued integrity of public accounting.*[21]

The mere indication of this continuing interest in the profession on the part of Congress is sufficient to cause the profession to examine and reexamine its practices and institutional structure for possible improvements. A major effort in this direction is under way. A joint committee of NASBA and AICPA members has been formed to study the issue of regulation in all its facets.

Professional Organizations

Since professionals provide services rather than products, relationships with clients are intensely personal, and depend for success upon the individual skills of the practitioner. Interposition of third parties into that relationship is difficult. However, although individual behavior is crucial to the delivery of professional services, institutional guidance and control of that behavior likewise is necessary. This provides professionals with the expectations of their peers, and with a framework for discipline in the case of failure to meet those expectations.

One of the attributes distinguishing a profession from an occupation or business is the element of self-regulation. This self-regulation is both personal and institutional, and is made necessary by another attribute of a profession -- that its practitioners are expert in a body of specialized knowledge not available to the laity.[22] Thus, a professional's peers, themselves possessing such knowledge, arguably are those best qualified to establish behavioral patterns and to discipline transgressors.

The AICPA

The AICPA now is the principal professional organization of certified public accountants in the United States. It and its predecessors (the first of which was organized in 1887) over the years have served as a forum for professional concerns, a focal point for self-regulation, and a mechanism for the development of professional ethics and standards of accounting and auditing practice. There are, of course, other accounting organizations in the United States -- for example, the American Accounting Association -- but the AICPA represents most public (i.e., professionally practicing) accountants, and in that capacity has been at the forefront of the turmoil of recent years.

Of the AICPA's over 331,000 individual members [1997] some 40 percent are in public practice; the balance are employed in business, education and government or were retired.[23] Although in the past members were only individuals (not firms), in 1977 a new Division for CPA Firms was established to provide for membership of practice units (firms). The Division includes two sections, one for firms having or expecting to acquire clients subject to the jurisdiction of the SEC (the SEC Practice Section, SECPS) and one for firms with privately held clients (The Private Companies Practice Section, PCPS). Many, but not all, firms have elected to become members of both Sections.

Important technical activities of the AICPA include issuing authoritative pronouncements on auditing standards, quality control standards, and accounting and review services; providing commentary to the Financial Accounting Standards Board (FASB), the SEC and others on accounting standards; and issuing and enforcing ethical rules and interpretations. The AICPA also devotes significant time and resources to preparing and grading the semiannual Uniform CPA Examination for all CPA candidates; maintaining relations with educators and with federal and state agencies and legislators; preparing and distributing courses for use in continuing professional education; and dealing with the practice problems of CPAs in areas outside the attest function such as management advisory services, income taxation and, most recently, personal financial planning.

The Division for CPA Firms

The formation of this Division in 1977 was one of the most important steps ever taken by the profession to implement its program of self-regulation. It was taken in recognition of the fact that public practice is carried out mostly by and in the names of firms, not individuals, and that some means was required to provide assurance regarding the quality of that practice. The effective operation of the Division has been critical in responding to the concerns expressed in congressional hearings in 1976 and 1977, and to subsequent SEC oversight activities. Given customary institutional inertia, the speed and decisiveness with which the Division and its activities were put into place were breathtaking.

Disciplinary control over member firms is exercised by (a) requiring adherence to stringent membership provisions, (b) checking adherence to those provisions and to prescribed internal quality control measures through a mandatory peer review every 3 years, and (c) in the SEC Section, by investigations conducted by the Quality Control Inquiry Committee (QCIC).

Each Section of the Division is administered by an Executive Committee, which establishes membership requirements and, where required, assesses disciplinary penalties. Each also has a Peer Review Committee (PRC), which prescribes standards and procedures for conducting such reviews, schedules and administers them, accepts review reports and makes them publicly available. In order to provide credible assurance that the public interest was being protected through these organizational changes, an autonomous Public Oversight Board (POB) was formed with membership comprising respected individuals with a broad record of distinguished public service to observe and report publicly on the activities of the SECPS.

Membership requirements of the two Sections are similar in that they require the annual reporting of a broad range of information about each member firm and the completion every 3 years of a peer review of the firm's system of quality control for its accounting and auditing practice. There is no reason why such reviews should not be extended to every facet of a firm's practice, but the more immediate objective and the one immediately addressed was to increase credibility for the attest function. Each section also requires members to adhere to the pronouncements of the AICPA's Quality Control Standards Committee.

Members of the SEC Section have certain additional requirements, including (a) rotating audit partners and making concurring partner reviews of reports on SEC engagements, (b) refraining from performing certain kinds of services, such as psychological testing, for SEC audit clients, and (c) reporting to a client's board or audit committee specified information such as nonaudit services and the fees therefor, and certain disagreements (if any) with management over accounting or auditing matters.

A troublesome fact in the past has been that not all practice units belonged to the Division, and therefore were not subjected to peer review. Some nonmembers have audited the financial statements of SEC registrants, and suggestions have been put forth looking to mandatory membership in the SEC Section for such firms.[24]   The new Code of Professional Conduct, approved in 1988, now will provide for some type of quality control (peer) review of AICPA members who perform attest services, even though their firms are not members of the Division. The professional impact of these reviews promises to be widespread and profound. The AICPA and the various state CPA societies are actively setting standards and organizing to handle the expected flood of quality control reviews to come. Some state boards of accountancy have similar quality control review programs.

Peer Review. As noted above, each Section has a Peer Review Committee and requires each member to undergo a peer review every 3 years. The objective in each case is for the reviewer to form an opinion whether (a) the reviewed firm's system of quality control meets the objectives of the AICPA's quality control standards and was being complied with during a specified period (usually a year) to provide the firm with reasonable assurance of conforming with professional standards, and (b) the reviewed firm otherwise was in conformity with the particular Section's membership requirements. The peer review reports are available publicly.

The peer review consists of two elements. First, a consideration of the quality controls in the nine functional areas of independence, assigning personnel to engagements, consultation, hiring, supervision, advancement, professional development, acceptance and continuance of clients, and inspection. Second, a review of selected professional engagements. These engagements are reviewed to test the output of the functional controls, i.e., to see whether there is reasonable assurance that performance in the field conforms to professional standards. Significant failures in either area can result in a recommendation by the PRC to the Executive Committee for the imposition of sanctions. Suggestions by reviewers to reviewed firms regarding deficiencies in controls or their application are furnished in a "letter of comments" at the conclusion of each engagement. These letters, together with the reviewed firm's responses, are filed with the Section's PRC, and are publicly available.

The SEC on numerous occasions has stated that the profession's efforts at self-regulation will turn on the success or failure of the peer review process. It therefore has been particularly sensitive to all of the performing and reporting details of the peer reviews and made numerous suggestions while those details were being worked out.

Quality Control Inquiry Committee.   The peer review process is not directed to seeking out "problem" engagements (although occasionally these surface and are dealt with on an ad hoc basis); rather the review is directed to evaluating the efficacy of the reviewed firm's system of quality control. Review teams, in fact, are instructed that an appropriate reason for eliminating a particular engagement from those selected for review is if litigation is pending or threatened. Further, the AICPA's ethics enforcement practice also is to defer investigations until litigation is complete. Although the legal rights of firms and individuals should not be prejudiced, the need also is pressing in the establishment of a credible posture of self-regulation to address what may be perceived as audit failures promptly and effectively. The QCIC was established within the SEC Section for this purpose.

The QCIC consists of nine partners or former partners of different member firms; its charge is to:

> . . . *make such investigation as it considers necessary to determine whether alleged audit failures indicate a possible need for corrective measures by the member firm involved or indicate that changes in generally accepted auditing standards or quality control standards need to be considered, and to recommend to the executive committee, sanctions when deemed important.*[25]

SEC Section members must report to the QCIC regarding certain litigation or publicly announced regulatory agency proceedings involving their firms in connection with an audit of the financial statements of a present or former SEC client, or alleged violations of federal securities laws in connection with nonaudit services to such clients.   Although the findings of the QCIC so far have been confidential, it reviews reported situations involving member firms and decides whether to dismiss, continue to monitor, or actively to investigate them. The SEC reviews summaries of closed cases.

Public Oversight Board. The POB was established as a part of the SEC Section of the Division for CPA firms to, among other things:[26]

> *Monitor and evaluate the regulatory and sanction activities of the peer review, and executive committees to assure their effectiveness.*

> *Determine that the peer review committee is ascertaining that firms are taking appropriate actions as a result of peer reviews.*

> *Conduct oversight of all other activities of the section.*

It has been very active and positive in carrying out this charge, delving into every aspect of the SEC Section's operations and making recommendations thereon, monitoring and participating (as an observer) in peer reviews, considering such matters as the propriety of nonaudit services by CPAs, and generally serving as a sounding board when critical issues regarding the self-regulatory process are being resolved. The Board publishes an annual report on its activities and those of the Section.

The POB, although funded by the Division, otherwise is completely independent, appointing its own members and being supported by its own staff. The board consists of a chair and four others with distinguished records of public service. Although the SEC has been reluctant to relax its perceived oversight functions over the activities of the profession, the POB indeed seems to have served to bring an appropriate degree of credibility to self-regulation, and to assure the Congress and others that self-regulation in this case at least has not represented self-interest.

Ethical Behavior and Self-Discipline

Self-regulation in the accounting profession requires the existence of an effective mechanism, first, for establishing and promulgating standards of behavior and, second, for exposing substandard performance and taking appropriate disciplinary action. Individual members of the AICPA are bound to follow the provisions of its Code of Professional Conduct.

Although failure to observe the Code is the only basis for discipline of individual members, it (the Code), among other things, requires compliance with professional technical standards. Thus, it reaches technical as well as behavioral violations. Enforcement is provided through the Professional Ethics Division, which establishes investigative files from various sources such as news reports and complaints against members. If litigation involving a particular issue is pending, and a member's legal rights might be prejudiced by an ethics proceeding, active investigation is suspended until litigation is terminated.

This policy has been criticized by those who believe quicker action is necessary to demonstrate the AICPA's dedication to self-discipline. One purpose of the QCIC (Quality Control Inquiry Committee described above) is to provide evidence of that quicker action. However, the effect of the litigation itself on the member's current and future behavior should not be overlooked; furthermore, as a practical matter, the AICPA cannot take any action that might prejudice personal rights, and appropriately would be prevented from doing so in any event by defense counsel.

Once litigation, if any, is completed an ethics investigation is initiated and carried forward with appropriate attention to due process. Initial determinations are made by staff and an assigned representative of a technical standards, independence, or behavioral standards subcommittee; final disposition may be made by the Trial Board unless the member agrees to a proposed disciplinary action at an intermediate point. Penalties may range from a private censure to suspension or expulsion from the AICPA, with attendant publicity for more serious actions.

Since state societies have similar ethical codes and take similar actions for ethical violations, the AICPA has entered into a Joint Ethics Enforcement Program (JEEP) with most of them. Under JEEP, investigations may be carried out either by the AICPA or by state ethics committee representatives. This program not only avoids the question of double jeopardy, that is, two investigations of the same event, but greatly expands the ability of the profession at large to pursue such actions. In the past, the AICPA has reserved to itself those cases perceived to be of broad or national interest.

State CPA Societies

Although not affiliated in a corporate sense, the various state CPA societies complement and reinforce the AICPA's activities at the state and local level; most AICPA members also hold membership in their respective state societies. With some generally unimportant differences, the AICPA and the state societies have in the past adhered to the same code of conduct. It is to be presumed that the latter in due time will conform their ethical codes to those adopted in 1988 by the AICPA. Some have done so already; others do so automatically where their bylaws so provide. Both the AICPA and the various state societies contribute heavily to the continuing professional educational and other activities of their members.

Setting Accounting Standards[27]

Prior to the turn of the century, accounting practices (it seems pretentious to refer to them at that stage as principles or standards) were developed, ad hoc, by business enterprises and their accountants to meet perceived business needs. These practices initially were influenced by Scottish or English accountants who came to this country following investments made by entrepreneurs from the United Kingdom. In no real sense, however, were they organized into anything resembling a theoretical pattern, and it is doubtful whether initiatives at the time went much beyond bookkeeping techniques.

Increased industrial and financial activity in the early twentieth century, and the growing necessity to report to shareholders and other third parties, began to put pressure on accountants to consider the theoretical underpinnings of their craft. Legislation relating to income taxes, banking, and antitrust matters had a definitive effect upon the accounting profession, which now was required to set methods to be used in handling legal reporting requirements. Early encounters between the accounting profession and emerging regulatory agencies over establishment of accounting principles clearly left the former in charge. "What the practicing accountants got was . . . disciplinary control over their profession . . . and rejection of a uniform system of accounting that would have reduced their control over accounting practices and thus reduced the value of their services."[28]

An interesting exception to the profession's domination of the standard setting process was the Interstate Commerce Commission, which promptly exercised its authority by establishing a uniform system of accounts for railroads. The rigidity and theoretical infirmities of this system have been cited as prime examples of the dangers of allowing accounting matters to be handled by a bureaucracy.[29]

The dominance of the private sector in the establishment of accounting standards continued, and was legitimized in 1938 with the issuance of ASR No. 4 by the SEC, wherein that body stated that financial statements would be considered misleading unless prepared in accordance with accounting principles having "substantial authoritative support." It was intended that such support be developed and expressed by professional accounting bodies, and the AICPA undertook that task. A Committee on Accounting Procedure (CAP) began to issue Accounting Research Bulletins (ARBs); these were pronouncements on specific accounting problems drawn to the attention of the Committee, and did not pretend to be issued within any coherent theoretical framework. Before its demise some 20 years later, the Committee issued 51 ARBs; a companion Committee on Terminology issued four bulletins on its topic.

In 1959, the Committee on Accounting Procedure was succeeded by the Accounting Principles Board (APB), which was expected, with the support of a new research capability, to develop a theoretical framework within which particular accounting problems could be addressed. In the event, the APB badly fumbled its early pronouncements and quickly was drawn into the same pattern as the old CAP of dealing with emerging problems without being able to integrate its decisions. The APB did not issue a pronouncement until 1962 (on depreciation) and suffered the indignity of having its second opinion (on the investment credit) in effect overturned scarcely a month after issuance by the SEC in ASR No. 96. This defeat was acknowledged a year later by the Board's fourth opinion, negating the position taken earlier in the second opinion.

Several studies were published by the research staff,[30] but were never incorporated into the APB's agenda. The APB issued 31 "Opinions" and 4 "Statements" (on broad accounting topics) before being supplanted, in turn, by the Financial Accounting Standards Board (FASB) in 1972. Since the FASB is an independent agency, the APB actually was supplanted in the AICPA by the Accounting Standards Executive Committee (AcSEC), which from time to time issues "Statements of Position" representing the members' consensus on a matter.

The Financial Accounting Standards Board

The apparent inability of the APB to deal with fundamental accounting issues, and growing criticism in the 1960s of accounting practices related to increasingly complex and innovative business practices, led the AICPA to initiate a study of the standard-setting process itself. At a conference to discuss this matter, the then president of the AICPA observed: "If we are not confronted with a crisis of confidence in the profession, we are at least faced with a serious challenge to our ability to perform a mission of grave public responsibility."[31]

Shortly thereafter, at the direction of the AICPA's Board of Directors, a study group of seven was appointed under the chairmanship of Francis M. Wheat, an attorney and former SEC Commissioner, to consider the whole issue of the institutional structure by which accounting principles should be determined. Included in the study group, in addition to the chairperson, were three CPA-practitioners, and investment banker, a corporate financial vice-president, and an accountant-academician. The recommendations of this group led to the formation of the Financial Accounting Foundation (FAF), an organization separate from all existing professional bodies, which appointed a full-time Financial Accounting Standards Board (FASB) to issue pronouncements on accounting standards,[32] and a Financial Accounting Standards Advisory Council to work with the FASB in an advisory capacity.

The structure and organization of these new entities has been the subject of much attention over the years, and changes have been made from time to time to accommodate developing views on the formulation of accounting standards. Most recently, at the urging of the SEC, the composition of the FAF has been altered to increase the number of "public" members from three to five, thus providing for more input from nonprofessionals.

The FASB was recognized as the appropriate authority for the formation of accounting standards by the AICPA, which designated Statements on Financial Accounting Standards (SFASs), as the FASB's pronouncements were called as being enforceable under the institute's Code of Ethics. The SEC followed in 1973 with ASR No. 150, reiterating that agency's support for private-sector accounting standard setting and noting that the FASB's standards would be recognized as representing "substantial authoritative support," while contrary principles would have no such support. Notwithstanding this reaffirmation of support for the private sector, upon rare occasions the SEC has overruled FASB pronouncements, with at least some diminishing effect on the prestige of the latter body.[33] It is clear that the ultimate authority in such matters lies with the SEC, should that agency choose to exercise it.

Although not untouched by controversy, the FASB has in the main been successful in its mission. It has issued a number of pronouncements on a variety of difficult questions, and the routine by which it does so (including exposure of proposed SFASs for comment and public hearings) is designed to provide for due process and input from reporting entities and financial statement users.

Public or Private Standard Setting?

Notwithstanding the private sector's continuing control over the determination of accounting principles, challenges to the current state of affairs continue to arise. These challenges seem to come from those who are understandably upset with accounting abuses, alleged cases of audit failures -- particularly where major corporate bankruptcies are involved -- and similar instances that are pointed to as representing an inability of private institutions to deal with matters of public interest. Criticism coming from federal legislative bodies focuses also on the asserted improper delegation of the SEC's authority in this area to private bodies such as the FASB.

The most important of such charges came during congressional hearing in 1976 and 1977 held by subcommittees under the direction of Senator Metcalf and Congressman Moss, and have resurfaced again in calls for subcommittee investigation by Congressman Dingell. The issue of public versus private determination of accounting principles was addressed directly in the Wheat Report. Reasons cited for public control included the belief that (a) accounting matters are too important to be left to a body not responsible to Congress, (b) that conflicts of interest (between standard setters and reporting entities) can only be avoided through the interposition of governmental agencies, and (c) that accounting principles have the effect of law and should only be established by bodies charged with responsibility in this area and following all procedures prescribed for rule making.

The report, however, came solidly down on the side of continuing standard setting in the private sector. Principal reasons for this decision were the fear that (a) otherwise accounting principles would be set primarily to accomplish political goals, (b) rules would be inflexible and unresponsive to emerging problems, (c) such a move would sap the vitality of the profession, and (d) the focus of the rule making body necessarily would be on reporting by public companies and to governmental agencies, whereas the true domain of accounting is significantly broader.

Summary

This chapter has included a discussion of the regulation of the profession of public accountancy by federal and state administrative agencies, and the bases for such regulation. Licensing of CPAs and disciplinary actions by state boards of accountancy against practitioners violating state ethical or other rules are important in this respect, although the SEC has exercised an influential role in developing proper professional standards of accounting and auditing. Further, Congress has on several occasions conducted investigations of the profession that have resulted in profound changes in the structure of professional organizations. Finally, the courts have exercised their function by defining professional duties and responsibilities in particular circumstances.

In this chapter we also have considered the various self-regulatory (private sector) means by which the accounting profession is regulated and its activities directed to best serve the public interest. The place of professional organizations and their rules of conduct in this process was described. The AICPA and its Division for CPA firms is an important element here, what with triannual peer reviews, the POB and the QCIC in place to add credibility to the process. Finally, the topic of the appropriate mechanism for the development of accounting standards was considered. This responsibility so far has rested with the private sector (now in the form of the FASB), although there are those who believe that this responsibility is misplaced and should ultimately rest with a governmental or quasi-governmental agency of some description. This discussion is likely to continue.

Discussion Questions

1. What do we mean when we talk about "regulation?"

2. Has the accounting profession been forced into changing its behavior by outside forces (reactive) rather than taking the initiative in doing so (proactive)? Is this a good or a bad thing?

3. Why do even members of otherwise autonomous occupations often actively seek governmental intervention in their activities?

4. What are the three, often conflicting, concepts driving regulatory agencies? What are the implications of this to the accounting profession? Discuss how each of these may be reflected in the activities of the SEC, of the various state boards of accountancy.

5. What is the relationship between the accounting profession and the SEC?

6. Why has the SEC been so interested in the structure and operation of the SEC Section of the AICPA, and particularly in the peer review process?

7. Why should private companies, not registered with the SEC, be concerned with the activities of the SEC in accounting and auditing matters?

8. How does the SEC's authority in the development of accounting principles differ from its authority in the development of auditing practices?

9. Discuss the implications of the varying requirements for attaining the CPA designation among the states. Why is it important to resolve these differences? What proposals have been offered to do so? Why is it important to consider the implications of these matters in international trade and commerce?

10. Does your state board have a "positive enforcement" program? How does it work?

11. Review the accountancy act and the rules of the board of accountancy in your state. Attend and report on a meeting of the board or its disciplinary committee.

12. Consider the challenges to the authority of the several state boards of accountancy, and the implications thereof to the future of the profession.

13. Should CPAs be allowed to practice and hold themselves out to be such in an organization not in itself licensed by a board of accountancy? Do you distinguish between attest and nonattest function in this regard?

14. Is there a difference between regulation of the technical aspects of a profession and its commercial aspects? Should there be? What effect has the consent agreement between the AICPA and the FTC had on the practice of public accountancy?

15. Describe the organizational structure of the AICPA, the Division for CPA firms, and the place of the peer reviews in the self-regulatory process.

16. What are the two sections of the AICPA's Division for CPA Firms, and how do they differ?

17. Why were the AICPA's Committee on Accounting Procedures and its successor, the Accounting Principles Board, ultimately replaced by the Financial Accounting Standards Board?

18. Outline the principal arguments for and against setting accounting and auditing standards in the private sector. What changes, if any, would you make to this process as it now exists?

Endnotes

[1] Buckley, John W., and Weston, J. Fred, eds., *Regulation and the Accounting Profession* (Belmont, Calif.: Lifetime Learning Publications, 1980), editorial comment in Chapter V, 197.

[2] Objective of the establishment of the Massachusetts Medical Society in 1781. Quoted by Starr, Paul, *The Transformation of American Medicine*, Basic Books, Inc., New York, 1982.

[3] Cannon, James G., Presentation at Annual Banquet, *Twenty-First Anniversary Year Book*, The American Association of Public Accountants, New York, 1908, 120.

[4] See, for example, McCraw, Thomas K., "Regulation in America: A Review Article," *The Development of SEC Accounting*, Gary John Previts, ed. (Reading, Mass.: Addison-Wesley Publishing Company, 1981).

[5] Ibid., 268.

[6] In most states, public accountants (PAs) are accounting practitioners who are licensed as such, but who have not otherwise complied with the full educational and examination requirements established for CPAs. This class of individuals usually consists of those who were in practice at the time accountancy acts were adopted and who were "grandfathered" in with the expectation that no further PA licenses would thereafter be issued. In a few states, however, a two-tier system prevails in which the PA license is a license to practice granted to CPAs after they have completed specified experience or other requirements not initially necessary for the issuance of the CPA certificate.

[7] ASR No. 4 (April 25, 1938) expressed the SEC's view that financial statements will be considered misleading unless they are prepared using accounting principles having "substantial authoritative support." A reference to ASR No. 4 in ASR No. 96 (January 10, 1963) stated that "this policy [was] ... intended to support the development of accounting principles and methods of presentation by the profession. . . ."

[8] Burton, John C., "The SEC and Financial Reporting: The Sand in the Oyster," *University of Florida Accounting Series, Number 11*, University Press of Florida, 1980.

[9] ASR No. 19, *In the Matter of McKesson & Robbins, Inc.*, December 5 ,1940.

[10] American Institute of Certified Public Accountants, 1995-1996 Annual Report, p.5.

[11] NASBA *State Board Report,* January, 1997.

[12] NASBA/AICPA *news release*, February 11, 1997.

[13] NASBA *State Board Report*, February, 1997.

[14] Ibid., December, 1996.

[15] *Ibanez* v. *Florida Dept. of Business and Professional Regulation, Board of Accountancy,* 114 S.Ct. 2084 (1994).

[16] AICPA, *The CPA Letter*, January/February, 1996.

[17] Arizona State Board of Accountancy, *ASBA Update,* Fall/Winter, 1996.

[18] *Fischer* v. *Kletz*, U.S. District Court for the Southern District of New York, 266 F. Supp. 180 (1967).

[19] Statement on Auditing Standards No. 82, *Consideration of Fraud in a Financial Statement Audit,* AICPA, effective for audits of financial statements ending on or after December 15, 1977.

[20] *Improving the Accountability of Publicly Owned Corporations and Their Auditors,* Report of the Subcommittee on Reports, Accounting and Management of the Committee on Governmental Affairs, United States Senate, Lee Metcalf, Montana, Chairman, (Washington, D.C.: U.S. Government Printing Office, 1977). *Federal Regulation and Regulatory Reform,* Report by the Subcommittee on Oversight and Investigations of the Committee on Interstate and Foreign Commerce, House of Representatives, John E. Moss, California, Chairman, (Washington, D.C.:U.S. Government Printing Office, 1976).

[21] Commerce Committee Democrats, Congressman John D. Dingell, Ranking Member, news release September 24, 1966.

[22] Formal definitions of a "profession" focus on these and certain other characteristics. For an early and careful consideration of such matters, see Roy, Robert H., and MacNeill, James H., *Horizons for a Profession* (New York: AICPA, 1967), Chapter 3.

[23] AICPA *1995-1996 Annual Report.*

[24] In February 1990, the AICPA membership adopted a by-law change requiring that a member practicing with a Firm with one or more SEC clients may retain that membership only if the firm is a member of the SEC Practice Section (and the firm therefore becomes subject to the triennial peer review membership requirement).

[25] *SECPS Manual,* (New York: AICPA, 1986), 7-6.

[26] Ibid, 1-14.

[27] The terms **principles** and **standards** are used more or less interchangeably today. "Standards" connotes perhaps a somewhat higher level of authority, but the auditor's standard report still refers to conformity with generally accepted accounting "principles."

[28] Chatov, Robert, *Corporate Financial Reporting: Public or Private Control?* (New York: The Free Press, 1975); 50.

[29] See, for example, Spacek, Leonard, *A Search for Fairness in Financial Reporting to the Public,* (Chicago: Arthur Andersen & Co., 1969): 22-23.

[30] *E.g.,* Moonitz, Maurice, *The Basic Postulates of Accounting,* Accounting Research Study No. 1, (New York: AICPA, 1962).

[31] Report of the Study on Establishment of Accounting Principles, *Establishing Financial Accounting Standards,* (New York: AICPA, 1972): 3. (Usually referred to as the "Wheat Report," after the chairman of the group.)

[32] A companion and similar agency, the Governmental Accounting Standards Board (GASB), began operating in 1984, also under the aegis of the Financial Accounting Foundation. The GASB establishes financial accounting and reporting standards only for state and local governmental units.

[33] For example, in 1978 the SEC issued ASR No. 253 (financial and reporting requirements for oil and gas producing activities) directly overturning SFAS No. 19,

which had previously been developed by the FASB at the SEC's request to meet a congressional mandate to develop standards in this area.

CHAPTER 6

Personal and
Professional
Responsibilities

*The essence of a profession in the traditional sense is
found in the grant by society of a special franchise in
return for which the practitioners of that profession
accept responsibilities to provide a degree of
regulation and enforcement through expert advice
and persuasion, thereby relieving society of the burden
of providing that control by other means.*[1]

Robert K. Mautz

Introduction

Various efforts have been made from time to time to describe a "profession" and to
distinguish it from other forms of occupation by citing such characteristics as
education at higher levels and licensure by a governmental agency. Although
differing in some particulars, all of these descriptions include reference to a system
of self-regulation based in a code of ethics (conduct). This undertaking of self-
regulation by a profession is in exchange for the grant by society of a franchise, or
exclusive right to practice in a particular area of expertise. It is the hallmark of
professionalism.

The focus of attention on ethical behavior and professional self-constraints
regarding this matter in the past has been primarily on the responsibilities of those in

the practice of **public** accounting. Nevertheless, the realization has been growing in recent years that those CPAs in academe, corporate practice, government, and other occupations necessarily cannot sever their ties to the "CPA Profession" in a larger sense. They still are professionals and cannot therefore shed their training, their ideals, and their responsibilities merely because of their immediate occupational calling. The AICPA has recognized this in the introduction to its Code of Professional Conduct:

> *The Code of Professional Conduct was adopted by the membership to provide guidance and rules to all members -- those in public practice, in industry, in government, and in education -- in the performance of their professional responsibilities.*[2]

Some have interpreted the responsibilities imposed by professional behavioral norms as overriding other considerations, such as a perceived loyalty to a corporate employer, for example. The resolution of seemingly contradictory requirements in such circumstances leads to painful choices, often with career-choice and legal implications.

Whether CPAs are practicing public accounting or carrying out professional duties in another arena, three fundamental forces influence and direct their behavior -- laws (which may be ambiguous, but which express the will of society regarding a particular class of persons), institutions (self-regulating organizations of professionals), and personal integrity. Since one of the principal attributes of a professional's relationship with a client or an employer is that it is above all an individual one, of all three forces, personal integrity is the most fundamental and the most important. Professionals are nothing without personal integrity, without an inner commitment to a course of action in which conflicts are resolved in accordance with the best and highest traditions of their calling -- and their own conscience. In a very real sense, professionals hold the welfare of others hostage to their own knowledge and good judgment; this is a fiduciary relationship.[3] It is in the individual that the focus of training, expertise, and judgment come to bear on a professional problem.

> *Integrity requires a member to be, among other things, honest and candid within the constraints of client confidentiality. Service and the public trust should not be subordinated to personal gain and advantage. Integrity can accommodate the inadvertent error and the honest difference of opinion; it cannot accommodate deceit or subordination of principle.*[4]

Laws enacted by society regulate professionals and convey to them the franchise of practice; they provide the social contract by which the professional is entrusted with the public weal in a particular area of expertise. But practice is by a person, an individual representing one's profession, and it is on that individual that the burden falls to carry out the mission. Laws can circumscribe behavior and punish transgressions, but when decisions are made, individuals make them — and their clients or employers suffer the consequences or reap the benefits.

Self-regulatory institutions and their ethical rules assist the individual in deciding the best course of action in particular circumstances. These rules are developed by peer groups from the collective experience of the profession and are always being modified as that experience accumulates. They provide a supporting framework for individual decisionmaking, but such institutions cannot and do not participate at that critical juncture when the decision is made and the die is cast. Although constituting a necessary support system, the very existence of institutional codes of conduct, or rules, may for some provide at once minimum *and* maximum standards of behavior. Ideally, the professional should strive always to exceed prescribed norms and live up to the spirit, not just the words, of ethical codes. Not all do so. The danger was described by columnist Edwin Yoder thus:

> *Most of the important safeguards of propriety, as of liberty, depend on unwritten laws, enforced by a sense of shame, to which principled people adhere. Ethics laws as a genre add little of value to the unwritten rules, and may well undercut them with people who think that if you're not in jail or on the way there you're clean.*[5]

Individuals fail in their duties to clients and others if they fail to acquire **and maintain** those skills necessary to accomplish that which they undertake, that in which they claim to be expert. A species of fraud is committed if that expert knowledge and skill are, in fact, missing. Although a CPA license granted under state law conveys some indication of at least a basic knowledge in the field, and membership in a professional organization conveys some recognition of collective influences on behavior, only professionals themselves can judge their ability to perform a particular task. This means that true professionals not only recognize and have confidence in their skills, but, just as important, recognize and will not undertake those tasks for which they do not have the necessary skills. Schools can train, and professional bodies and state boards can license and discipline miscreants, but only the individual can control the unknown ground between apparent qualifications and disaster. Limitations unrecognized, indeed, are prescriptions for disaster.

This personal responsibility has ramifications in several areas, not the least of which is the one of continuing professional education. Who wants to be treated by a physician who has not yet heard of antibiotics? It also leads to the necessity for participation in professional society activities, exposing individuals to the mainstream of developments in their specialty (or enabling them to acquire a new one). State licensing boards recognize this responsibility by adopting continuing professional education requirements as a prerequisite to periodic relicensing. Even here, however, the trappings (e.g., completion of specified training courses) do not of themselves evidence necessary skills. Judgments as to competency still must be made by the professional.

Individuals are aided in their development of competence and skill by the growing practice of specialization in particular areas within a discipline such as accountancy.   Clients and/or employers of CPAs also can more easily and confidently identify specialists if some method (such as "board certification" in the medical field) is available to them for this purpose. Specialization and scope of practice are related here to the professional's personal and individual responsibility to offer those services, and only those services, where a representation of expertise is justified.

This chapter discusses the process by which individuals are exposed to and trained in the ethical concepts essential to the practice of public accounting -- primarily through employment by professionals who serve a support and instructional role. Also considered is the role of the AICPA's Code of Professional Conduct. These concepts carry over as CPAs move from public accounting to other occupations. The murky implications of breaking ethical imperatives, such as the requirement for confidentiality in the face of perceived "higher" responsibilities to society at large, are discussed. In every case, however, the individual must understand and apply institutional ethical rules regarding practice as a CPA, recognizing that these rules are but minimums and that minimum behavior may not be an acceptable objective. The development of a personal approach to problem solving is suggested herein, and is presented together with an illustration of the intractable nature of problems the professional must solve in the face of uncertainty and the competing claims of parties at interest. Professional "failure" is defined and discussed, as well as the methods by which the profession and society deal with it.

The Process

Individuals do not spring full-blown into professional life, ready at once to take on all challenges in a discipline such as public accounting. They first acquire some basic technical knowledge through formal training, and perhaps some hint of appropriate behavior in varying circumstances from academic role models or others. Ethical imperatives, of course, come from many sources, not the least of which may be family or religious codes and habits. These carry over into professional life and enhance an individual's ability to function with integrity and self-confidence.

But the patina of self-confidence and its justification of underlying skill takes time to acquire. Experience and the guidance of mature professionals are the next essentials. These are acquired in various ways, depending upon whether the aspirant is employed by an individual or a firm, enters into practice alone (if state laws permit), or otherwise is occupied prior to actually embarking on a professional career.

The Firm

A professional firm furnishes the initial exposure of an aspirant to the working environment, whether that association is with a large firm of CPAs or with an experienced sole practitioner. The scope and range of services to clients may differ markedly across the spectrum of practices, but the ethical milieu ideally is the same. In any case, such a milieu comprises written and unwritten rules of conduct, attitudes toward clients, dedication to the profession itself, and most of all, encouragement in the development of a sense of individual responsibility. Firms have the duty to provide this support, and aspiring CPAs have a right to demand it. The extent to which these conditions are present in employment outside of public accounting firms varies tremendously, but the necessary environment of dedication to responsible and ethical behavior is the same.[6] A pattern of "professional" behavior should be the norm whatever the actual situation in which CPAs find themselves.

This early phase of a CPA's development usually comes under the rubric "on-the-job-training," and indeed that is what it is. But the process is more subtle than just instructions from superiors regarding how to do this or that. It comprises at once social control and social support -- "social" in the sense of an environment steeped in the culture of practice. It is during this period that aspirants are judged and their careers shaped, technically and ethically.

The necessity for, and the extent of "experience" that should be required for the CPA license has been the subject of much debate, probably linked to an underlying suspicion that such a requirement seeks only to limit access to the profession, not to assure quality in its performance. The essential element here being discussed, "integrity," or an individual's inner set of ethical guidelines, most likely is difficult to develop outside of exposure to supervisors who are sensitive to and take positive steps to reinforce appropriate behavior in a professional setting -- in a word, experience.

The supervisor, charged with guiding the development of a subordinate, has a delicate and sensitive task. Whether explicitly recognized as such or not, this task is essentially threefold: technical, ethical, and supportive.[7] First, the aspirant must be judged regarding technical knowledge, and that knowledge enhanced and furthered in a working environment. Second, the aspirant must be judged regarding ethical conformity to a professional norm on at least two levels-institutional (ethical rules) and the personal standards of the superior. Lastly, since failure of the aspirant to measure up to either technical or ethical norms in some degree is to be expected from time to time, the supervisor must evaluate the seriousness of deviations, correct errors (rescue the client or customer from the novice), and support the development of self-confidence in the face of momentary failure.

Of course, ultimate failure on the part of some is a necessity if professional practice properly is to be limited to the qualified. An essential part of the judgment exercised by superiors is whether a particular aspirant should succeed, or whether a budding career should be terminated. This part of the process is ill-defined, and the results ragged as struggling aspirants either leave the profession or find themselves lacking in its practice. If the screening process here described is ineffective, this burden falls on the profession's self-regulatory mechanisms, the states' licensing process, or corporate disciplinary activities as professional failures are surfaced and handled. Public accounting, as all professions in recent years, has been subject to critical attack for alleged lack of vigor in disciplining practitioners.

Technical errors are always going to be made. If they are made by aspirants performing conscientiously, but in areas where their skills fall short of the task, the lapses usually can be overlooked -- particularly if they are acknowledged, surfaced, and nonrecurring. Furthermore, technical errors offer an opportunity for more experienced professionals to school the aspirant. Inability to acquire higher technical skills is and should be a limiting factor in a career. On the other hand, moral "errors," violations of written or implicit canons of behavior, are more serious since they are an indication of inability to establish proper priorities -- to the ultimate degradation of the fiduciary relationship between professional and client or professional and employer. A concealment of a technical error, an inability to work through ambiguities in relationships and duties, or a refusal on the part of an aspirant to acknowledge written or unwritten codes of behavior, are fatal to a professional career and should be treated as such.

The Individual

The relationship between a professional and a client or a professional and an employer can be characterized as a fiduciary one, since the client's or employer's affairs are entrusted to the skill of the professional in a specialized field of knowledge. Therefore, the individual practitioner must develop an inner sense of the meaning and implications of such a relationship. This development initially is aided and guided by others, but as we have seen, the final responsibility lies with the individual; it can neither be forced into being nor shared in its application. In another context, Thomas P. Holland has suggested five essential ingredients of a fiduciary relationship: honesty, competence, diligence, integrity, and discretion.[8] These certainly correspond in intent if not in specifics to ingredients desired by CPAs in their relationships with clients and employers.

Listings of ethical rules and personal attributes and qualities that should be developed by practitioners cannot, of course, provide the professional with clear guidelines in the inevitably murky and ambiguous situations found in the "real world." CPAs, as other professionals, usually must make decisions where knowledge of circumstances may be incomplete, and where uncertainties exist regarding outcomes. Yet, decisions **must** be made; the question is how to do so in a responsible manner.

Many suggestions have been offered for guidance in such matters, but most include some structure for isolating problems and weighing alternative solutions. It is worth repeating that such structures do not **solve** problems; they only provide some coherence to a consideration of them, and they may be used consciously or unconsciously to assist the professional in doing what in the final analysis only the professional can do -- make the final decision.

It is important to be as sure of the facts as is possible. It was the financier/philosopher, Bernard M. Baruch, who is reputed to have offered the thought that every man has a right to his opinion, but no man has a right to be wrong in his facts. This is particularly relevant to the process of deciding ethical questions. Then, those with an interest in the outcome should be identified; these often are referred to as "stakeholders," and usually include the individual professional and/or his or her firm or employer as well as stockholders, creditors, regulatory agencies, and perhaps the general public.

Alternative courses of action next can be specified, and consideration given to the possible effects of each alternative on each concerned party. Ethical concerns and values such as "fairness," "rights," "legality," "conformity with technical requirements," and "protection against financial harm" must be weighed in making the final decision, and it is likely that tradeoffs will be necessary in balancing the concerns of all stakeholders. This is usually what is referred to as a "zero sum" calculation; benefits to one may well result in damages others. It is also a process of setting up a value framework -- *value* being defined as that which is perceived as good.[9]

Whether the views of constituencies should be solicited ("participatory" decision making) may depend upon the nature of the problem posed. It is likely impracticable in most cases to do so, particularly since ultimate decisions are the purview of professionals, in light of their trusteeship relationship with a client. Further, most decisions in a professional -- as opposed to a commercial or social -- environment are not properly subject to a vote, but in any event depend on the exercise of the professional's skill and judgment. Solutions preferred by interested parties (e.g., a client) enter into the professional's consideration if offered, but cannot be decisive if objectivity is to be maintained.

The last and most important question deals with priorities, and here the inner integrity of the true professional is most critical. What factors are important in a decision, and which of the CPA's constituents should come first in assessing the benefits and/or penalties attaching to a particular course of action? Theoretically, in a purely commercial setting, cost/benefit calculations could be made on the assumption that the maximization of gain is of most benefit to the party most at interest -- the business entity. More realistically, the collateral effects of any decision on other parties may be just as or more important, and the individual professional must be able to assess and assign priorities to these effects. Benefits to one party ordinarily will involve costs to another. The individual's value system -- personal and professional -- then is critical to this process.

It is impracticable to explore all the ramifications of this thought, but, for example, should a client be permitted to follow a marginal (but currently acceptable) accounting practice that will maximize share prices, thus benefiting current officers and shareholders? More difficult, does the CPA have a professional responsibility to inform the client of the existence of this option even if then arguing against its use? Should the practice be allowed in the face of a perceived trend leading to the possible future withdrawal of professional approval for the practice? Do the interests of the investing public at large, and particularly potential investors who may be affected by such possible changes, weigh heavily or lightly? The answers to these questions cannot be supplied in the abstract, but the dilemmas they so obviously pose are illustrative of the focus on the professional public accountant and the value system that the individual necessarily must have or develop.

Professional Failure, Institutions and the Law

Some attention needs to be given to enforcement mechanisms that serve to protect society in the event of failure by a practitioner. First there is the question of defining a "failure," next of surfacing it, and finally of the appropriate action to be taken and by whom. These issues arise only because professionals are human, and fallible as a consequence. A principal criterion of professionalism is expertise in a specialized field of knowledge; but this does not either imply or guarantee perfection. Hence, except for breaking legal minimums, some perhaps ill-defined higher standard is imposed, ad hoc, the breach of which should lead to action against the professional.

Describing professional failure in any definitive sense is difficult. Professional rules, laws of the state, and institutional standards of behavior all should be viewed as minimums that the practitioner ideally should strive to exceed in every case. Violations of such higher standards may not in the event be punishable, except insofar as they lead to lack of success through lack of excellence, rather than to any reprehensible technical or moral aberration that causes damage.

There is room for honest differences of opinion on technical matters, areas in which there is no clear consensus, and problems arising from interpretation, analysis, and opinion. The fact that experts disagree, therefore, is hardly cause for action. The fact that damage to a client or others does or does not result likewise is not a determinant of a professional failure, but may be taken into account with other factors in deciding on disciplinary action. A somewhat vague and perhaps unsatisfactory reference to "standards of the profession" may be the best measure to be applied in defining failure, and indeed this is in effect the standard applied in the event of litigation. Experts (other professionals) usually are called upon to establish those standards in particular circumstances.

Although "damage" may not be an indication of failure, it usually is the method by which possible failure is brought to the surface. A client complains, an investor is injured, or other parties allege improper performance by a CPA, and an inquiry is launched or a lawsuit is filed. Other less visible means are employed as some state boards of accountancy launch positive enforcement programs, routinely investigating and monitoring the performance of licensees. The peer review concept applied by the AICPA and other professional societies is another evidence of this activity.

An interesting and, some say, perverse development is beginning to arise where professional bodies themselves attempt to respond to outside criticism by setting and enforcing standards. In May, 1988, the U.S. Supreme Court ruled that hospital peer review committees are not immune from antitrust suits brought by doctors they penalize, and reinstated a lower court antitrust award. In this case a physician claimed the other doctors acted against him because he was a competitor.[10] This cannot but exert some chilling effect on self-regulatory efforts in any profession.

Once defined, surfaced, and investigated, professional failures call for action if the public interest is to be protected. This can take many forms and result in a range of penalties, from a simple cautionary warning by a professional society or a state agency, to loss of license to practice and/or damage awards as a result of legal action by an injured plaintiff. Voluntary actions by professional societies may be followed by more severe penalties in any event, as the knowledge and implications of failures become known.

AICPA Code of Professional Conduct

An entirely rewritten Code of Professional Conduct was adopted by the AICPA on January 12, 1988, and most recently was amended January 14, 1992. This Code consists of two sections, one setting forth "principles," or behavioral objectives, the other setting forth "rules," or enforceable behavioral norms. The latter serve to govern the performance of professional services, and provide a basis for disciplinary action where necessary. These rules include those requiring compliance with professional technical standards (e.g., Rule 202, "Compliance with Standards"), and therefore a violation of a technical standard is, by definition, also an ethical violation.

Other guidance is provided to CPAs by ethical "Interpretations" and "Rulings." The former are issued by the professional ethics division's executive committee to amplify and explain particular rules and their implications. The latter are formal rulings made by the executive committee to determine the application of particular rules to particular factual circumstances. Members who depart from rulings in similar circumstances may be required to justify such departure. Both interpretations and rulings are made only after exposure to state societies, state boards of accountancy, practice units, and other interested parties. The Code emphasizes the essentially personal nature of institutional ethical constraints, stating: "Compliance with the Code of Professional Conduct, as with all standards in an open society, depends primarily on members' understanding and voluntary actions...[and only secondarily on peer pressure and disciplinary action]"[11]

Section I of the Code, setting forth the principles of ethical behavior, deals with the responsibilities of professionals to (1) exercise appropriate judgment in their activities, (2) serve the public interest, (3) maintain a high sense of integrity, (4) preserve objectivity and freedom from conflict of interest, (5) exercise due care in the performance of professional duties, and (6) observe the principles of the Code in determining the nature and scope of services provided clients. Section II of the Code, setting forth enforceable rules of conduct, covers matters of (1) independence, (2) integrity and objectivity, (3) general standards (of behavior), (4) compliance with promulgated (technical) standards, (5) compliance with accounting principles, (6) confidential client information, (7) contingent fees, (8) acts discreditable (to the profession), (9) advertising, (10) commissions and referral fees, and (11) the form and organization (of practice). The Code in its entirety is included as Appendix A to this volume.

From the beginning, the profession's codes of conduct have dealt with what might be classified as "ethical," i.e., moral, matters, as well as with what might be classified as "commercial," i.e., materialistic, matters. The two long were thought to be inseparable, since such commercial activities as advertising and bidding were believed to impinge on the professional's commitment to provide quality service regardless of economic gain or loss, and on the client's need to select a CPA on the basis of that quality, not on the basis of price. The basic issue is one of assuring that the client's welfare -- both economic and substantive -- is best served. Is the selection of a professional advisor on the basis of price, for example, preferable to the selection based on quality of service? If the latter, how is the client to measure "quality," and to be protected against price gouging by unscrupulous practitioners?

For many years, the accounting profession, as with other professions, was believed to be exempt from antitrust (anticompetitive) constraints. Sometime in the late 1960s or early 1970s, however, the Federal Trade Commission (FTC) began to consider whether such laws should not also apply to the professions, and began to pressure for the relaxation of professional ethical rules against allegedly anticompetitive activities. Then, in 1975, the U.S. Supreme Court determined that the provisions of the federal antitrust laws applied as well to professions. In the *Goldfarb* case, the Virginia State Bar Association's minimum fee schedule was held to be illegal price fixing, in violation of the Sherman Act.[12] The FTC promptly then proceeded to move against ethical constraints imposed by professional bodies that were perceived to inhibit free and open competition in the marketplace.

After extended negotiations, in 1990 the AICPA entered into a consent agreement with the FTC, which thereupon issued a complaint and order[13] requiring modification or repeal of a number of ethical rules. In particular, the AICPA agreed not to interfere if its members wished to accept contingent fees from nonattest clients, accept disclosed commissions for products or services provided by third parties to nonattest clients, engage in advertising or solicitation, make or accept disclosed referral fees, or use trade names. Further, the AICPA cannot discourage or prevent, among others, such practices as self-laudatory or testimonial advertising, advertising that some might consider "undignified," or in-person solicitation of prospective clients. However, it may issue ethical guidelines prohibiting solicitation, advertising, or the use of trade names reasonably believed to be false or deceptive.

Ethical Dilemmas

Although, broadly speaking, any situation involving choices among competing interests could be characterized as an "ethical dilemma," the focus here is upon two of the traditional ethical constraints binding CPAs, and the pressures being brought upon them by today's rapidly changing financial and economic environment. These are the rules dealing with the concepts of independence and confidentiality. An extraordinary expansion of the number and types of services provided by those practicing public accounting has been taking place in response to worldwide demands for auditing, accounting, tax, and consulting skills of all kinds. This has created unprecedented and unanticipated strains upon rules adopted in a simpler time. Another important factor here is that, prior to the adoption of the present Code of Professional Conduct in 1988 (as amended in 1992), the principal ethical concerns were with CPAs in public practice, and most particularly with those performing the attest function. Since the new Code now specifically envelops CPAs in corporate practice, academe, government, and other nonpublic occupations, suddenly relationships and loyalties previously unchallenged are coming under scrutiny.

Independence

The concept of independence is grounded in the notions of a CPA's objectivity, impartiality, intellectual honesty, and avoidance of the subordination of judgment to the importunities of others. This has its roots in the performance of the attest function, by the exercise of which a CPA adds credibility to the representations of others (issuers of financial information) for the benefit of third parties (users of financial information). Credibility is crucial to the efficient functioning of a free private enterprise economy, wherein investors must rely on such financial information in making judgments about alternative investment opportunities and relative risks.

Traditionally, a CPA's "independence" has been said to have two facets: independence in fact and independence in appearance. Since independence in fact is a state of mind, it cannot be observed or evaluated by others, and so over the years the emphasis in the profession has been on preserving the **appearance** of independence. Thus financial and other relationships between CPAs and their clients have come under microscopic scrutiny, and those conceivably clouding a CPAs independence in the view of an objective observer in possession of all the facts have been forbidden. Rule 101, Independence, requires that:

> *A member in public practice shall be independent in the performance of professional services as required by standards promulgated by bodies designated by council.*[14] [Emphasis supplied]

Although CPAs not in public practice (or, indeed, those in public practice not fulfilling the attest function) sometimes need not or cannot maintain the appearance of independence, the ethical requirements to maintain integrity and objectivity still apply. Rule 102, Integrity and Objectivity, states:

> *In the performance of any professional service, a member shall maintain objectivity and integrity, shall be free of conflicts of interest, and shall not knowingly misrepresent facts or subordinate his or her judgment to others.*[15]

The implementation of these deceptively simple and seemingly straightforward propositions has resulted in the proliferation of an ever-increasing and ever more complicated set of rules, rulings, and interpretations. Regulators, aided by professional bodies, have sought to develop specific guidelines for every conceivable circumstance. As of June 1, 1995, the AICPA had issued 98 ethical rulings (some of which have been repealed, replaced, or amended) on independence, integrity and objectivity, and 15 pages of interpretations of the rule on independence. The SEC, which is charged with the responsibility to enforce the statutory requirement that financial statements filed with that body be certified by *independent* accountants, frequently releases findings regarding factual situations brought before it for resolution. The net result of all this scrutiny is a bewildering web of guidelines to be applied to factual situations that are ever new and ever changing. Not all of the "solutions" arising from this process are effective; in fact, they often serve to forbid relationships that on balance are beneficial to all concerned or those that clearly meet the test of common sense but not the complexities of some inflexible finding.

A number of proposals have been made to halt or slow this apparently inexorable process of complication. One of some interest has been proposed by Steven M. H. Wallman, currently an SEC Commissioner. Although Commissioner Wallman speaks only for himself, and not the Commission or others in the administration, his views are important in this search for what some would call sanity and common sense in defining the independence issue. Commissioner Wallman, bypassing all the detailed rules regarding what behavior or relationships are suspect, focuses instead on what he calls the real issue, not of **independence**, but of **dependence**. Is a situation such that the auditor (or attestor) is dependent on the client? It is that dependency which is the potential corrupter of integrity.

Although this distinction initially may seem a matter of semantics, it is more substantive than that in judging particular circumstances. Under Commissioner Wallman's proposal, the focus would be on: "(1) [T]he individual, office or other unit of the firm making audit decisions, (2) whether a relationship or activity has the potential to create a dependency that could bias auditing judgments, (3) whether the potential for dependence is such that independence can nevertheless be maintained through reasonable measures, and, if it cannot be, (4) whether the benefits to the audit process of the relationship or activity outweigh the potential independence concerns."[16] This would introduce some measure of common sense into the equation. At least it would provide for flexibility rather than rigidity in judging circumstances. It might also be observed here that this flexibility is abhorred by those who are fearful that it will be misused. Of course the possibility of misuse exists! The question is whether flexibility, combined with responsibility for results, or rigidity best serves the objectives of the rules.

Prior to the turn of the twentieth century, in discussing the Civil Service Reform Act of 1883, Senator Hawley of Connecticut said it well:

> *Do not let us indulge an idea that we can make a perfect system and eliminate all evils or possibilities of evil. We can lay out some general lines....[and] say generally....'we hold you....responsible for the thorough administration of all affairs....under these general rules.'* [17]

The appearance of independence in the case of a CPA in an employer/employee relationship is of course impossible to maintain, but the similar constraints imposed by Rule 102 regarding integrity and objectivity still apply. In such circumstances, however, the extent and effectiveness of any outside monitoring process is likely to be minimal, and the burden of compliance rests even more heavily on the individual than is the case in the public arena.

As attractive as Commissioner Wallman's approach may seem, it still would be subject to the same infirmities as all attempts to define such behavioral patterns have been -- interpretation and implementation. Whether an appeal to "dependence" rather than to "independence" can survive the attacks of rule writers remains to be seen, but some approach involving common sense cries out for recognition.

This problem has become so intractable, and the concerns arising from consulting and other nonattest services offered by CPA firms so pervasive, that the

SEC and the AICPA agreed on a new forum for setting independence standards. It will be modeled after the Financial Accounting Standards Board, that is, it will be a separate panel charged with the responsibility to issue pronouncements on independence matters, and those pronouncements will be accepted as authoritative by both the SEC and the AICPA.[18]   While the Board's authority is directed only to matters involving public companies, the Independence Standards Board (ISB) will be housed in the AICPA's SEC Practice Section.

The new ISB is comprised of four members from the profession, including the President of the AICPA, and four "public" members, one of whom serves as chair. The Board's authority will pertain only to auditors of publicly owned companies; independence and other ethical standards for auditors of other entities remain the responsibility of the AICPA's professional ethics executive committee.

Confidentiality

CPAs In Public Practice. Any professional relationship depends for its success on the willingness of both parties to establish and maintain an open and uncritical dialogue, in which all pertinent facts and circumstances are freely disclosed. A medical doctor cannot be expected to make an accurate diagnosis unless the patient is forthcoming with symptoms; a lawyer cannot mount a client's case without a full airing of all the circumstances -- including, if applicable, knowledge of guilt; a CPA cannot judge the propriety of accounting or reporting practices without being fully apprised of a client's or employer's financial circumstances and plans. The candid exchange of information, advice, and views on a particular matter ultimately depends also on the belief by each party that the discussion will be held in confidence. Any suspicions to the contrary inevitably will degrade the quality of the relationship and the effectiveness of the advice. It is a serious question whether a professional should allow a relationship to continue under such circumstances.

Rule 301, Confidential Client Information, states in part:

*A member **in public practice** shall not disclose any confidential client information without the specific consent of the client.*[19] [Emphasis supplied]

This rule has a number of exceptions. For example, a member is not relieved of the obligation to follow applicable standards for carrying out professional engagements, including appropriate reporting regarding a client's conformity with generally accepted accounting principles. Further, since the confidentiality constraint is only a professional ethical rule, it generally has no standing at law, as does a lawyer's "privileged" communication with clients (disclosure cannot be forced by outside agencies, including the courts). Accordingly, an accountant can be required by appropriate court summons or subpoena to disclose otherwise confidential information regarding a client's affairs. This was underlined by the U.S. Supreme court in a prominent case granting access to the auditor's working papers by the

Internal Revenue Service. The Court focused on the fact that the business of accountants, unlike that of attorneys, clergymen, and physicians, is to prepare disclosures of information for the investing public and regulatory agencies. It said:

> *To insulate from disclosure a certified public accountant's interpretation of the client's financial statements would be to ignore the significance of the accountant's role as a disinterested analyst charged with public obligations...*[20]

This decision led to much soul-searching on the part of auditors, who were concerned that they be afforded access to all information necessary to form an opinion on a client's financial statements. The clients had to deal with the possibility that what they told auditors might be forced into public view. A pragmatic balance has been reached in this particular case, as the IRS administratively has been careful not to upset what is recognized by all to involve public policy issues beyond the immediately perceived need to gain access to working papers. Nothing fundamental really was changed by the case, since the public responsibilities of CPAs have long been recognized by the profession: "A distinguishing mark of a profession is acceptance of its responsibility to the public."[21] It initially may have been disconcerting to practitioners to see this high-minded and self-proclaimed obligation so clearly affirmed in writing by the highest court in the land.

What since has been happening, however, in public accounting as elsewhere, is a growing concern to answer the question whether it is ever appropriate for one privy to otherwise confidential information unilaterally to disclose it to third parties in the name of a "greater good." Whatever the individual's personal answer to this question, there is a growing pressure to force such disclosures over the objections of some practitioners. For example, in the 1995 amendments to the securities acts,[22] an auditor who becomes aware that a client has or may have committed an illegal act must:

1. Inform an appropriate level of management, and assure that the audit committee of the board of directors (or the board) is adequately informed.

2. If management or the board does not take "appropriate action," and the failure to do so reasonably would lead to a qualification in the auditor's report, the auditor must promptly so inform the board.

3. The board, within one business day of receiving such information, must inform the SEC, with a copy to the auditor of its notice to the Commission.

4. If the auditor fails to receive a copy of such notice within the one-day period, he must either (a) resign the engagement, or (b) furnish the Commission directly a copy of the report to the board.

5. In the event of resignation, the auditor still must furnish the Commission

directly a copy of such report.

CPAs offering tax and consulting services are covered by the same Rule 301 applied to those offering attest services, although the public policy aspects of the former relationships are more compelling in favor of extending protection to confidential information because of the lesser degree of third-party interest. A separate argument may be offered for providing "privilege" (protected communications) in the case of tax advice or tax return preparation. The attorney-client privilege has long been a part of Federal law; clients of CPAs performing the same or similar services are afforded no such protection.[23] In order for privilege to be invoked, an accountant must work through an attorney, an awkward and seemingly unnecessary complication. Whether working directly with an attorney or an accountant, a client should have the confidence that the full and free disclosure so necessary to competent advice will not result in a disadvantage if one or the other professional is chosen.

Although not directly related to the pressures to disclose client information, another example of changing social attitudes toward violations of confidence is the web of secrecy being woven around the newly "secure" CPA examination. Since the beginning, the CPA examination has been open; questions were regularly published by the AICPA, along with unofficial answers. These were available to all who wanted to study them and/or to prepare for future examinations. Beginning in May, 1996, the examination became "secure," meaning that no questions or answers would ever be published. A number of valid technical reasons led to the decision to make the examination secure, and certain rules were adopted that were thought necessary for the security to be effective. These imposed some unusual requirements on everyone associated with the examination. For example, each candidate now is required to sign the following declaration:

> *I hereby attest that I will not divulge the nature or content of any question or answer to any individual or entity, and **I will report to the board of accountancy any solicitations and disclosures of which I become aware**........ I understand that failure to comply with this attestation may result in invalidation of my grades, disqualification from future examinations, and possible civil and criminal penalties.*[24] [Emphasis supplied]

Consider the implications of this undertaking. If a candidate is approached by **anybody**, innocently or otherwise, with a question even remotely bearing on the examination, the candidate is **obliged** to report the approach to the state board of accountancy -- on pain of possible civil or criminal penalties and other dire consequences. The inquirer also presumably faces similar actions. One can appreciate the need to provide for the security of the examination and still question the need for draconian measures to preserve that security. Is a student required to report an instructor who asks after the examination: "How did it go?"?

CPAs in Corporate Practice, Government, Other Employment, or Academe. As stated above, independence in appearance is impossible to attain in an employer/employee relationship, but the requirements for objectivity and personal integrity still pertain. Here the principal issue, and ethical dilemma, is whether "other" considerations can or should override loyalty to an employer to the point where the employee is justified in breaking a confidentiality barrier, say, to report a perceived breach of an accounting principle to the SEC. This general problem comes under the rubric of "whistle blowing," and discussion of it has generated a great deal of heat in the accounting profession, as well as in other occupations. We all perhaps still have a vestigial memory of what it means at a grade school level to "snitch" on a member of a group or class. We don't like "snitches," and whistle blowers are a modern version of that persona. And yet there is indeed a public responsibility borne by a CPA, a responsibility not to participate in a deception. Medical personnel have a legal responsibility to breach the confidentiality barrier to report gunshot wounds, and perhaps also certain diseases perceived to offer public dangers. Is there not a similar obligation for CPAs?

What is "whistle blowing"? Whistle blowing is a direct and blatant violation of any precepts of confidentiality. Whistle blowers sound an alarm regarding the very organization in which or for which they work, aiming to spotlight neglect or abuses that threaten the public interest. Several assumptions in this definition require comment. The "blower" takes the moral high ground in the name of "public interest." Although he or she may have misjudged that interest or the facts being disclosed, there is an underlying conviction that the good done by the exposure outweighs the damage potentially inflicted on the entity -- or indeed on the individual's personal career. There is a conflict here that only the individual can resolve, in the light of all that individual's life training and convictions. In any event, the matter is brought into better focus for CPAs by an interpretation of AICPA Rule 102 on Integrity and Objectivity. Interpretation 102-4 states, in part, that a member (not in public practice) who concludes that his or her employer's financial statements could be materially misstated, and appropriate corrective action is not taken, should:

> *...consider any responsibility that may exist to communicate to third parties, such as regulatory authorities or the employer's (former employer's) external accountant...*[25]

This imperative seems at first blush to be at direct odds with the provisions of the Standards of Ethical Conduct for Management Accountants, promulgated by the Institute of Management Accountants (IMA). These standards require management accountants to "Refrain from disclosing confidential information acquired in the course of their work except when authorized, unless legally obligated to do so."[26] It is not clear what "legally obligated to do so" means, nor what constitutes "authorization" to disclose confidential information. A further admonition in the Standards does nothing to clear the problem. Under the caption "Resolution of Ethical Conflict," the instruction is given that: "Except where legally prescribed, communication of such problems to authorities or individuals not employed or engaged by the organization is not considered appropriate."[27]

This would seem to create a conflict of loyalties that cries out for resolution. It may be that such resolution will come from an action filed against an employer by a CPA, one Albert C. Reeves. Mr. Reeves, formerly employed by Aetna Life and Casualty Co., contended he was fired in January, 1995, for publicly disclosing an alleged shortfall in the company's mortgage portfolio reserves.[28]   It was his contention, among other things, that Aetna forced him to violate his professional code of conduct (as a CPA), and thus opened the possibility that he might lose his license to practice, as well as his membership in professional organizations. The competing pressures of company loyalty, public interest, and professional imperatives thus come into focus. As of the date of this writing, no resolution of this particular issue has been forthcoming, but the dilemma is clear. How it will be solved in individual cases is a matter for individual conscience.

Summary

Personal integrity is the most important attribute of any professional. This chapter has dealt with the development of a personal code of behavior for a CPA, and the factors that guide and influence it. Ways were suggested to think about ethical problems, and to establish priorities in circumstances where there are competing claims to be resolved. Institutional ethical codes were viewed as minimums, and as not necessarily representing the best measure of proper activity in particular circumstances. Indeed, reliance on codes or laws to establish proper norms tends to reduce all judgments to the lowest common denominator; such reliance is the final refuge of those who have failed to reach for the higher standard that is the hallmark of the true professional. This in the final analysis is a personal problem, and the solutions can only be personal, as each individual weighs the values of competing interests and the effects of choosing one against the others.

Discussion Questions

1.   What are the principal forces directing the behavior of all professionals -- CPAs included?

2.   What do we mean by "personal integrity"?

3.   How does the relationship between a professional and a client differ from the relationship between a salesperson and a customer? In what ways may the two be the same?

4.   Who is to judge whether a professional is able to perform the services that he or she holds out to the public as being able to perform?

5. Would CPAs and their clients be better served if the profession had no articulated rules of conduct? Why or why not?

6. Why has the new AICPA Code of Professional Conduct been extended explicitly to cover CPAs not in public practice?

7. To what extent is it necessary or desirable that a candidate obtain "experience" under the direction of a CPA before being granted a license? If so, should that experience be in a particular area of expertise, such as performance of the attest function, for all candidates?

8. Discuss the three areas of responsibility falling to a supervisor in guiding the experience of a CPA candidate.

9. Describe from your own experience a situation involving ethical choices, and consider how that situation might have been resolved using the approach described in the text. Would you have reached the same or a different answer?

10. Develop your own definition of professional "failure." How would you surface and deal with it in the best interests of the public served by the CPA?

11. Why does the AICPA Code of Professional Conduct contain both "principles" and "rules"?

12. Has the elimination of rules forbidding antitrust activities engaged in by CPAs been in the best public interest? Best for clients? Best for professionals?

13. Select one of the Code's "rules" and trace the changes in that rule over time, as influenced by professional and legal developments affecting CPAs.

14. Several of the rules (e.g., Rule 101, Independence) refer to compliance with "....standards promulgated by bodies designated by Council." What is the significance of this reference? What are "bodies designated by Council"?

15. How do you think standards and rules regarding independence should be formulated and enforced?

16. What are the public policy aspects of the ethical rules regarding confidentiality for a CPA in public practice? For those CPAs in other circumstances?

17. Is it ever acceptable to break the confidentiality barrier when dealing with a client? When working in an employee status for an employer? In the case of a former employer? Be specific.

18. Should communications between CPAs and their clients have the same protected ("privileged") status as those between a doctor and patient or a lawyer and client? Why or why not?

Endnotes

[1] Mautz, Robert K., "Public Accounting: Which Kind of Professionalism?," *Accounting Horizons,* September, 1988, 122.

[2] AICPA Code of Professional Conduct, adopted January 12, 1988, amended January 14, 1992.

[3] The use here of the term "fiduciary" to describe a professional relationship is not meant in the literal sense of turning one's affairs over to another to manage, but only to indicate an arrangement in which one party willingly agrees to abide by the skill and good intentions of another party in dealing with a problem.

[4] Article III, *Integrity*, Section I, *Principles*, AICPA Code of Professional Conduct, adopted January 12, 1988, amended January 14, 1992.

[5] Yoder, Edwin, syndicated columnist, quoted in *The Wall Street Journal,* editorial page, August 4, 1988.

[6] Laws dealing with the qualifications necessary for the granting of a CPA certificate vary widely from state to state in the amount and nature of required experience in public accounting or under the direction of an individual already holding a certificate. Some states have dropped the experience requirement entirely, and grant the certificate based only upon educational attainments and the passing of the uniform CPA examination.

[7] The authors are indebted for some of these notions to a study of social interactions in a medical training environment. Bosk, Charles L., *Forgive and Remember, Managing Medical Failure,* The University of Chicago Press, 1979.

[8] Holland, Thomas P., "The Social Worker," *The Power of the Professional Person* (Lanham, Md.: University Press of America, Inc.) 1988.

[9] A philosophical discussion of what constitutes "good," in the realm of public accountancy or elsewhere, certainly is beyond the scope of this work, or indeed the capabilities of its authors. Suffice to say that the highest ideals attributable to the profession by its leading spokesmen and practitioners can serve as a working definition of the term.

[10] As reported in *Professional Ethics Report,* American Association for the Advancement of Science, Spring, 1988.

[11] AICPA *Code of Professional Conduct,* New York, 1996, p. 3.

[12] *Goldfarb* v. *Virginia State Bar,* 421 U.S. 773 (1975).

[13] Federal Trade Commission, Docket No. C3297, Complaint and Order: *In the Matter of American Institute of Certified Public Accountants,* July 26, 1990.

[14] *Code of Professional Conduct,* American Institute of Certified Public Accountants, New York, 1996.

[15] Ibid.

[16] Wallman, Steven M. H., *The Future of Accounting, Part III: Reliability and Auditor Independence,* Accounting Horizons, December, 1996, p. 76.

[17] As quoted by Howard, Philip K., *The Death of Common Sense,* Random House, 1994, p. 76.

[18] MacDonald, Elizabeth, *The Wall Street Journal* (June 18, 1997): A8.

[19] *Code of Professional Conduct,* American Institute of Certified Public Accountants, New York, 1996.

[20] *United States* v. *Arthur Young & Co.,* 465 U.S. 805 (1984).

[21] Article II, *The Public Interest,* Section I, *Principles,* AICPA Code of Professional Conduct, adopted January 12, 1988, amended January 14, 1992.

[22] Title III - Auditor Disclosure of Corporate Fraud, *Private Securities Litigation Reform Act of 1995.*

[23] Some states have provided for accountant-client privilege in tax matters, but this protection does not extend to Federal cases.

[24] American Institute of Certified Public Accountants, *Information for Boards of Accountancy, Implementing the Nondisclosed Uniform CPA Examination,* January, 1996, p. B-7.

[25] American Institute of Certified Public Accountants, *AICPA Professional Standards,* June 1, 1995, p. 4426.

[26] National Association of Accountants (now the Institute of Management Accountants), *Statements on Management Accounting: Objectives of Management Accounting, Statement No. 1B,* New York, N.Y., June 17, 1982.

[27] Ibid.

[28] *Wall Street Journal,* August 4, 1995.

The Marketplace for CPA Services

CHAPTER 7

The Economics
and Business of CPA
Practice

*"...information about money
has become more
valuable than money itself."*
Walter Wriston[1]
Citicorp

Introduction

"Wall Street leads the world" proclaimed the center banner headline of The *Financial Times* weekend edition in mid June 1997. Pretty heady stuff![2]   The Dow Jones Industrial average, a benchmark of stock list performance begun in 1896, had just surpassed 7700 and was continuing to move upward.   Free enterprise, market-based capitalism and the contract law system of profitable employment of private property seemed to soar effortlessly in the post-Cold War business world.   Just five years before the Dow had closed at a record 3201 in early January 1992. The editors of *U.S. News & World Report* had given this feature story the title "A Market gone wild." Indeed to what is such activity attributable? Is it the strength of the system or mostly fortunate circumstances per se? [3]

The transformation of social and economic order again, for the populace of a century which had experienced three world conflicts, one in the second decade, one in the fifth decade, with a prolonged conflict over another four, ending in 1989, seemed to be setting the world up for new levels of competition and economic growth, reordering the factors of production on an even more integrated global scale.

The wrenching reality of corporate "downsizing" or "rightsizing" left many industrial era workers and voters disoriented. Transportation and communication costs, spiraling downward, have made travel and information communication around the global nearly as inexpensive as former local activities along these lines.

The Economics of Practice

Disclosure, Information rights, and the cost of capital

The justification for this global information role for the information profession is in part macroeconomic and in part political in that the supply of high quality objective information for investing, measuring, and evaluating performance is needed to achieve a higher standard of living for all members of a global village society--just as maintaining a high level of social investment in a medical profession's proficiency is necessary to achieving longer and healthier life spans. A more significant macroeconomic justification for the scope of capital market information services which CPAs offer to the global investment community is based on efficiency. These global forces play themselves out in a variety of ways. "The global village concept," said Arnold McKinnon, a top executive of the Norfolk Southern Corp. in 1987, "creates pressure for fast and efficient transportation world-wide (and) market forces favor consolidation of modes under one management for improved efficiency and service."[4]

Similarly, one should observe that global village efficiency and access to capital and information about capital and the performance of capital investment creates pressure for global ability to delivery and provide "one stop" shopping for decision information. The market forces would seem to favor organizations and professions which can meet this demand for reliable and relevant information.

What has empowered the CPA profession to undertake the challenge of becoming the premier profession in this market for information needed by the capital markets is its tradition, reputation and organizational capabililty to employ technology and experience effectively on a global scale of economic activity. This effectiveness is demonstrated by facilitating the flow of capital among nations by providing information flows which correspond to the needs of investors. Managing the process of providing, assessing, and analyzing such flows requires "political skill" not readily identified with the "old" CPA community—so unfairly bound with negative image stereotypes. But the profession has been in fact quietly involved in politics from the earliest days of income tax legislation in the first decades of this century, through the Securities and Exchange Acts of the 1930s, in wartime emergency legislation, through inflationary times and upto the moment, with laws involving business and professional tort reforms. Indeed a recent "political responsiveness" report card on the profession was issued in September 1996 by the United States General Accounting Office. The study reported: "GAO's analysis of the actions taken the accounting profession in response to the major issues raised by the many studies from 1972 through 1995 shows that the profession has been responsive in making changes to improve financial reporting and auditing of public companies..."

"However," the study continues, "findings show that the actions of the accounting profession have not been totally effective in resolving several majors issues."[5] Indeed with inflation concerns in the 1970s, pension fund failures associated with closings of "rust belt" industries during the 1980s, the savings and loan crisis thereafter, and most recently the specter of "derivative" investments, the profession has had a series of major challenges adapting to the world since the "book-end" events of the oil crisis of the 1970s and the fall of the Berlin Wall in 1989.

A Nation of Investors-The United States in the next Century

While President Calvin Coolidge may have said "The business of America is business," it is well to understand that without the steady flow of trusted investment, performance and operating information provided, in the main, by the CPA Profession, America might very well be "out of business." Surely, you say, such is too much of a claim. But challenge yourself by asking how much capital **you** are willing to put at risk without the ability to obtain trustworthy information about it once it leaves your checking or bank account? Like many of the great "utilities" of our way of life, accounting is taken for granted. Now envision global transfers of your hard-earned capital (perhaps as represented by a 401 [k] or mutual fund investment) moving across national boundaries to other continents, where the languages and traditions are far different. This is what is happening today! The United States as a nation of investors is increasingly involved in providing capital for the development of enterprises to serve the "global village." Can there be any greater role for a profession than to have to provide consistent, comparable, and timely information to assist in maintaining the financial health and stability of those resources which in turn provide the basis for our physical well being and quality of life? If a system of capital market information to support investment can be reduced to the level of the lowest possible cost for capital, the greatest opportunity to improve the quality of life in the "global village" can be achieved by making the scarce factor of production, investment capital, available to all who need to employ it.

| **Table 7.1** | International Investment |
| | Per Capita Fund Investment by Country in U.S. Dollars |

Country	Amount
United States	$ 12,429
France	8,375
United Kingdom	3,125
Japan	3,075
Germany	2,047

To understand the demand for CPA services in this truly global market one must relate to the public interest goal, the broader goal, of raising the standard of living for all. This can be enhanced by information that aids making efficient decisions about scarce resources in a world populated by billions. This is the public interest policy goal and a role which justifies the title of "CPA profession." We are reminded of this in the remarks made by former AICPA President, Phil Chenok. "I am sure that if I asked members why they became CPAs, they would say, ` I did it to earn a living.' There is nothing wrong with that; all of us need to earn a living to take care of our families and ourselves. But I believe that in serving the public interest we put ourselves in an even better position to meet our other responsibilities."[6]

Between the Lines: A CPA Business Model

How a particular firm's activities will fit into the broader global market for CPA services will probably depend upon case-by-case decisions over a long period of time. An individual firm's cost benefit and risk preferences for providing the service will dictate decisions in particular local, regional, national, and global markets. The economic benefit of growth to a practice unit can be evaluated both in terms of contribution to the top line (revenues), and/or the bottom line (income). The top line characterizes the size and critical mass of the firm and may influence the ability of the firm to specialize to the high degree necessary in larger marketplaces. Therefore a firm's decision to "grow by the top line" may reflect important strategic (market share) options about the type and variety of services that are to be offered, which are in turn based upon the size of the economic unit itself. Often these are considerations related to economies of scale and the efficiencies of maintaining headquarters office and image at a target level of operation (national, etc.) or specialty support and overhead functions, including technical research and support, firmwide training, and continuing education. The combination of Ernst & Whinney and   Arthur Young, for example, was projected to produce a firm with annual worldwide revenues in excess of $4 billion.[7] The merged firm was foreseen as having more than 6,000 partners worldwide and more than 68,000 personnel. At year end 1996 the firm reported its annual worldwide revenues at $7.8 billion, up 13.6% over 1995.[8] If one of their merger objectives was to achieve strategic global mass and position to achieve growth, it could be argued that they have been successful at the "top line."

Outsourcing

Speculation about such growth, in the face of a "mature" if not shrinking, market for audit services, indicates that the growth of nonattest services [NAS] has developed into a dominant element of public practice.   The analysis of the range of services now included in public practice follows in a subsequent chapter.   It is worth emphasizing, however, that an important rationale which has been supportive of this trend in public practice has been "outsourcing" of previously provided corporate staff level services.   "One does not buy the cow, when it may be rented more conveniently" is a parody on a related axiom.   But when companies began the process of rightsizing for global growth, the cost of support staff being purchased or hired as needed, favored hiring from outside versus adding to staff inside.   Firms which could readily provide the "one-stop" staff service equivalent were given the opportunity to tap into a growth market.   The economics of this phenomenon and the fact that public practice firms are reformulating their own costs by becoming capital versus labor intensive, suggests that an efficient combination and leveraging of these factors of production will dictate much of the economics of business practice in CPA firms at all levels in the years to come.

Profits and Public Interest

Each professional service firm or corporate support service element must contribute to the bottom line [income] of the entity's economic interest.   Professional accountants worthy of this designation are not, of course, expected to elevate the bottom line to the level of the be-all and end-all of their existence. Indeed true professionalism involves placing the interest of those relying on one's skill and judgment before one's own self-interest. So, allowing for the lack of perfection in the human instrument of professionalism, there is appeal   identified as to the proper balance between self interest and the public interest in the oft-quoted query: "If not for yourself, who is? If only for yourself, what are you?"

Along with the relentless competitive pressures for increasing global market share, and achieving reduction in production costs, businesses that found attracting capital now involves institutional sources representing large communities of individual investors, many seeking retirement security.   Americans had become a nation of investors, no longer solely blue-collar or white-collar workers.   The rise of individual tax qualified 401 [k] plans for retirement investing and the discovery of the mutual fund as a vehicle to parley stock market funds had transformed the average person into an "investor," whether or not they fully appreciated the meaning, risk, and responsibilities of that role.[9]

In the macroeconomic sense, within a global capital market transacting trillions of dollars of exchanges per day, a CPA can be expected to contribute to creating the highest possible service value by reducing transaction costs and reducing the risks due to inadequate or unreliable information. The CPA profession will justify its role in the economic equation of global investment and competition by continuing to enhance the efficient allocation and utilization of a scarce, valuable, and highly sought-after resource—information. With the interaction afforded by technological advances, global investment communities including Europe, Asia, and the Americas can be expected to demand a consistency and comparability of performance from information providers. This will have a substantial influence on the market for information services of the quality and value level required to permit efficient allocation of investment capital. The global demand for capital shifts as does the product cycle, which itself transforms in response to the cost of the factors of production. The classic product cycle following the post World War II period was: "America would invest in a new high tech product and learn to mass produce it. Gradually the product would shift to being a mid-tech product produced in ....mid-wage countries, when it would eventually move to a low-tech product in a low wage country."[10]   However, it has been disrupted by the changes in technology and geopolitics in the post-Cold War period in ways which still defy complete description. New global market competition even more dependent upon information is now attempting to sort the allocation of resources on a scale never before encountered in human history.

CPA services in this post-Cold War market must be provided on a timely basis if capital investments are to be attracted and sustained. These services, those which are new and those which are more traditional, must be relevant and reliable as well as objectively determined if they are to provide added value to decision making and performance evaluation processes.

The justification for this global information role for a CPA information profession is in part macroeconomic and in part political in that the supply of high quality objective information for investing, measuring, and evaluating performance is needed to achieve a higher standard of living for all members of a global village society--just as maintaining a high level of social investment in a medical profession's proficiency is necessary to achieving longer and healthier life spans. A more significant macroeconomic justification for the scope of capital market information services which CPAs offer to the global investment community is based upon a more fundamental precept than competitive efficiency or economic demand alone. Services must be related to the broader goal of raising the standard of living for all. This can be enhanced by information that aids making efficient decisions about scarce resources in a world where rhetoric about achieving a "living wage" is insufficient, but the achievement of such a lofty goal represents an ultimate challenge.[11]

The Public Accounting Profession and Its Transformation

It is difficult to be precise regarding the size and composition of the CPA profession, as represented by organizations such as the AICPA and State CPA units. As to public accountancy, all indications point to a steady and increasingly rapid growth, particularly after the midpoint of this century. The growth of the largest public practice firms gives some idea of the expansion of the marketplace for public accountancy generally. Professional personnel (United States only) in these firms in the aggregate increased by 35%, from 61,200 to 82,900, in the mid-1980s.[5] This growth shows no sign of abating, particularly in the new phase of outsourcing induced growth. The sheer size of some firms raises questions whether some practical limit may not exist, given the characteristics of the practice and of those individualists who offer its services. Certainly the management challenges in such circumstances are formidable. The reasons for expansion include the necessity to follow the growth of business, particularly global, post-Cold War business; the demand for a variety of services related to the CPAs expertise in accumulating, processing, presenting, and verifying business information; and, of course, ever more complex tax laws.

There were more than 331,000 members in the AICPA in 1997. At the turn of the century only 92 members existed; there were 16,000 in 1950 and 112,500 in 1975. Of this number, as has been mentioned, about 45% are in public practice. An increasing number of CPAs are now found in corporate and government practice and now comprise the majority of AICPA members. Accounting graduates in the process of fulfilling their experience requirements, and employees of accounting firms who are specialists in various aspects of tax or management advisory services, also practice public accountancy, but may not be CPAs.

Well over one-half (59%) of AICPA members are with firms of less than 10 members; and slightly less than one-half of those (23% of the total) are sole practitioners. The 25 largest firms include about 20% of the total AICPA membership.[12] Thus the vast majority of public practice units comprises small to medium-sized firms. Of the largest firms, six generally in the past have been considered as a separate group because their size, individually and in the aggregate, is substantially in excess of that of the next "tier" of firms.

Competition in Public Accounting

The issue of competition in the public accounting profession is a complex one. On one hand, in our free private enterprise economy, competition in all its forms generally is viewed as a desirable device to assure the delivery of the very best in goods and services to the consumer at the lowest price; in short, competition stimulates the producer to this end and to everyone's assumed benefit. Laws, both federal and state, have long been in effect to assure that such competition is maintained and is fair. However, sometimes these laws appear to conflict with ethical imperatives which look to the overall perceived best interests of the client rather than to the precise method by which those best interests are achieved. This may require a professional balancing of purely competitive benefits with other considerations.

The advent of competition in the professions, in accounting no less than in medicine and law, has brought sweeping changes to the practice, its structure and its character as well as its economics. Hospitals and doctor's offices have become HMOs. Lawyers work out of "Legal clinics." To a significant degree, this competition has been forced upon practitioners by the actions of federal government agencies such as the Federal Trade Commission and the Justice Department. These agencies, sometimes prodded by private suits by practitioners impatient with behavioral constraints and sometimes by legal and social pressures, have increasingly viewed ethical canons of the professions dealing with commercial behavior as improperly anticompetitive.

The focus of efforts to increase competition is largely on pricing, and the professional view always has been that this is a perverse incentive since it is based on money and not on competence. Further, price pressures in the view of many inevitably lead to a diminution of quality, to the ultimate degradation of a trusting relationship that must be nurtured between professional and client.

The pressures of price competition within the public accounting profession itself are accompanied by competition with other providers of nonattest services--tax and consulting. Particularly in the consulting field, this competition is leading to changes in the way public accountants organize and conduct their practice. The division of the profession into two elements, attest and nonattest, has as yet unforeseen consequences, but these are likely to be significant and highly visible. The appropriate balance between unrestrained competition in public accounting and traditional concepts of professional behavior is yet to be reached, as is the point at which the welfare of the client is most likely to be maximized. We will see much in the way of change in the years to come--not all of which will rest comfortably with practitioners.

Some commentators have expressed a fear that competition, particularly price competition, and related NAS provided on attest professional engagements, have together: 1) undermined auditor independence, and 2) diminished attest quality.

There are no comprehensive responses to such persistent concerns. However, as to the former, it must be remembered that the notion of independence, like the Constitution in our government, is continually subject to reinterpretation. As to the latter, fears remain largely unsupported by substantial evidence. For example, a blue ribbon study group concluded in that:

> . . . *time and budget pressures frequently cause substandard auditing . . . we believe one probable cause [of time and budget pressures] is excessive price competition--that is, excessive competition among firms to offer lower fees-- but the Commission has been unable to document this relationship*[13]

Effective and beneficial competition in the commercial, financial, or industrial economy depends in large measure on the ability of the consumer to evaluate the quality of competing products or services and their prices, and to make a rational choice among them. In the case of a profession, because of the very nature of the service offered, the consumer may not be able to make such evaluations--at least to the same extent. If this is true, competition in the professions must have different meanings and measures than in purely commercial endeavors.

This observation, of course, is not universally valid. If a consumer has no expertise in a field, quality sometimes can be judged from the expressed satisfaction of other users of services, and that judgment can be confirmed or denied by subsequent personal experience. Yet it is unlikely that this can be foreseen or evaluated in advance from claims supported only by advertising or fee considerations. Should a decision regarding the proper physician to be selected for brain surgery be based on minimum fees and published claims regarding skills?

The critical question to be answered, of course, is who is to guard the welfare of the consumers if they cannot fend for themselves in choosing among professionals offering what may appear to be essentially the same service (e.g., an audit). One proposal is to overlook the differences between professional and commercial activities and to insist on precise legal safeguards and impartial regulatory experts. Regulation by such agencies, it is argued, is needed where competition per se is limited because of consumer lack of knowledge. It is this proposal that has driven much of the controversy with those who believe that, if applied blindly, the bad effects will outweigh the good.

Elaborate ethical constraints against professionals participating in such activities as bidding and advertising seem somewhat quaint and even archaic when viewed from today's perspective. Most of the old patterns have been swept away, largely in the name of competition. Actions by agencies (e.g., the Federal Trade

Commission being most notable for CPAs)[14] have been rationalized to apply antitrust and similar laws to the professions, challenging some former ethical barriers, which were erected in the name of competence when it was a seller's market and there was no need to truly compete. Thus it is not realistic to take the position that the introduction of more modern concepts of competition into the profession has been entirely negative. For example, such a move no doubt has been instrumental in improving audit efficiency as firms seek ways to mitigate fee pressures and still maintain performance quality.

In 1985, J. Michael Cook, now CEO of Deloitte & Touche, stated: "Five years ago if a client of another firm came to me and complained about the service, I'd immediately warn the other firm's chief executive. Today I try to take away his client."[15] Competition among public accounting firms for clients may be the most visible aspect of this matter, but there also is competition between accounting firms and nonaccounting-firm providers of management advisory services and, probably to a lesser extent, with providers of tax services. Further, the seemingly ever-expanding portfolio of services in public accounting firms in turn has fueled the demand for personnel. The need for both those with experience and those coming directly out of college has led to intensified recruiting activities, monetary support for select academic programs in colleges, and extensive efforts to create a favorable on-campus image.

Competition with nonaccounting providers of nonattest services such as taxes and consultancy has led to significant changes in the structure of CPA firms in the profession, as well as the way in which they deliver their services and manage the customary kinds of services (attest, tax, and consulting).[16] This general turmoil in the profession manifested itself in the late 1980s, in highly publicized events involving the internal struggles of large accounting firms to manage swiftly growing consultancy practices.[35] One firm later announced a major restructuring of its practice, quite obviously in an attempt to deal constructively with these swift professional developments.[36]

Obtaining clients via competitive pricing of services may be the most obvious and contentious, but is by no means the only, or perhaps even the most important aspect of competition. It is central to the matter of obtaining business, and is the arena most often considered in discussing competition--competition for clients. Competing for personnel, however, may be just as crucial to the ultimate well-being of any firm, for without competent people a service organization such as a public accounting firm has no hope of success.

Seeking Clients

Public Relations. This is no longer new to the practice of public accountancy. It describes the active search for and development of a client base, and includes advertising, solicitation of clients, and the development of a public image and reputation. A 1980s survey sampled firms belonging to the AICPA Division for CPA Firms and questioned them regarding their practices in three areas: mass media (advertising), social communication (client newsletters, community activities), and internal communication (employee newsletters, meetings).[17]

Somewhat surprisingly, in view of the controversy over the use of advertising by professionals, surveyed firms were found actually to have made relatively little use of mass media advertising. About one-half (48%) reported occasional use; but almost as many (46%) stated they never used paid advertising. Nevertheless, examples of advertising in local and national publications are not hard to come by. Super Bowl advertising by major firms, and frequent print and television campaigns, are now common. Soon after the AICPA's ethics rule regarding advertising was amended, *The Wall Street Journal* reported:

> *Deloitte ... has been touting its expertise in such publications as* The Wall Street Journal *and* Inc., *a magazine for small business. Others, such as Peat Marwick Mitchell & Co., ... and Coopers & Lybrand, have been promoting specific services in publications including* Business Week, Forbes *and trade journals. Price Waterhouse ... is advertising a computer-based program to help oil and gas companies do windfall-profits tax returns.*[18]

Most recently, in 1995, the AICPA began a multiyear, multimedia, multimillion dollar campaign with the tag line "The CPA. Never Underestimate the Value." This effort, the second by the AICPA, the first in the late 1980s, was short-lived, is a carefully developed program to work on changing the image and perception of the services and value of the CPA, not only in customary public practice, but across a wide variety of functions.

Use of advertising as a tool is consistent with the practice of at least one major firm in its early years. After the American Institute first enacted a ban on advertising in 1929, and in direct defiance of that ban, Ernst & Ernst continued to place ads in national publications such as *Fortune* magazine as late as 1931. However, from 1929 to 1978, the rule against advertising was included in the AICPA's ethical code and in the codes of several major state CPA societies and state boards of accountancy. By and large, it was observed, if not always scrupulously. Today we once again employ information dissemination as a means of identifying new areas of service as well as renewing messages about traditional practice. Advertising is now accepted public policy and business practice for CPA firms. It serves to give notice to potential clients and the public about the newly available as well as established services. It places other firms in the same market on notice that they cannot take their client base for granted as may have been the case in years gone by when there was more than enough business for everyone. This increasing awareness on the part of CPAs that they no longer have a market which they can take for granted adds additional incentives to performance which will benefit the public, or at least this is what is hoped for by those supporting this view of the value of competition to allocate market share.

All of these efforts--advertising, and the various forms of external and internal communication without and within each firm--have other unstated but important objectives, such as to develop a firm image. Such an image can create instant awareness in the global, national, or local market community of a firm about the services it provides, thus increasing the likelihood that prospective clients will respond positively. Where other methods of communication (public relations) are used, it is the credibility (image) of the individual or the organization, not the medium used, that is the critical factor.

Mergers and Acquisitions. In the 1980s the big news was the merger of Peat Marwick Mitchell & Co. with KMG Main Hurdman reportedly creating then the world's largest accounting firm, followed in 1989 by a combination of Ernst & Whinney and Arthur Young.[19] Thereafter, even the culturally differentiated firms of Arthur Andersen & Co. and Price Waterhouse held merger discussions, but could not come to terms. In addition, the major firms absorbed some smaller accounting and consulting firms. Thomas Doorley, in a 1989 *Wall Street Journal* column, reported that ". . . the Big Eight public accounting firms acquired about 45 other accounting firms and nearly 40 consulting firms in the past two years."[20]

And if mega-mergers are no longer making headlines in the financial press, new combinations, offering the CPA to a broader retail market, are giving new meaning to the word "buy out." [21] Mid-size and smaller practice units are responding to offers from publicly held entities such as American Express Financial Advisors, Inc., to acquire the nonattest and financial advisory service base of firm practices. This tactic, it is presumed, affords AEFA access to the reputation of "CPAs" and access to individuals with funds to invest in instruments such as the mutual and investment fund mediums of American Express. Building retail volume into these money management funds yields an annual stream of revenue which is characteristic of long-term income annuity. In brief, once the money is brought in house to be managed it yields a percentage income to the manager over the long term. A similar attempt to leverage CPA reputation into investment management was attempted by H. Vest and his firm many years earlier. However their arrangement was essentially fee based, and not a derived as a percent of assets under management. American Express, however, as in the case of Vest, is still in the process of proving the profitability of this approach. As a financial services analyst at Goldman Sachs pointed out: "American Express faces tough competition."[22]

Marketing. In the mid-1970s it would have been unheard of for public practice units to employ the word "marketing" let alone employ marketing professionals. Today, with new value added services to be developed in the global information setting, "marketing" is the watchword of every established and aspiring firm's business development plan.

By the early 1980s, writers like Tyebjee and Bruno had outlined four steps for an accounting firm in developing a marketing strategy: identify the needs of current and prospective clients, partition the market into segments with similar needs, select one or more as the targets of business activities, and design services that will convey benefits to prospects.[23] These describe succinctly the process followed in one form or another by most firms. What perhaps was new was the organized effort being made to do this, including the hiring by some of public relations firms to assist in the process.

A very visible part of this effort by some firms is the marketing (selling) of how-to guides, particularly in the tax field. Although the revenue aspect of these guides is not inconsiderable, their purpose is not to generate income but to build image and attract clients. Several of the major firms now sell tax guides, The Ernst & Young version is among those well recognized. Regional firm alliances produce similar tax guides which they give away to clients and others. "We believe in that kind of promotion," averred a representative of one of the producers of these tax guides. "The idea is to attract the accounting business of individual taxpayers. . . whose [financial] prospects are on the upside," said another.[24]

Another example of marketing efforts is the concentration of many CPA firms on emerging business entities—new companies and small companies, which can be expected to grow in the future, perhaps issue shares to the public, and otherwise become good long-term clients. In this arena, large CPA firms are competing with small CPA firms. And in some instances smaller and regional firms prearrange access to larger firms for such client services at the point of an IPO [Initial Public (stock) Offering]. "Fastest-Growing Private Entities Want Good Service; Hire Local Firms Most," reads a headline in *Public Accounting Report*.[25] This suggests that larger firms are not always the first choice of developing companies.

On the other hand, the large firms are aggressively seeking such clients. When two corporations merge, and the 1990s have seen a watershed of such consolidations, there is usually one firm remaining, and one firm with a lost client. "After years of kowtowing to the largest corporations, the Big Six is finding it hard to expand . . . . The accounting firms—because their clients aren't growing--aren't getting anywhere either. They need small business."[26]

Big Firms---Little Firms. The competition between large and small accounting firms permeates many areas of the professional environment, not just in seeking out emerging businesses as clients. Large firms offer economies of scale and a spectrum of expertise not possible in a small firm (no small firm could audit General Motors, for example). By the same token, training and other overhead costs in a large firm make price competition with smaller firms difficult. Small firms contend they are better able to handle the problems of small businesses, and to offer a personal relationship with a client they say is difficult for a larger firm to provide. The differing perspectives and scope of services offered by firms of varying sizes suggest that the profession is far from monolithic, and units within it have different needs.

Product Differentiation. The perceived necessity to project a distinctive image has driven firms to find various ways to distinguish their product (even though sometimes that product may seem to others to be indistinguishable). A decade ago "Arthur Andersen & Co. trumpeted its TFA (transaction flow auditing), Coopers its CAAG (computer audit assistance group), and Touche Ross, now Deloitte & Touche, had its TRAP (Touche Ross audit process); but to clients, an audit is an audit." [28] More importantly, firms now have developed and organized practices around their industry expertise, which may well be one of the most effective devices for acquiring clients. Clients and potential clients generally like to employ the experts in their particular field. [29]

But is an "Audit an Audit" regardless of which CPA undertakes it? If auditing is a routine, mandated/compliance, low-value service, it resembles a commodity; a term the profession views with no little horror. Nevertheless, efforts to dispute it have been notably unsuccessful. Although not always held to be the case, an audit report sometimes is believed to be the same in the eyes of the user whether signed by one firm or another, and fees often are more important to a client than the identity of the signer. Further, the number of companies requiring or needing audits is limited or finite, and, except for emerging companies and those in certain other special fields such as municipalities that now must be audited, most entities already have retained auditors. Thus the market for audits is relatively mature or stable, and new clients generally are acquired by one firm only at the expense of another. This and the "outsourcing market" mentioned above are among the reasons for public accounting firms to have aggressively expanded their practice in other areas of nonattest service.

Fees. CPAs have believed that client service, promptly and expertly delivered by competent professionals, should be the only legitimate basis for competition. Because of the nature of the knowledge base necessary for such service, fees were never a long term factor—or should not have been. You got what you paid for; a cut-rate fee likely would produce a low-quality performance.

The removal of the ban on competitive bidding by the AICPA in 1972, particularly when combined with the pressures arising from the growing belief in the audit as a commodity, opened the floodgates. Further, work for governmental bodies and agencies was becoming important, and the solicitation of bids for such work often was mandated by law. Bidding by CPA firms became commonplace. However, bids significantly below any reasonable measure of cost or profitability (lowballing) generated publicity and criticism. Whether this practice was widespread, or if so, whether it was inconsistent with the new emphasis on competition, is a continuing debate.

Companies that otherwise were satisfied with their public accountants now have the opportunity to satisfy economy-minded stockholders and others by negotiating fee reductions, often by throwing the annual audit open for bids. This resulted more and more frequently in auditor changes. Early surveys of companies changing auditors disclosed that 36% did so to get a break on audit service fees. This represented an increase over previous experience.[30]

Opinion Shopping. A dark side to competition in the field of public accountancy shows up in recurring inferences that auditor changes sometimes take place because of disagreements over accounting principles or other professional matters as to which the present CPA's position is unsatisfactory to the client. For example, given a particular set of circumstances, the client may hope that a new firm would be able to issue an unqualified audit report, whereas the current one refuses to do so. Such inferences, needless to say, are treated with contempt by practitioners because of the tacit insult to their integrity. It would be ingenuous to assert that this never happens, but countervailing pressures (such as the possibility of litigation) preventing it for the ethical practitioner are enormous.

The issues are further complicated because of the indefinite boundaries set in marginal cases by generally accepted accounting principles, as to which opinions legitimately may differ. Further, situations where there are auditor changes may also involve disputes over fees, allegations of unsatisfactory service, lack of a particular skill on the part of the CPA, or that old standby, personality differences. These may be difficult to untangle.

In order to bring some coherence to these matters, at least for the CPA with a public client, the SEC requires that auditor changes be reported by a the CPA firm's client (the registrant) on Form 8-K. This report must disclose significant disagreements with the auditor, and the auditor must file a separate letter stating concurrence (or lack thereof) with the client's assertions on a very timely basis. The period for resolving these agreements has become increasingly shorter in the past decade. Further, there are now requirements wherein auditors of public companies may be compelled to blow the "whistle" on unsatisfactory client response to concerns about material fraud in the financial statements of a publicly traded company client.[31]

A number of 8-Ks filed each year indeed disclose auditor-client disagreements, but it is not clear whether auditor changes resulted in more favorable treatment by succeeding auditors. In any event, despite cries of foul from the profession, the suspicion that this is the case persists, being intrinsically difficult to prove one way or another. A typical reaction is one expressed by a prominent accounting professor: "Auditors rarely sell their souls but they do sometimes shade their souls." [32]

Following concerns identified in 1993 by then SEC Chief Accountant Walter Schuetze, issues about the role of auditors in the entire spectrum of corporate governance were addressed in a special report of the Public Oversight Board in September 1994. The report, authored by a group led by former FASB Chairman Don Kirk, emphasized that the auditor works best in a public company environment involving a strong board of directors and audit committee. This is an "evergreen" issue which the profession will have to continue to work hard to overcome. Recent legislation specifies steps for auditor action in cases of material public company fraud--detailed below, and since 1989, members of the SEC Section of the AICPA's Division for CPA Firms have been required to confirm the termination of an SEC client/auditor relationship by letter to the client within five days, with a copy to the chief accountant of the SEC. [33]

Seeking Personnel

The core asset of a service business, such as a public practice firm, is its people. It is not strange, therefore, that firms take steps to seek out the best and most talented individuals available.   This means active, selective   recruiting of university educated men and women who are acculturated to the ideals of the profession and can   be expected to mature into true professionals. Direct hiring of specialists and experienced personnel may be an alternative or a supplement to university   recruiting particularly in those areas of taxes and management advisory or consulting services where an academic grounding in accountancy is not as essential as are other skills.

In competition with one another, all large firms, most medium-sized firms, and many small firms have organized college recruiting activities and cultivate the academic community in a variety of ways. Funding of chairs of accountancy, sponsorship of faculty internships and meetings of faculty   members from leading universities, grants for advanced study and for research projects, and contributions to university programs are common.

The total supply of college and university accounting degrees (graduate and undergraduate) was stable at approximately 54,000 throughout the period 1980-1991, although there were slight changes both up and down between the number with bachelor's degrees and those with master's degrees. Public accounting firms hire about one-third of this group. Many pursue other careers, or use the undergraduate degree as a solid foundation to enter law or professional management study or enter corporate practice directly. International students being trained in the United States and returning to their home countries also comprise a growing portion of this number. With the gradual implementation of the graduate equivalent or 150-semester hour requirement for AICPA membership and for state qualification taking effect in the year 2000, a pronounced shift in graduate hires may occur. However, students will also have the option of obtaining this additional coursework on a part-time basis, and it is expected that a substantial number of individuals and firms will select this approach. While overall the increase in new hires with advanced degrees is small, the trend may be significant in the light of the expansion in the breadth of knowledge necessary to practice as a CPA professional, and the demands of specialties such as taxation, SEC and regulatory reporting, financial planning, and business valuation. Public accounting firms also hire graduating students with nonaccounting degrees. Seven percent of new hires in 1987-1988 hold degrees in such related specialties as law and management information systems or computers. [34]

Regulatory Agencies and Professional Behavior

An overhanging and contentious issue regarding ethical behavior in the practice of public accountancy is the existence of rules of behavior thought to enhance the delivery of services in a proper manner to clients, but which are alleged to inhibit competition in apparent defiance of laws (such as federal antitrust statutes) designed to maintain a competitive environment in our free, private enterprise economy. Here there is a conflict between canons that seek to limit professional activities in areas that seem to be commercial rather than moral, and statutes proscribing such limitations. Clearly, ethical rules pertaining to bidding, advertising, and solicitation, offers of employment to employees of other accounting firms and the like, deal with business practices that are morally neutral, in themselves neither good nor bad; it is only their probable effect on other behavioral imperatives (such as independence) that the professional has sought to mitigate. Regulators disagree—in the name of competition. In effect they intervene in a profession's self-regulatory process to "deregulate" in favor of competition, that is, an external agency "employs" competition to determine what services are to be offered and what type or manner of payment is acceptable. This view it is argued "empowers" the consumer to choose the means of payment while causing the provider to compete for the consumer. Consider the following examples:

Bidding. Effective March 6, 1962, the AICPA adopted Rule 3.03, which prohibited competitive bidding as follows:

> *A member or associate shall not make a competitive bid for a professional engagement. Competitive bidding for public accounting services is not in the public interest, is a form of solicitation, and is unprofessional.*[35]

About this time, however, concerns were starting to be expressed that prohibition of activities such as competitive bidding might conflict with antitrust laws. The March, 1965 version of this rule, therefore, was identical to that adopted in 1962, but contained the following footnote:

On the advice of legal counsel that Rule 3.03 subjects the Institute and its representatives to risks under the Federal antitrust laws, the Institute's executive committee, Council and committee on professional ethics have decided that the Institute will continue to refrain from taking any disciplinary action against any member or associate under Rule 3.03 until there has been a change in circumstances that would justify a different opinion on the legal status of the Rule.[36]

This concern was justified when, in 1972, the AICPA, in response to a suit filed by the federal government, agreed to delete the competitive bidding rule from its code of ethics. In 1975 the Supreme Court stated that it "could not find support for the proposition that Congress intended" to exclude the learned professions from the reach of the Sherman Act. And further, that "The nature of an occupation, standing alone, does not provide sanctuary from the Sherman Act."[37] This case pertained specifically to the attempt on the part of the Virginia Bar to publish and enforce a fee schedule for certain services, but the clear denial by the Supreme Court of any protection afforded professions from the Sherman Act served to open the door to other attacks on ethics rules perceived by regulators to be anticompetitive.

Commissions and Contingent Fees. The power of the federal government to influence the ethical behavior of professionals was illustrated again in the controversy over CPA traditional rules against accepting commissions and contingent fees (C & CF). The Federal Trade Commission (FTC) in the 1980s addressed an issue which was from an independence "appearance" perspective was more sensitive. Because of prior views on independence, the CPAs in public practice who had developed their attest and other practices on a hourly/fee-based economic basis, resisted this modification of C & CF rules. The prohibitions were continued in the code of professional conduct in January, 1988 in the face of ongoing investigations and actions taken by the FTC.

However, the FTC persisted, and in August, 1988, officers of the AICPA were authorized to sign an agreement with that agency. This agreement arranged for the AICPA to prohibit acceptance of contingent fees or commissions, from clients for whom a CPA member performs audits, reviews, certain compilations, or examination of prospective financial statements. This, it was hoped, would preserve the essence of the independence requirement where it is most important--in the attest function. The agreement also would permit the acceptance of commissions, but would require the member to disclose that fact to the client; acceptance of commissions may, however, be prohibited for attest clients during the period of the attest engagement and the period covered by any historical financial statements involving such attest services. This revision of Rule 302 and a subsequent interpretation, effective in 1991, provide the contemporary framework for the AICPA's response to regulatory pressures.

State Legislation. These developments have raised questions in the minds of many practitioners regarding the effect on their responsibility to serve the public properly. Resistance, at the State regulation and legislation level was forthcoming. CPAs, regulators and legislators in Texas and Florida, for instance, undertook changes to bolster the traditional views challenged by the FTC. [38] Thus licensees could be following acceptable AICPA behavior and be found to violate State regulation or law. Since under the U.S. Constitution such state legislative enactments are beyond the reach of the FTC, this development may serve to inhibit that agency's initiatives, at least in the states taking such action. The effect of a state-by-state enactment of similar prohibitions may or may not be seen as beneficial, but is likely to make compliance difficult for firms having operations in several states. However, given the 1997 approval by AICPA Council of the proposed version of the Uniform Accountancy Act (UAA) establishing "substantial equivalency," this point may be moot. This version of the UAA follows the AICPA Code with regard to such matters. That is, CPA firms continue to be prohibited from accepting commissions and contingent fees from attest clients. However, even these firms will be permitted to accept commissions and contingent fees for services from clients for whom they do not perform attest services.

Competition With Others

Because CPAs have a franchise, or a social contract or a license from the state to be the exclusive providers of one service in a specific area of practice--expressing opinions on financial statement--competition with those outside the profession in the fulfillment of the attest function is rare or nonexistent. The profession's state monopoly in this respect is buttressed by laws such as the federal securities acts, which provide that only a licensee, an independent public accountant, may examine and express opinions on financial statements. There may be some ambiguity in state laws which allow the attest function to be performed by a nonlicensee as long as there is no holding out to be a CPA or PA, but the effect probably is negligible in terms of competitive position. The situation regarding tax practice is quite different, and that regarding management advisory services is radically different. One begins to appreciate, as we next consider the continuously evolving scope and range of services provided by the CPA Profession, the challenge of balancing services which are both mandated under a franchise and those which are determined substantially or solely by the market.

Summary

The role of information in the capital markets is influenced by its value in making important allocation decisions which affect all the factors of production. Information about money, is especially today, in a truly global investment economy particularly important. Financial capital seeks its highest and best use, and investors and owners in a property system are empowered by the information rights related to their capital and rely on the CPA Profession to provide a timely, relevant and reliably social reporting process as to operating and investment performance. In a free enterprise system the role of its trusted and valued information profession involves a variety of functions, occupations, and services. The next chapter describes the established and evolving services that CPAs provide to society through public and corporate practice, government and nonprofit positions and in education.

Discussion Questions

1. How does the CPA profession establish a claim to professional status today?

2. How do consumers/clients purchasing professional services to evaluate whether they are receiving appropriate value for their money? To what extent should this be assured by legal mandates? By professional rules? By market competition?

3. Are global public accounting firms too large? What are the considerations for determining the economic size of such a firm? Should these firms compare in size and manner to the way law, medicine, and engineering firms practice?

4. Why were advertising and bidding for engagements by CPAs considered u n professional activities? Why did this view change? Should these types of activities be restricted in any way? How?

5. Critics often are suspicious that CPAs serving as auditors sometimes bend the rules on accounting matters to obtain or keep a client. What factors mitigate against such actions? What, if anything, do you believe should be done about the situation?

6. By accepting payments in the form of commissions and fees on a contingency basis for nonattest clients, are CPAs forfeiting a public trust? Some in the profession resisted these changes; why?

7. Public accounting firms compete with non-CPA consulting firms. How and why is this affecting the structure of CPA firms?

8. How has low-cost, computer information technology affected the way CPAs meet the global demand for information used in the capital markets?

Endnotes

[1]Donkin, Richard, "Value and rewards of brainpower," *Financial Times* (June 13, 1997): *I.*

[2] Coggan, Philip, and Dunne, Nancy, "World markets power ahead," *Financial Times* (June 14,15, 1997):1.

[3] "A market gone wild," *US News & World Report* (January 13, 1992):60.

[4] "Who's News," *The Wall Street Journal* (February 19, 1987):34.

[5] United States General Accounting Office, *The Accounting Profession: Major Issues: Progress and Concerns,* (Washington, D.C.: GPO, 1996):4.

[6] "The Public Interest Must Come First," an address by Philip B. Chenok, *Journal of Accountancy* (February, 1996): 63.

[7] "Who's News," *The Wall Street Journal* (May 24, 1989).

[8] MacDonald, Elizabeth, "Accounting Firms Post Strong Rise In 1996 Revenue," *The Wall Street Journal* (February 3, 1997).

[9] In its July, 1997 issue, *Nation's Business* reported that 401 [k] assets have grown from zero in 1984 to over one trillion dollars today. Further that amount is expected to double in less than 5 years. Defined contribution plans, since 1984, are now nearly twice as numerous as defined benefit plans. The former now cover over 40 million workers.

[10] Thurow, Lester, "New Rules for Playing the Game," *Phi Kappa Phi Journal* (Fall 1992) *10.*

[11] Blumentstin, R., and Solis, D., "GM's Mexican Houses on Shaky Ground," *The Wall Street Journal* (June 20, 1997):A15.

[12] "Expanding Horizons," AICPA Annual Report 1994-1995,

[13] *The Commission on Auditors' Responsibilities: Report, Conclusions and Recommendations,* (New York: AICPA, 1978): 109-110.

[14] "FTC ISSUES FINAL ORDER AGAINST AICPA CONCERNING RESTRAINTS ON CERTIFIED PUBLIC ACCOUNTANTS," *FTC NEWS,* Federal Trade Commission, Washington, D. C., (August 7, 1990) Docket No. C-3297.

[15] J. Michael Cook, as quoted in *The Wall Street Journal* (September 20, 1985).

[16] MacDonald, Elizabeth, "Andersen Appears to Rule Out Breakup," *The Wall Street Journal* (December 23, 1996):A2.

[17] Pincus, Karen V., and Pincus, J. David, "Public Relations: What CPA Firms Are Doing." *Journal of Accountancy* (November, 1986): 128-138.

[18] Yao, Margaret, *The Wall Street Journal* (March 18, 1981).

[19] *The Wall Street Journal* (January 5, 1989).

[20] *The Wall Street Journal* (April 24, 1989).

[21] "Accounting's New Corporate Giant: IDS challenges the profession," *Public Accounting Report* (February 28, 1994).

[22] "Heard on the Street," *The Wall Street Journal* (October 11, 1996): C1-2.

[23] Tyebjee, Tyzoon T., and Bruno, Albert V., "Developing the Marketing Concept in Public Accounting Firms," *Journal of the Academy of Marketing Science* (Spring, 1982): 165-188.

[24] Knoffo, Anthony Jr., "Publications Offer Tax Advice," *The Phoenix Gazette* (December 21, 1988).

[25] *Public Accounting Report* (June 1984).

[26]Richard A. Connor, Jr., as quoted by Sammons, Donna, "Accounting for Growth," *INC.* (January 1984).

[28] Bernstein, Peter W., "Competition Comes to Accounting," *Fortune* (July 17, 1978).

[29] Ibid.

[30] Klott, Gary, "Auditors Feel the Heat of a New Scrutiny," *The New York Times, Business,* May 13, 1984.

[31] Under Title III (Auditor Disclosure of Corporate Fraud) of the Private Securities Litigation and Reform Act of 1995, after the auditor satisfies investigation and reporting steps, including reporting said fraud to the board of directors of a public company, a notice of said report is to be sent by the board to the SEC within one business day of the notice. If the board fails to notify the SEC as required the auditor must either resign or furnish the Commission with a copy of the report.

[32]Lee Seidler, as quoted by Klott, Gary, op. cit.

[33]Update 9 (March 17, 1989) to the *SECPS Manual,* (New York: AICPA, 1986).

[34] Data from: *The Supply Of Accounting Graduates and The Demand for Public Accounting Recruits,* (New York: AICPA, 1988) and *Accounting Education: A Statistical Survey, 1992-1993* (New York: AICPA, 1994).

[35] *By-Laws, Code of Professional Ethics,* AICPA, 1962, 32. (Previous AICPA rules against bidding prohibited this activity only if it would conflict with local professional society or state board rules.)

[36] *Code of Professional Ethics,* AICPA, March 4, 1965, 7.

[37] *Goldfarb* v. *Virginia State Bar,* 95 S. Ct. 2004 (1975).

[38] *Today's CPA* (Texas Society of Certified Public Accountants, March/April, 1989).

CHAPTER 8

The Scope of CPA Services

"Information is the life blood of the capital markets. CPAs as information preparers, auditors, and analysts of operations and performance are principal suppliers of that information."
Barry Melancon, CPA[1]

Introduction

The needs of society and users of business information constantly change; therefore, the nature, scope, and domain of CPA services is constantly subject to change within the bounds of competency. So the CPA profession has to be able to continue to "reposition" itself to those places where the highest and best use of its social and professional product are to be employed. The phenomenon of "outsourcing" mentioned previously, and further developed below, is a contemporary example of one which evokes "repositioning." This also has been accented by the increasingly global need for cost beneficial disclosure about corporate control[2] and performance measurement information which will affect the price and availability of an important factor of production, **investment capital**. Practitioner competence to perform a given service is perhaps an initial factor to be considered when evaluating the scope and domain of CPA services. Attention to competence is market-derived and focuses on making public practice responsive to user needs. [3]

It may be a truism for CPAs to say " We are what we do!" But, by examining the types of things CPAs do, especially when such activity is a typical endeavor, we will know more about what it means to be a CPA. In a global internet and computer information age, the existing and future scope of CPA services reflects the influence of technology upon a judgmental and therefore labor intensive profession. CPAs in public, corporate, and government practice are professionals differentiated by specialized functions including report preparation, performance and investment analysis, as well as consultancy, tax, and traditional attest functions. These are the general "product lines" which comprise the CPA profession's scope of services. These functional product lines are further distinguished by the specific business or industry to which they are applied, for example, agriculture, transportation, communications, retail, banking, health care, and so forth.

The competencies involved in developing and managing the practice domain of the CPA are many. By means of entrepreneurial effort, leadership, economic assessment and organizational form, CPAs, individually and in their practice units, determine the extent of their services at a point in time and this, compounded by multiple unit experience, gives identity to our profession. The domain of CPA services is based upon fundamental competencies. The knowledge, skills, and abilities underlying these competencies, in the past, have been based upon and associated with accounting and attest services for a clientele of private and corporate organizations, governmental, and nonprofit institutions, as well as a variety of users of performance information about business operations and competitive activities. Nearly every group of decision makers potentially may be involved, be they managers, employees, investors, creditors, owners, corporate managers, government officials, and private individuals in this country and around the world.

To state that the domain of CPA practice is truly global seems appropriate, although this clearly implies a vision and understanding beyond what is held by those who entertain a mere double-entry view of the disciplines employed in CPA services.

Research and commentary on the evolution of and debate about the scope of services can be found in several major studies, including Briloff (1965), the Public Oversight Board of the AICPA (1979), Previts (1985) and R. H. Parker (1986), as well as, summaries including a report to the Treadway Commission by James B. Edwards (1986), a century-long perspective by Mednick and Previts (1987), and forward-looking views by Mednick (1988, 1991), Wallace (1990), and *The Public Accounting Profession: Meeting the needs of a Changing World* (1991).[4] Professional research periodicals and journals, including *Research in Accounting Regulation* and the *Journal of Accounting and Public Policy,* feature studies and policy discussions about aspects of the subject.

"Scope of Services" has become the term commonly applied to the public practice activities of the CPA profession. It was popularized by the series of Congressional hearings in the late 1970s based upon the congressional staff study mentioned previously, *The Accounting Establishment.* Scope of services became a euphemism for the debate over the extent to which CPAs, who served as principal external auditors for publicly held companies, could undertake nonattest services (NAS), including tax and other forms of advisory and consulting work, without affecting the independence of thought and action expected by the public and required under federal securities laws. In the 1990s, as dramatic shifts in the demographic patterns of CPAs into corporate career positions occurred, combined with outsourcing induced shifts into consultative services, and the reduction in demand for audit services, the term has evolved a new meaning, indicative of the repositioning of the CPA community as the premier information profession to service decision makers in global capital markets.

Following AICPA membership endorsement of the concepts of self-regulation set forth in George Anderson's Committee plan to restructure professional standards, there was an increased awareness that the CPA's scope of professional services, which traditionally focused upon public practice, must also consider issues related to CPAs in other areas such as corporate and government practice. AICPA members in corporate practice areas had become a majority. Other important, although smaller components of the CPA community included practice in government units or not-for-profit entities, and teaching and conducting research in educational settings. These CPAs, while fewer in number than those in public and corporate practice, complete the CPA profession's profile and image in those major sectors of society where government, education, and nonprofit entities affect the lives of countless people.

To the extent that the authority of law influences practice, there may be other political issues to address to resolve scope of service issues. For example, CPAs and lawyers negotiated for nearly two decades at the national level, through the 1950s, to establish which aspects of complying with federal tax law were authorized versus unauthorized from the point of view of the legal profession contention that all such tax practice was the practice of law.[5]

As mentioned, the term scope of services acquired increasing significance in the 1970s. It was shortly after the Congressional hearings of this period that the Securities and Exchange Commission promulgated two Accounting Series Releases (ASRs) which required that proxy statements of publicly held companies contain information disclosing the percent of audit fees represented by NAS fees paid by the company to the CPA firm that conducted the audit.[6] This requirement had what professionals called a "chilling" effect on CPA ability to present their case for providing NAS to attest clients, since only the fees paid to auditor-CPAs for such services were subject to this disclosure. If the services were provided by competitors, including CPA firms that were not the auditors of record or non-CPAs, who are a significant percentage of NAS competition, no disclosure was required. Many clients, audit firms argued, saw this disclosure as an additional cost, decision, or burden which could easily be avoided by not engaging the auditor to do such work.

Extensive and seemingly repetitive studies to evaluate the issue have not established that the potential conflict of NAS with audit services causes a compromise of independence. Persuasive arguments, including those by a former chief accountant of the SEC, assert that such expanded services in fact are in the best interest of the client, given the need for efficiency and for "one stop shopping for information related professional services".[7]   Furthermore, the public is best served, given proper safeguards to independence, by permitting the full skills of CPAs to be employed in concert with market forces. Yet criticism in the media, some warranted, and some from potential competitors, and in Congress and government agencies is likely to continue, if only because of the increasingly competitive arena for such activity.

Practice Environment

Without much debate, the traditional view of the scope of service of CPAs has meant the practice of public accounting firms. "Real CPAs" were traditionally identified with auditing, and tax practice, and client services such as compilation or review of private company reports. Now the domain and scope of CPA services is broader than public practice alone, while retaining the recognition of the unique core public practice franchise, the attest function. Furthermore, CPAs practice inside corporate entities as well as in practice firm units, just as physicians, lawyers, and other established professions may be found in private medical practice or with a law firm or on staff as in-house corporate legal counsel, or serving as a physician in a company clinic.   So the entity of practice is not the defining aspect. *A physician is a physician, a lawyer is a lawyer, and a CPA is a CPA, regardless of the practice environment.* The public responsibilities of a CPA who serves as chief financial officer of a major corporation, or in the office of the Comptroller General of the United States, positions commonly held by CPAs, are as significant to the concerns of society as are the responsibilities of CPAs who are external auditors or advisors to an operating company. As Melancon points out in his banner quote opening this chapter, CPAs participate in the lifeblood function of capital markets, producing, auditing, or analyzing decision information. Maintaining this informational infrastructure as the basis of measurement and disclosure in the capital markets is as essential to the public's well-being as a fair and effective court system.

This broad domain of scope of services rests on a corresponding view that CPAs are expected to conduct themselves as CPAs in each of the principal practice occupations, as reflected in the expanded recognition of duties and responsibilities for American Institute members in its code of professional conduct.[8] CPAs in all practice environments, public, corporate, government, and so on, are required to follow reporting standards, to maintain their expertise via continuing education activities, and new entrants must meet the post baccalaureate educational requirements that will become effective over the next few years. And all CPAs are expected to reflect the positive values of integrity, objectivity, and competence in their chosen roles.

Public, Corporate, and Government Practice

Public Practice Scope of Service   Striking changes have occurred in the composition of services offered by public practice units of all sizes. The trend to achieve growth from market-based user needed services in contrast to seeking growth from mandated service products lines (attest and tax services) is a fact of life today in public practice. Many of these services relate to single event, often long term, projects. Their economic characteristics are not like mandated service which have an annual "annuity" fee structure. Therefore the need to continually obtain new project income requires skills in developing valuable knowledge and marketing it as well. Further accelerating the shift from traditional services is the availability of relatively inexpensive, user friendly software to facilitate preparation of reports and returns. Thus the changing structure of costs, the competition for experienced staff with greater amounts of formal education leads to the necessity of constantly responding with high value added service which will support a structure of professional fee income.

Consultancy and advisory services have flourished in this way, due in part to the outsourcing phenomenon and the need for firms to develop new value added services based upon their professional skills. Available data points out that outsourcing, a $135 billion dollar market [1997] "...trend began with the outsourcing of such ancillary functions as building equipment maintenance, and progressed to support services, including payroll and data processing.[9] Companies now "outsource" internal audits"[10] and large companies, including British Petroleum and Mobil are seeking to cut as much as $5 billion from a joint venture by "outsourcing many financial task to international accounting companies." [11] Financial Service firms such as J. P. Morgan have identified a 7-year $2 billion transfer of its computer staff to outside suppliers. The rationale for much of this outsourcing is not mere staff cutting but the elimination of functions which the company cannot do better than someone else. . . that is, non-core competencies. Core competencies, in about one-third of recently studied companies include such activities as business strategy, information technology strategy, and new product development.[12]

The long-term outsourcing trend, of course, is uncertain. Some say that it must reach its limit soon. Their view is reflected in a 1997 Supreme Court decision, that independent and other contracting arrangements cannot sustain popular and judicial concerns if merely a tactic to slash wages and benefits.[13] Others believe that outsourcing is the start of a even more permanent trend in delivery of services which will be outlined in the next chapter.

The strategic implications for public practice firms, corporate CPAs, and the entire CPA profession are obviously significant. If outsourcing is carried to its "core" extreme will only generic providers of outsourcing services exist? Will all corporate staff be pared to individuals involved in strategic functions with all other activities contracted for in the marketplace? And if so, how does one determine true core versus service competencies? Is the maintenance function of an airline a contracted service or a core function? If control of service quality is a significant factor in transportation, does outsourced maintenance afford quality control? Obviously finding the balance point between internal and external sourcing is not clearly defined. Similar questions relate to our field. If most all CPA functions are outsourced does the corporate CPA become extinct? How does that prospect equate with the phenomenon of the growth of AICPA members not it public practice, who now comprise the majority of its members?

Audit, Attest, and Assurance Services

Audit and Attest. The rationale for CPAs receiving the attest franchise is related to the explosion of industrial development in the United States during the decades preceding World War I. Historians of the CPA profession have documented a progressive movement, in search of a "community of the competent" achieved legislation creating a new profession.[14] CPA laws, beginning in 1896, in the State of New York, were in existence in all States by the mid-1920s.[15]

As the mix of public practice services has changed in recent years, revenue from "core" attest services (annual audits, quarterly reviews, compilations, etc.) has become a smaller percent of total fee income (see Chapter 2, Table 2.3).[16] From his vantage point, the SEC's Chief Accountants, Michael Sutton sees profound effects for public practice firms. "By the year 2000," says Sutton, "revenues from consulting services could constitute more than two-thirds of CPA firms' total revenues."[17] Further, the SEC's chairman has cautioned that CPAs should view auditing as " `the very soul of the public accounting profession,' and not stray too far from its core job of policing corporate financial statements."[18] He has further remarked that "he shares the concern, expressed by two recent private sector studies, that `auditing firms are becoming more focused on consulting and other services, at the expense of the audit function.'"[19]

(The studies to which the SEC Chairman referred are (1) the report of an AICPA Special Committee on Financial Reporting, named the Jenkins Committee, after its chair, Edmund L. Jenkins, who is now Chairman of the FASB.[20] and (2) the report by a panel appointment by the Public Oversight Board, issued in September

1994, which addressed the role of the auditor in public companies, especially with regard to corporate governance and the audit committee.)[21]

The subject matter of these reports, (1) attention to the needs of financial statement users, and (2) relating the role of the auditor to the corporate governance structure, were among the principal reasons for the formation of the Independence Standards Board (ISB) in 1997. The board, previously described, will be expected to develop both a conceptual framework and practical guidance to assist firms addressing the concerns raised by the SEC, it will be assisted by an Independence Issues Committee (IIC).

The ISB may likely pursue its role, at least at the outset, by asking a central question? *What do we know about auditor behavior and independence?* It will take an organized program and research to obtain the types of responses which will be useful. Independence is often evaluated on the basis of "appearance" and not as a matter of "fact." By avoiding matters such as financial involvement with a client, membership on client's board of directors and other potential financial and personal conflicts of interest of this order, the auditor manages to avoid the "appearance" of a lack of independence. The "fact" of independence, that is, whether or not the auditor truly behaves independently, is much more difficult to assess. Absent an individual's admitting being compromised, assessing independence *in fact* would seem to require the ability to measure the inner workings of another's mind. Researchers in the field of audit decision behavior now conduct studies and build models which can be used to assess such complex issues.

The advent of a separate board to oversee auditor independence affects all sizes of practice units who have public company clients, but has been most visible in the professional press which covers large- and medium-sized firms. Furthermore in 1997, the AICPA firm ownership rules were again modified to increase the recognition of the ownership right of other non-CPA professionals. This acknowledgment is likely to support the expansion of the breadth to the scope of services in practice units by involving individuals with skills needed in the marketplace but not traditionally found in firms.

Assurance Services. In late 1996, culminating two years of work, the AICPA Special Committee on Assurance Services [The Elliott Committee], reported out its findings as to the future of this "product line" of CPA services. The report was disseminated via linkage to the AICPA's web site [www.aicpa.org] instead of being printed and distributed in the typical fashion of such documents. The delivery of the report itself was a message, as orchestrated by Committee Chair, Robert K. Elliott of KPMG Peat Marwick. The new form of communication is the electronic page! Elliott's committee's work was also pathbreaking in a perhaps even more significant way. Not only was it successful in completing its charge, it served as the model for the organized CPA profession to conduct research into new areas of potential service in order to determine how and what could be provided from the existing and likely skills consistent with the "permissions" or roles which society identifies with CPAs. This process, which was research based, encourages experimentation and adaptation has formulated a "research and development" process for the AICPA to employ which is unique to the modern era of our profession.

Assurance services, are defined as "independent professional services that improve the quality of information, or its context, for business or individual decision makers." The committee also emphasized that such services are not confined to financial statements or conventional reports. The committee also identified several areas where this potential new "product line" can be marketed.

Table 8.1   High Potential Assurance Services[22]
                   The Elliott Committee - AICPA

1. Electronic commerce assurance
2. Health care performance measurement
3. Entity performance measurement
4. Information systems quality
5. Comprehensive risk assessment
6. Elder care assurance

The efforts of the Committee, and its foresightful chairman, seem to be very much on target judging from recent press reports on employers in the United States helping staff to care for elderly parents, and a proposal by the U.K.'s Securities and Investments Board calling for "certified web sites" to assist investors.[23]

Compilation and Review. To many public accounting firms whose principle client base is privately held companies, the term "A&A" signifies "core" services. Accounting and Auditing (A&A) likely will remain the majority service fee income base for many such firms. The valuable "accounting" service provided to such clients is subject to professional standards, just as with auditing. Accountants involved in compilation and review services practice under Statements on Standards for Accounting and Review Services (SSARS). SSARS #1, 1978 issued by the AICPA's senior technical committee, the Accounting and Review Services Committee of the AICPA, is titled *Compilation and Review of Financial Statements.* The statement contains standards for performing either of two levels of service on unaudited financial statements of nonpublic companies—a compilation or a review, and specifies wording for the accountant's report to be issued in each case. To date over a half dozen such standards have been released. The appropriate audit application of SSARS is guided by the hierarchy of generally accepted accounting principles elaborated by a Statement on Auditing Standards issued in 1992[24] The importance of this guidance, particularly with regard to small, closely held, private enterprises is to assist practitioners in planning applications of standards in ways which will minimize the concerns about "standards overload" and or duplication. The cost of complying with standards is an issue with CPAs whose compilation (write-up) work raises service cost in comparison with non-CPA providers, including commercial, publicly held entities now appearing in the market. The Technical Issues Committee [TIC] of the Private Companies Practice (PCPS) section of the AICPA, the unit which supports public accounting firms which serve only private companies, continues to seek resolution of standards overload issues by presentations at standard setting meetings, and by informing member firms of emerging issues.

Critics, Concerns, Conflicts: Questions and Responses

It is not reasonable to expect to undertake the magnitude of change involved in the era of outsourcing, and to adapt to the opportunities identified in the assurance service market without criticisms and legitimate concerns being raised.[25] How will CPAs maintain their competencies across such a varied portfolio of services? Is the CPA examination properly structured for this new age? Is the domain of service manageable in a global context? When financial calamity and political fallout occur, alleging conflicts of interest, how will these be sorted out without gratuitous litigation sapping energy and resources?[26] Will new services endanger other or older "permissions" awarded to the CPA profession by society and the marketplace?

Since inception, the practitioners of accountancy have been challenged to accept greater financial responsibility for a crisis which occurs on their watch, in short to become insurers of the validity of disclosures. No one, of course, has the resources to back the bets of the entire capital market, yet at times it seems that no less would be satisfactory to the most ardent critics. Part of the organized profession's reaction to concerns and conflicts with regard to major public concerns has been to invest in projects, commissions, or special committee efforts. The endnote citations which detail the passages in the text below present a general literature of many episodes involving resolution of litigation, fraud, insider trading,[27] manipulation or other collusive acts, or cases where audit failures are alleged or suspected, leading to investor or market loss.[28] As recently as 1987 the [Treadway] National Commission on Fraudulent Financial Reporting[29] completed a major study of the phenomenon of financial fraud and continues to act to carry out its recommendations through COSO, a follow-up organization, the Council of Sponsoring Organizations. Yet from the episode of the South Seas Investment Bubble in Britain prior to the industrial age, through frauds including McKesson[30]in the 1930s, Equity Funding[31]in the 1970s, ESM Securities[32]in the 1980s and to the host of recent debacles, involving Orange County,[33] Barings Bank,[34] and the gold stock fraud Bre-X, [35] one begins to understand that in dealing with humankind there can be no complete protection against misdeeds. There is a certain predictability and timelessness about such misbehavior. Popular press accounts of "cooked books,"[36] of Michael Milken,[37] of multi/mega million dollar settlements by public practice firms related to Savings & Loan engagements,[38] of large jury awards against auditors (Miniscribe), [39]of sleazy banks (BCCI),[40] of a convicted corporate officer (Phar-Mor)[41]or auditor (ESM Securities/Home Savings Bank), have been disturbing in frequency, even in a bull market setting.[42]   And, of course at the next market downturn "that question" will again be asked: "Where were the auditors?' (Perhaps answer will be: "They were not out there all alone.")

Corporate Governance. A first response anticipating "that question" came in September 1994. Following expressions of concern about auditor independence, the Public Oversight Board of the AICPA's SEC Practice Division issued a report which recommended, among other actions, that client board audit committee charters be modified to contain a statement which places both the audit committee and the auditor on notice that the board and not the management, is the client of the auditor. [43] The tactic of explicitly identifying the audit committee and the auditor in this relationship responds to the growing interest on the part of Institutional investors, who generate over half of equity market's capital, that active board participation in the oversight of the external auditor function is a role of corporate governance. [44] The auditor alone cannot craft a policy and procedure which will insure a cost beneficial system of internal review and control.   Indeed preventing corruption, fraud, insider trading, and other illicit acts must be understood to be a duty of those on the board, in management and in professional staff positions such as internal audit as well. [45] (The auditor should not be out there alone!)

Financial Statement Fraud. Another response, recognizing a public expectation that auditor's affirm and define their responsibilities to detect fraud in financial statements, the Auditing Standards Board of the AICPA issued Standard No. 82 in February 1997.[46]   It had been expected that perhaps part of the political bargain to achieve federal tort reform legislation would be an explicit action by the organized profession to state clearly its role in the detection of financial statement fraud. SAS 82 uses the word "Fraud" explicitly ... acknowledging that in the process of the financial statement audit the auditor has a responsibility to plan and perform the audit to obtain reasonable assurance about whether the financial statements are free from of material misstatement, whether caused by error or fraud.[47] By repositioning itself with regard to the previous standard (SAS No. 53), the new standard requires auditors to ask management about the risk of fraud and whether they have knowledge that fraud has been perpetrated on or within the entity. If the entity under audit has a program that includes steps to prevent, deter, or detect fraud, the auditor will inquire of persons overseeing that program as to whether the program has identified any fraud.[48] Early academic survey work on small firm reaction indicates that "The new SAS is a double edged sword. The SAS will become the minimum level of acceptable professional care ... although the auditor has the same responsibility regarding fraud detection as under SAS 53, the new SAS provides detailed implementation, documentation and reporting guidance." And while the auditor is not required by the standard to discover all fraudulent occurrences at a client, the new standard makes clear that even minor fraud findings discovered are to be brought to management's attention.[49]

Forensic Audits/Special Procedures. As early as 1912, Robert Heister Montgomery, a founder of the firm Coopers & Lybrand in the United States, made the important distinction often dismissed by individuals unfamiliar with the traditional limit of a financial audit, namely the distinction between an "audit" and an "investigation." "Investigations," Montgomery wrote, "are usually undertaken in connection with the sale of a business to a corporation or other purchaser for the purpose of obtaining special information relative to finances or general affairs, or with respect to alleged fraudulent transactions, or into the profits derived from manufacture of infringing articles, etc." [50]

Modern accountants who profess to practice this particular skill, of forensic auditing include Price Waterhouse's Warren McInteer. Called in to investigate the collapse of tycoon Robert Maxwell's publishing empire, in the midst of concerns of manipulation of employee pension funds of Maxwell Communications Corp. McInteer discovered a classic Ponzi scheme. "Maxwell had about 50 bank accounts ...[F]rom March to October 1992, he made about 2,000 bank transactions worth well over one million pounds each."[51] Eventually Maxwell became very desperate, notes, McInteer, and "Desperate people will usually do desperate things."

Today forensics, or "sleuthing" is big business in the Big Six and in other firms, large and small. Since 1992, Price Waterhouse has doubled its forensics ranks to 500; Coopers & Lybrand has increased its forensic staff more than fivefold to 380.[52] Among the investigations in which Big Six forensic auditors have become involved relates to the review of accounts at 450 Swiss banks searching for dormant accounts and other assets deposited by victims of the Jewish Holocaust. It may be that as forensics becomes more widely known it will be recognized for its special role in contrast to the financial statement audit and the latter will be better understood as to its focus to business and financial reporting.

Education. A portion of the 1987 Treadway Commission Report (Appendix E)[53] also sought to engage the community of higher education to better prepare prospective CPA auditors. By supplying cases which portrayed environments in which fraudulent activities might be suspected, cases encouraged role-playing by faculty and students to enforce the meaning and events of the case. Several of the major firms, and the AICPA now sponsor case writing or provide case training materials for classroom use. However this flow of material still seems minimal given the growing dimension of practice scope.

Perhaps even more important in this process is the matter of attitudes and expectations about learning, in the university environment prior to the beginning of one's career, and then during the life-long experience of practice.   The current model for selecting and measuring competence over time involves education, testing and experience at the entry level, and then continuing education thereafter.   The adequacy of former concepts in these models is now being reviewed.   The content of the CPA Examination also is the subject of study by the [David B.] Pearson Committee of the AICPA.   Continuing education is being reevaluated in terms of learning achievement and life-long learning models which seek to add value and knowledge on a basis other than "hours" attended in a classroom.

Client Selection: Managing Audit Risk. Litigation exposure and involvement with distressed firms, obviously, does not enhance a firms reputation. For example, Unitech Industries, a Scottsdale, Arizona maker of telephone accessories discovered, for example that a Big Six firm chose to resign the engagement due to "insufficient internal controls."   The pullout of the firm left the client without sufficient resources, they claimed, to develop reliable financial reports.[54] Start-up and troubled companies will find it difficult to engage an auditor with sufficient "risk aversion" to accept the potential exposure. Business risk analysis has become a more visible aspect of client management techniques in the face of an aggressive plaintiff's bar and class action suits.   The business decision and long-term public interests here at some point may be at odds. There are those who fear that the businesses who most need expert assistance will be too risky for the firms to engage. A potential solution may be some type of equivalent of a "public defender" model, wherein groups of professionals, funded and insured by capital market and/or government sources or institutional investors, take up the business as part of a compensated public service activity.

Test of Review and Conflicts of Interest.   The concept of a test of review, the origin of peer review, can be traced to the 1960 writings of Robert Trueblood. In brief, the concept called for systematic review by reasonable persons capable of ascertaining the facts and drawing conclusions about matters such as a CPA's independence in audit work or about other phases of CPA activity.[55] Undergoing a test of review was to subject oneself to review, examination and criticism by fellow practitioners--i.e., in one form, a peer review. A peer review involves an evaluation of a practice unit's procedures and working papers, selectively, by an individual or a team of CPA peers as a means of assessing the practice management and technical competence of the firm under review. At some time in the future it may become common practice to peer review the quality of the nonattest services offered by CPAs. Such a program, at least initially, would provide the public increased assurance not only in matters of integrity and objectivity, but also in the particular NAS competencies of the subject firm. Alternatively, involving the client's audit committee and or board in any major consultancy engagement decisions at inception, as well as during and at the end seems a reasonable and prudent action. It may involve substantial preparation and consultation with senior management and firm personnel, but the long-term quality of the engagement certainly will be affected by such an arrangement in any event. Suggesting the inclusion of such a provision in the audit committee or board charter could be an added service to the client. Furthermore, from the firm point of view, there is as much client retention risk involved from an unsatisfactory consultancy as from poor service in tax or in attest service.

At present the processes in place among firms which have associated with self-regulating organizations, such as the AICPA division of firms, require that certain services, (e.g., executive search) be proscribed and that there be an annual reporting of NAS fees. The fee data in turn is publicly available, and usually constitutes the basis of rankings supplied by the firms and published in trade magazines.

At what point does a potential service become incompatible with the role of a CPA? As might be expected this is a difficult question.[56] As the profession continues to base itself on the personal integrity and responsibility of each member, and as peer reviews become more broadly used to assess the meeting of such responsibility, answers may gain more meaning. For the present it can be asserted that when an actual or proposed service conflicts with independence requirements (in appearance or in fact) observed in rendering a related or potential attest service to the same client, the service may be inappropriate and warrants careful evaluation. There are no perfect guidelines for this type of judgment. The following may be of some value, however:[57]

1. If the service presumes a competency at the supervisory level of practice (such as a knowledge of specialized industries) which is not available among the equity holders of the practice unit, then the service may be inappropriate.

2. If the assignment requires acting in the capacity equivalent to a member of management or employee the service is inappropriate.

3. If the service requires having the ability to access, control or assume custody of client assets the service is inappropriate.

4. If the service requires assuming the role of a promoter or underwriter the service is inappropriate.

5. If the services to be provided are not subject to review by competent individuals within the client organization, so as to determine and evaluate results, the service is inappropriate.

6. If multidisciplinary service entity proposes to offer an inappropriate service using the auditor as a conduit, the service remains inappropriate.

7. If the service impact on a workload or schedule configuration is such as to reduce or eliminate proper resources to conduct other engagements the service may be inappropriate.

8. If the service is voluntarily proscribed by rules of a professional organization, the service is inappropriate.

With regard to the latter, the AICPA division for CPA firms has membership requirements which limit practice activities that are inconsistent with the firm's responsibilities to the public or that consist of the following types of services such as psychological testing, public opinion polls, certain types of actuarial services and certain types of management recruiting. Knowledge of how these are currently interpreted and common sense practice safeguards provide guidance in determining whether to initiate a service for an attest client. Some suggested common sense safeguards include questioning services which:

1. May cause a violation of professional practice standards.

2. May be difficult to provide with consistent quality on a timely basis.

3. May be perceived as incompatible with a CPA's occupation; recent interpretations suggest that in such cases, full public disclosure would strengthen the case to permit offering the service.

Certain aspects of tax practice and evolving services such as litigation support and financial advice all have a characteristic which is in contrast to a central culture of the attest service in that these are "advocacy" services.[58] Here the professional "advocates" a particular point of view in support of the employing party, whereas in attest-based service, the third party user of the statements is relying on an independent opinion supplied by the CPA professional. In all cases the fundamental premise that underlies either advocacy or independence roles is that CPAs offer each service with integrity objectivity and competence, and further, under the evolving peer standards in the area, disclose clearly to each client their professional role in a service.

Final Solutions. As mentioned in an earlier chapter, human institutions, like professions, are incomplete and imperfect, because of the nature of the agents involved. If private sector attest services are to be preserved as a part of the free enterprise system there must be a political willingness to acknowledge such human limitations. The most vocal critics of perceived failures or abuses related to conflicts of interest cannot be satisfied short one of "final solution"---governmental control of the corporate audit function. This may seem far fetched at a time where the known limitations of timely government service are legendary...considering tax audits and other activities as an example. Accepting private sector service also has limitations. There is a price to be paid in political terms for cost-effective and timely auditing of publicly held entity financial reports. And while wholesale failure of the capital market process, as was experienced in the 1929 market crash and subsequent depression, may seem implausible, history reminds us to be prepared. Even the "unexpected" has a way of recurring!

Taxation: Planning, Compliance, and Advice

In tax practice, competition involving non-CPAs, broadly speaking, is either with those who perform compliance work (the filling out of tax return forms by tax preparers and the like) at one end of the spectrum, and with those who do tax planning at the other. Some financial institutions, and firms specializing in mass tax-return preparation (e.g., H&R Block and more recently an American Express entity), offer continuing or seasonal services in this area. More overlap, and therefore more competition, may be present in the field of tax planning, where the same or similar services are offered by other professionals.

Tax planning involves the consideration of alternative courses of action leading to alternative or differing results in terms of the extent and timing of tax liabilities. Beginning with income tax planning, this field has expanded to encompass estate taxes, integration of tax strategy with the creation of wills and gifts of property, and the like. The whole field now has the potential to unify under the rubric of financial planning, which may include investment strategy as well as the tax implications of investment and other actions. Here the field is shared with attorneys and a new professional group, certified financial planners and various publicly held enterprises. The AICPA has increased its involvement in this area by development of an accredited specialty devoted to the needs of accounting practitioners in this area.

The overlap in tax practice between the profession of law and the profession of public accountancy gives rise to some gray areas at the margin, which, after some early disputes between the two groups, reached a balance as to federal matters. The US Internal Revenue Service automatically permits either lawyers or CPAs to practice before that agency, as well as enrolled agents, who must qualify by passing an examination. Not all tax advisors are fully equal in the eyes of the law, however. Many tax filers do not know that CPAs are not entitled to the "privileged disclosure" protection of attorneys.[59] Recent state level attempts to obtain privilege for CPAs in testimony would be of value, not in tax matters, but in litigation support.[60] Some form of CPA-client privilege exists in 24 states including 16 relating to testimonial privilege.[61]

Determining the degree of balance in state and local tax practice also seems to be a current issue. In March 1995, for example, the *Ohio CPA Newsletter* reported that the State Supreme court had rejected amendments to the legal professions proposal regarding the unauthorized practice of law. The proposal contained a "definition that would have greatly restricted the current practices of CPAs....the proposed rules would have restricted to attorneys the ability to represent clients before any administrative or governmental body; to give advice on wills, estate plans trusts marital property rights, mortgages and leases; and to advise clients on the organization or dissolution of a corporation, partnership, or other organization. In its July 1997 issue, the *Ohio Society Newsletter*, reported however, that the Supreme Court barred anyone but a lawyer from representing clients before county tax revision boards.

The availability of user-friendly software products, and the capacity for computers to rapidly process basic tax filings, has caused CPAs to consider repositioning themselves in the market for tax preparation.   In 1997, for example, the IRS announced that as of five weeks following the individual tax filing deadline for the 1996 year end (April 15th) nearly 114 million individual returns had been filed.[62] When state and local tax preparation is considered as a multiple of this activity the potential for devising cost-effective and rapid preparation support for just the individual market of returns becomes apparent. However the 1990s have marked a trend away from routine compliance work by CPAs in this market. The services which relate to structuring complex transactions and assessing tax consequences of business plans and contingencies are, on the other hand, increasingly becoming the focus of CPA services.

Consultation and Caveat Emptor

The field of advisory services (consulting) is where the CPA profession's competitiveness within the profession as well as with those outside the CPA profession seems keenest. Consultation provides a significant revenue stream to public practice firms, as well as balancing the scope of their practice in a logical way. The competition has significance to the very vitality and definition of the profession itself. In recent years it has become clear that the large accounting firms are also among the largest providers of consulting services.

A 1980s survey found four of the then Big Eight firms among the top ten consulting firms in the United States, with one (Arthur Andersen & Co.) being at the top ahead of such well-known consulting firms as Booz, Allen & Hamilton, and McKinsey & Co., Inc.   Ten of the top 25 consulting firms were large CPA firms. Andersen's consulting fees, worldwide, in 1988 were $1.1 billion, up from $838 million in 1987.[63]

Global rankings reported in the *Financial Times* tell a story of continued growth.   The information was taken from the World Survey by *Management Consultants International* confirmed in prior press reports and is abstracted here[64]

Table 8.2   Revenue Ranking-World's 16 Largest Consulting Firms

Firm	*FY 1996 Worldwide Revenue ($mill)*
Andersen Consulting	5,300
Ernst & Young	2,010
McKinsey & Co.	2,000
KPMG	1,836
Deloitte Touche Tomatsu Int.	1,550
Coopers & Lybrand	1,422
Arthur Andersen	1,379
Price Waterhouse	1,200
Mercer Consulting Group	1,159
Towers Perrin	1,001
Booz-Allen & Hamilton	980
AT Kearney	870
American Mgt. Systems	812
IBM Consulting [est.]	730
Watson Wyatt Worldwide	656
Boston Consulting Group	600

A review of the above rankings brings to focus the competition within the traditional CPA firm group, and among non-CPA firm providers. It also brings into sharp contrast the competition between siblings of Andersen Worldwide, the world's largest professional services organization, with total revenues of $9.5 billion.[65] In what the financial press termed a "face off" between consultants and accountants, the global Andersen entity of 2,700 partners was to settle a leadership succession and identity challenge of significant proportion as voting for the new CEO position was being undertaken in the Spring of 1997.[66] While the firm partners decided not to split off the consultancy arm, the choice of the new CEO was to be between a partner with accounting background versus one from the consultancy side. To the extent that the evolution of the Andersen firm, globally and in the mix of services, has served as a bell-weather for many other firms practice structures, the events at the firm are studied with interest and will continue to be.

Experimentation and innovation, of course, are not limited to any one entity in the competitive services markets. Some services, including an attempt to provide so-called "solvency" letters—that is, opinions about the fiscal future condition of a subject company—were an experiment with which several firms were involved and ultimately rejected as a line of service, in part, perhaps because of concerns over potential liability should subject companies indeed become insolvent following the issue of a positive solvency opinion.   Firms have also begun ventures in investment banking activities.   One major firm, however, recently withdrew from the business, dissolving its alliance with BayMark Capital LLC.[67] Another major firm, Coopers & Lybrand, has registered a securities entity with the SEC, not for the purpose of the sale of securities, but to provide merger and acquisition services, related appraisals, and so forth.   The firm, of course, faces restrictions involving audit clients.

The size of the consulting practices of CPA service firms has been a concern of legislators and regulators, who look to   the   possible effects on independence of performing nonattest services for attest clients. As mentioned earlier, this was one of the original subjects investigated in the late 1970s in the Congressional Committees and gave rise to two pronouncements (now rescinded) by the SEC on this specific point.[68]   However, the competitive battle ground has shifted from the legislation/regulation arena to the competitive marketplace. Rather than legislate the appropriate distribution of consultative resources public policy now allows the market to do so. So, let the buyer decide, and "caveat emptor." And if CPAs have "brand" advantage as the trusted information professionals in this competition wherein "caveat emptor" risk is a cost to business, that advantage should prove market valuable.

CPAs in other than Big Six firms would, in the past, consider this issue a big firm one only. Today the revenue distribution among medium-sized and smaller accounting firms suggests that consulting and advisory services, while on a smaller scale, now represent an essential service component to their   clients   often   not economically available from other providers. It is this important small business aspect of consulting services that, in part, also serves to persuade regulators and legislators to be cautious about imposing   hard   and   fast   scope-of-service limitations on the CPA profession at large.

Factors Affecting Consultation Structure

The future development of consultation has significance as to the very structure and practice of the profession at every level.   Among the several factors, in addition to the outsourcing marketplace, previously addressed, which will contribute to the development of consultancy, the following are further considered:

Professional culture.   There is a concern, often expressed by more experienced partners in firms, that the varied skills and increasing specialization necessary in consultancy affects, most say limits, the ability of this group of practitioners to acquire the background in the culture of integrity, objectivity, and competence needed in a service profession. Hence consultants are likely to be impatient with traditional constraints on practice imposed by the imperatives and positive goal oriented statements identified with such a culture. Such a culture even may be seen as an unnecessary impediment to competing with nonaccounting consultants not similarly professional. In 1981, when the SEC withdrew its requirement for proxy statement disclosure regarding nonattest services provided by the auditing firm there was a recognition of the fact that the issue of the effect of NAS on auditor independence was not subject to full resolution, but rather a "perennial will-o-wisp which continually eludes our ability to circumscribe it."[69] Further, there was a realization of a "chilling" effect alleged upon the market competition mechanism, which placed a cost or barrier on CPA providers, without substantial evidence of role risk to auditing,[70] and that self-regulatory activities by the firms and the AICPA provided additional assurances as to behavior. *The Wall Street Journal* summarized the SEC decision to withdraw the requirements as representing the view that "private regulation could be permitted to operate versus government agencies in the area."[71]

Sustainable Growth and Profitability. Consultancy appears to be providing much of the impetus for CPA firm growth and profitability over the past decade. This has led to some dissatisfaction as to proportionate distribution of profits (compensation). However, so long as the growth and profitability remain strong and the disaffected parties avoid an administrative or economic catastrophe, such dissatisfaction seems to be increasingly subject to management—especially in the face of less favorable economic circumstances reflected in legal services hinted at by decline in law school enrollment and by the concerns expressed about costs and compensation to physicians within the health care controversy. In sum, there are almost no CPAs and few consultants standing in unemployment lines these days. "If I could get 5,000 or 6,000 people, I'd take them tomorrow," said a Deputy Chairman of KPMG Peat Marwick.[72]

Litigation Risk. The considerable legal risks of providing attest services (and to a much lesser degree, tax services) have been seen as a financial burden not arising from consultancy practice, and therefore not willingly borne by it. This, of course, is a factor involved in the economics related to the structure problem in global service entities, such as Andersen Worldwide, mentioned above. There are signs, however, that litigation is becoming a factor in consultation. In 1994 for example, a $14.2 million dollar verdict was awarded against a major firm related to work in the litigation support area, which is described elsewhere in this chapter.[73] Even when the outcome regarding consultancy litigation is favorable in legal terms, the protracted activity, awards are but one cost of extensive court exposure which can be exhausting and distracting. The brief case study outline which follows is indicative of the course of litigation and an outcome that has both economic and legal consequences of substance.

In February 1996, following a Supreme Court decision in the State of Ohio, a case relating to a 1981 financial services engagement, was finally determined. In 1981, Scioto Memorial Hospital Association was building a retirement facility project. Financial projections for the project were reviewed by Price Waterhouse, and in 1982 the firm reported to Scioto that uncertainty about one of Scioto's assumptions—an important one, the rate at which units would retail in the market—

"does not permit a single most probable assumption regarding the timetable within which projected occupancy can be achieved." When a construction fire destroyed most of the project, the original timetable was upset, business conditions seemed to affect sales, and the project faltered.   The client filed suit in 1985 claiming the financial consultant's projections were negligently prepared.[74] PW argued the negligence involved was as much attributable to the client, and this comparative negligence factor should be considered. It was not, and PW lost the case at trial, with the jury awarding Scioto $15.8 million.[75] An appellate court decision was split and left both parties unresolved as to the key legal dispute issue, the accountant's right to invoke comparative negligence. The Supreme Court held that the defendant, Price Waterhouse "properly developed an appreciable body of evidence on the alleged acts of Plaintiff which would comprise all such affirmative defenses."[76] Accountants can now argue that negligence is not absolute but comparative. The court, however, awarded damages because it believed that in this case the lower court's decision was nonprejudicial.[77]

Practice Standards.   The determination of the proper standard of care to be employed in consultation may be the result not only of court rulings as above, but of professional regulation standards for CPAs as advisors, or both. In the Diversified Graphics engagement involving then Ernst & Whinney's provision of a "turnkey" computer system, the client sued. The CPA firm argued an ordinary standard of care was appropriate, but the court in deciding the firm had breached that standard, argued the firm was subject to a higher standard of professional care. The court referred to specific MAS Practice Standards (at that time MAS Practice Standards No. 1 – 8) adopted by the AICPA as being determining for this type of engagement.[78] Activities of the AICPA's Management Consulting Services Section now provide the information and materials which support improvement of consultation services. The cost-beneficial evolution of consulting guidance issued by the AICPA has evolved now to include Statements on Standards for Consulting Services introduced in 1991. These supersede certain earlier MAS standards and define categories of consulting service.

Regulation and Technology.   One example of regulation's impact can be taken from   the U.S. (1978);   The Foreign Corrupt Practices Act (FCPA). In an attempt to comply with the internal   control provisions of the act, large corporations sought senior auditing persons whose skill was at that time most likely to be in the employ of major public accounting firms. Demand for the skill rose as corporations built up their own internal audit staff capability. In order to attract the skill the corporations bid up the price. As demand rose and supply remained constant, auditing firms found fewer senior auditing personnel available. Also, as corporations utilized their newly acquired personnel on a full-time basis internally they found it possible to do some other NAS work heretofore performed by outside auditors, and so could cut back on outside services in this regard. A single law therefore changed the supply and allocation of one skill factor (senior auditors) and   shifted the demand for some   public accounting services.[79]   With the advent of outsourcing and "right sizing" firms are now considering this as a potential contract service, and once again labor markets for this skill may be reallocated—with increasing leverage due to the use of computer applications.

Accredited and Other Emerging CPA Services

As early as the 1960s interpretations of the AICPA's ethical precepts affirmed the propriety of organizing separate partnerships with non-CPA specialists[80] This was consistent with the intent of Council expressed in 1961 to encourage CPAs to perform the entire range of services consistent with their professional competence, ethical standards and responsibility.

Management and general consultancy have flourished along lines demanded by the global and technological developments of the 1990s. Complexity in certain functions bred practice specialization. This also created interest in distinctive recognition and identification of individuals competence to practice in these specialized activities. Specialty organizations formed by practitioners began to appear. The policy question faced by the AICPA, as well as by other mature professional organizations such as medicine and law, was the matter of managing this evolving practice phenomenon. In the last decade two accredited specialties have been authorized for award by the AICPA. The first, in 1988 was identified as a designation for personal financial planners[81] and in 1996 the AICPA Council approved business valuation as an area of accredited practice. These acknowledgments and institutional arrangements occurred relatively slowly at first but by 1994 the policy making Council of the AICPA approved a process granting formal standing to accreditation of specific services. One of the principal opposing concerns to the movement to establish accreditation was the concern over "fragmenting" the profession. Another related to the assessment of what constituted appropriate initial and continuing experience. In its process, the Council outlined a program of education, testing and experience to obtain and maintain an individuals accreditation.[82] Under the current policy individuals may continue to refer to themselves as "specialists" without having achieved an accredited designation. However use of the term "accredited by the AICPA" with regard to these practices requires successful completion of the approved program.

Financial Planning. By the early 1980s organizational activity among individual financial planning consultants resulted in organizations such as the Institute of Certified Financial Planners and a proprietary designator for such individuals, the Certified Financial Planner. [83] The growing public involvement in mutual fund and pension related investment programs, relative level of financial public literacy, and personal time to devote to managing investments seemed to justify a practice service to assist individuals in the development of a personal financial plan. Financial planning activities overall fit well into tax planning, estate planning, and advisory services already offered by many CPAs to middle and higher income earners. Federal and state oversight of investment advisors under the National Securities Markets Improvement Act of 1996 assigns to the SEC supervision of investment advisors who manage $25 million or more in client assets. Advisors who manage less than that amount are regulated by the states.[84]

Usually this service was undertaken on a traditional hourly rate or fee basis. Individual unit practitioners found that persons who specialized in personal financial planning tended to achieve some scale economies in their knowledge assets over time, as well as favorable public attention or publicity as a specialist. This combination of attributes soon drew entrepreneurs who attempted to franchise the investment advisory aspects of the service. Early advocates of such franchises found, however, that fee basis service was not sufficiently profitable. An income stream based on a percent of personal assets being managed was the practice in the investment industry. However, CPA and State Board rules placed limitations on acceptance of commissions and contingent fees. However, by 1997 as part of the movement toward achieving "substantial equivalency" to permit mobility of CPAs among States, such limitations are soon expected to be lifted in principal jurisdictions where they still apply.

The introduction of more commercial franchise and other organizations, such as those offered by American Express, has met with opposition initially. As individual legal and regulatory challenges have been studied CPAs are adapting well to this environment. The value which CPAs bring to the financial planning environment is reputational. CPAs are known to be competent and objective. Resistance, however, to commercially sponsored entities is likely to continue so long as concern remains about the commitment of such entities. This involves the need for employers to expect and support staff CPAs to perform this market service with integrity, objectivity, and competence. Groups of planners such as the National Association of Personal Financial Advisors, and the Licensed Independent Network of CPA Financial Planners have organized "fee only" planners to emphasize the traditional ethical emphasis of serving clients on that economic basis.

Consistent with all other areas of practice, AICPA members have adopted a process for establishing practice standards and have identified areas of responsibility which relate to engagements to include guidance when working with other advisors, and methods for monitoring and updating engagements.[85] More information about AICPA programs can be obtained at its website [www.aicpa.org]. Individuals wishing to learn about SEC policy should visit [www.sec.gov].

Accreditation in Business Valuation. As the economy recovered from the economic aftermath of the Savings & Loan failures of the mid- and late-1980s, federal legislation focused on the need for property valuations to be supported by appropriate expert evaluation in certain financial transactions relating to deposit insured financial institutions. Title XI, *The Financial Institutions Reform, Recovery* *and Enforcement Act of 1989 (FIRREA)* reads: "to promote the safety and soundness of insured institutions by requiring that real estate appraisals utilized in connection with federally related transactions be performed in writing in accordance with the uniform standards by individuals whose competency has been demonstrated and whose professional conduct is subject to effective supervision."

This mandate created demand for an even larger and more responsive community of experts than those already practicing. Perhaps as well in the minds of some legislators there had been concern that the former community had been tarnished by the fallout from the savings and loan crisis. Many "appraisers" also worked as inventory or business valuation specialists, the latter in the case of merger, estate, or combination situations. [86]

As leaders developed a proposal for an AICPA response to these new requirements they encountered many of the same concerns which were expressed about accreditation of financial planning. Will it lead to fragmentation? What are the requirements? Over the years alternative proprietary processes had come into being. For example, the Institute of Business Appraisers established in 1978, began offering a "Certified Business Appraiser" designation.

The AICPA program awards the Accredited in Business Valuation (ABV) designation. Requirements for AICPA members to obtain the ABV include that the candidate:

1. Be a member in good standing and hold an unrevoked CPA certificate or license issued by a recognized statutory authority.

2. Provide evidence of ten business valuation engagements that demonstrate substantial experience and competence.

To maintain the accreditation each credential holder is expected to:

1. Submit documentation at three year intervals demonstrating substantial involvement in five business valuation engagements.

2. Complete sixty hours of related Continuing Professional Education during the same three year period.

The first ABV examination scheduled for 1997 represented a final step in the development for this service designation.

Litigation Support Services. *"Litigation services are 'transaction services, in which the practitioner's function is to provide services related to a specific client transaction, generally with a third party."* [87] It has become commonplace for CPAs to serve as expert witnesses in business, commercial, and personal financial disputes.

Services include damage evaluation and computation, financial analysis, and when needed, expert testimony.[88] In working as a member of a team employed one by the parties in dispute, the CPA seeks to assist in achieving an equitable and where reasonable amiable solution under the law. In some instances, court testimony or deposition work is a major facet of the service. In some cases Alternative Dispute Resolution (ADR) procedures are employed. ADR techniques generally include three broad categories: (1) negotiation, (2) mediation and (3) arbitration.[89] The advocacy nature of these proceedings again distinguishes them from services traditionally identified with the attest service and the expectation for audit-like independence behavior. A recent AICPA Interpretation 102-6, "Professional Services Involving Client Advocacy" provides general guidance for service in this area. However expert witness work may be considered a "non-advocacy" engagement. The CPA supporting litigation must continue to observe the integrity and objectivity which provide value to the special competence and knowledge related to the issue. Authoritative guidance on the subject of litigation practice by CPAs advises practitioners to study each situation carefully. Usually, litigation service engagements are subject to the MCS Standards (i.e. relating to transaction services).[90] However, literally any standard could come into play in an engagement, some in turn related to authoritative and nonauthoritative literature.

A variety of consulting service practice aids have been developed in recent years to assist CPAs practicing in this area. They address construction of reports, engagement letter particulars, concepts including the tasks related to the discovery process, and skills employed in giving expert witness testimony. Noted earlier is the fact that CPAs do not, in some states, enjoy the equivalent of "client-attorney." The AICPA Code of Conduct requirement (Rule 301) does not protect CPAs in those states when CPAs are required to produce information requested with a valid enforceable subpoena. Working knowledgeably therefore in this area requires not only experience but an awareness of state law and AICPA guidance as it affects advocacy, confidentiality, and privilege.[91]

Government and Nonprofit Sector Practice. As Treasurer Secretary Regan moved to become Chief of Staff to President Reagan, he is said to have remarked to Secretary Baker, his successor: "It's really an easy job assets are on the left, liabilities on the right, and they must balance."[92] On a more serious note, given the significant portion of our nations assets and activities dedicated to the government and nonprofit sectors, the accounting function and the role of the CPA in these entities and operations may often be underestimated but recent events will help from it being overlooked. Much has changed, however, with regard to practice in this sector in part as a reflection of the activities over the 15-year term of Charles A. Bowsher as Comptroller General of the United States (1981-1996), and as a result of the formation [1984] and activity of the Governmental Accounting Standards Board.[93]

The vulnerability of nonprofit entities to fraud and misdeed has also been the subject of attention due to episodes of what is alleged to have been management excesses at the national United Way organization, and fraud in the dealings of the Foundation for New Era Philanthropy (New Era). [94]

The number of AICPA members identifying themselves as practicing in this area is about 15,000. When one considers that many CPAs in public practice, however are also involved in serving government and philanthropic clients, that number might easily be doubled. The size, therefore, is not so much the issue, as is the activity being accounted for by work of CPA professionals and the impact that quality government financial management has on the effective delivery of government service. The types of entities usually included in this category of practice, in addition to governmental units at all levels, include colleges and universities, health care providers, and voluntary welfare organizations. And yes, technically the FBI, which is a government agency and conducts forensic accounting activities, would be a branch of governmental auditing.

Substantial legislation directed by Bowsher includes the Single Audit Act, which Congress enacted in 1984. It added structure to the required audits of state and local government units which received federal funds. By that time nearly $100 billion annually was being spent by state and local government from Federal grants and programs. Revisions to this Act, signed into law in 1996, make clear that it applies to *all* nonfederal entities, not only state and local governmental units receiving more than a threshold amount in total funds (currently $300,0000) each year. [95] Other recent major legislation initiatives identified with efforts to improve the accountability of government include the Chief Financial Officers Act of 1990 which has resulted in an increase, to 24, of the number of Inspectors General [IGs] in federal agencies. Bowsher noted that IGs are responsible for conducting the audits of these agencies and "also for contracting with accounting firms to assist them in the audit process."[96] Other legislation, including the Government Performance Results Act (GPRA) and the Government Management Reform Act (GMRA) have made performance management a standard for government operations, setting the stage for a consolidated approach to governmental auditing. To insure conformity with uniform federal accounting standards, in 1996 Congress passed the Federal Financial Management Improvement Act. All told the movement toward financial management and disclosure improvement, including the establishment of standards, and programs, to include audits and activities by Inspectors General, has substantial improved the basis for the quality of federal programs and their effectiveness. [97]

State and local reports also have evolved during this period to support accountability through the design and issuance of the Comprehensive Annual Financial Report (CAFR) which is employed by government units at all levels. The momentum toward increased accountability now continues in a proposal of the Governmental Accounting Standards Board (GASB) to employ full accrual financial statements for governmental entities as a whole, while maintaining the essence of the current fund model for reporting. This so called "dual perspective" approach is controversial from the perspective of some preparers but reflects the perceived needs of the users of financial statements. GASB Board Chairman Tom Allen has commented that "The entity wide financial statements represent an evolutionary change in government reporting. This reporting has evolved first from fund-based only to combined statements, with the next step being entitywide statements. The Board believes that many unfulfilled financial reporting objectives can be met with the introduction of these statements without abandoning the traditional fund-based statements that many users find valuable."[98]

The evolving improvement in the application of financial management controls and planning which has been the signal event in governmental agencies now seems in the light of the New Era experience, to be of greater interest and value to philanthropic voluntary nonprofits as well. Professor Albert Meyer, who is credited with leading officials to investigate and thereby ultimately reveal New Era's pyramid, commented as follows: "There is simply no substitute for certified, audited financial statements..." as part of the due diligence which should be performed by voluntary agencies undertaking investments of any substantial amount.[99]

CPAs in Education. As with CPAs in government and nonprofit sector careers, CPA educators comprise a relatively small percent (2.4% in 1996, down from 2.7% in 1984), of the AICPA community. Unlike any other component of the profession, however, CPA academics are not trained to be practitioners. Indeed, one of the most telling transformations of the late twentieth century accounting professions has been the development of a cadre of full-time, fully qualified accounting academics. These CPAs educators, educated to the peer standard of their academic community, the Ph.D., are skilled in research, critical thinking, and communication and teaching. As educators first, the full-time demands of academic life often precludes ongoing full-time practice involvement for such individuals unless there is a plan and program of such involvement over time. This completely different style of career has resulted in past misperception by practitioners and continually finds expression in terms like "schism" which are used in attempts to describe the differences between academic CPAs and their practitioner counterparts.[100] In fact, the CPA profession, in contrast to law and medicine, remains the last of these three to have a significant difference in educational background requirements.

Currently CPAs can enter the profession [prior to the year 2000] with a minimum of a bachelors degree or equivalent. While increasing numbers are being employed with postgraduate degrees, even this de facto level of education is different than the accreditation standard for CPA academics, which is the earned doctorate. In both law and medicine the academic and practice communities are identified with professional doctorates as their qualifying formal education, that is, the J.D. and the M.D., respectively. As the CPA profession achieves graduate entry-level status over the coming decades, one important difference, the formal education gap between academics and practitioner, will be reduced.

These differences being noted, it is important to remark that if there were not these differences then academics would not be fulfilling their role. The significant shift in academic development was undertaken in the late 1960s when an agency charged with accreditation of business, management and accounting academic accreditation, with full support and involvement of the profession, increased the level of expected formal education for career academics so that the earned doctorate would become the standard for tenure track appointments in accounting programs. Previously a combined master's level degree and a CPA certificate were considered "terminal" qualification. If knowledge were to be incubated in the University as well as in the practice office, this added investment in the intellectual capital of the profession's education process would be needed. The costs of such a mandate fell on candidates who now must invest, ideally, in achieving practice experience and certification, as well as the doctorate—the latter usually requiring four years of study following the initial graduate degree. Clearly the economic sacrifice and the commitment required would not be attractive to everyone in the discipline. The challenge of finding the properly motivated and high quality individuals was resolved in part by the academic marketplace. Until only recently starting academic salaries for accounting Ph.D.s were consistently among the highest or nearly the highest relative to other campus positions.

Academic institutions are organized around the ideas and ideals required to provide students experiences to develop their scholarship, to learn, while supporting or serving the needs of the community. An academic with both professional experience and the earned doctorate, who accepts an initial appointment at age 30, will have as much as four decades of career management and development to undertake. The ability to obtain tenure, or assurance of continuing appointment as an academic is the organizational equivalent of achieving "equity/stock options" as a financial executive or partnership (ownership) status as a public practitioner. The equity of the academic in his or her tenured position can only be made more valuable by enhancing the reputation of the institution and its programs over time. At the end of that career tenure, having its risks and rewards as do all forms of equity, cannot be cashed in or sold as in the case of partnership units or shares of equity. Therefore the academic must seek to maximize rewards other than economic value. The return on intellectual investment of a satisfactory degree comes therefore from accomplishments in published scholarship, teaching excellence and/or institutional development. Academics chose to do their work just as other CPAs, usually first out of a sense of professional commitment to a career as an educator, and then to the chosen field of interest, in this case accountancy. Accounting academics face many of the challenges and dilemmas in managing their careers as do practitioners. In the current age of high cost tuition and declining demographics, CPA educators have also had to revise their roles. Non traditional students and life long learning programs are in many schools the principal focus of educational activity. The idyllic campus setting, with bonfires, football games, parties and uninterrupted strolls in contemplation around bucolic campuses are mythical to professors at graduate and doctoral degree granting institutions who are expected to operate at the pace of peer business executives.

Structure. An AICPA study of Accounting Education completed in 1992-1993 belies the changing structure of accounting faculty units. For example, over half of the surveyed faculty are organized in faculty groups of six or less individuals. This suggests that it is difficult, if not impossible for such groups to cover with substantial depth anything but the coursework related in preprofessional technical coursework. To become specialized, and address subject matters with increasing breadth would seem to require more individuals working in concert. To develop the various special aspects of a subject, for example, taxation, at the individual, partnership, corporate, estate, international, not to mention local and state, levels would challenge a single or even two person tax faculty within a group of six.[101] Yet this appears to be the situation in more than half of the cases. Thus by necessity of limited resources, smaller units often must self select into teaching fundamentals first and foremost. Where resources permit, however, limited staff, employing adjunct professors and nontenure track appointments are able to expand their research and teaching portfolios.

Accreditation. Accreditation of accounting programs, initiated in 1982 by the American Assembly of Collegiate Schools of Business (AACSB), now includes well over 100 campuses in the country. The Federation of Schools of Accountancy (FSA) includes among its membership almost all accredited accounting programs in the United States and Canada which offer postgraduate accountancy programs such as the Master of Accountancy or MBA/Accounting degree. The American Accounting Association (AAA), an organization of approximately 10,000 is comprised mostly of accounting academics from the United States and increasingly non-U.S. countries, and serves the general and faculty development needs of individual members of the accounting academic community regardless of their professional subject interest. As a voluntary nonprofit organization founded in 1916, the AAA offers programs which permit members to present and discuss research findings, curriculum developments, and program administration matters. Considered by many the premier organization of accounting academics, the AAA has recently completed a strategic planning process. It continues to support its multiple goals of improving teaching and research, but now has added a significant new objective of seeking to become a principal provider of lifelong learning and faculty development experiences for accounting professors.

Accreditation acts as a signal to the marketplace that the peer institutions of high quality in a discipline have reviewed the essential components of the education programs at a school and found them properly conducted, staffed, and supported by resources, as consistent with the declared mission of the school and the market for its students. Achieving accreditation is a means of communicating to potential employers that the faculty and administration of the school are sensitive to peer involvement and have measured up to it.

Quality education, of course for the sake of argument, can be achieved in settings where no formal education, let alone accreditation, is available. However, the assurance which is provided to a potential student or employer through accreditation seems to have value, if only evidenced by the fact that it has been successfully conducted since 1916 and has become adopted in other parts of the world as a means of peer approval. The statutes which have been enacted to support the 150-semester hour education requirement in most key states have received support from the legislative affairs staff of the AICPA. Many of these laws identify graduates of 150-hour accredited programs as being automatically accepted as candidates for the CPA examination

The AICPA plays several important roles in supporting and partnering with the academic community and its organizations. Through its Board of Examiners, who develop and assist the National Association of State Board of Accountancy (NASBA) and state boards in administration of the Uniform CPA Examination, the AICPA plays a significant role by emphasis and structure of the examination as to the content of the curricula. Most established programs of course consider the examination a factor in their curriculum, but only to the extent that it is a necessary, but not sufficient goal for accounting educational efforts. Producing individuals who value the learning experience, who have developed competency in technical skills, and who are effective communicators, careful thinkers, and capable of identifying and resolving problems, is likely to be the model objective for high quality programs in the future.

The AICPA's Academic and Career Development Executive Committee and the Education Division staffed by full-time administrative professionals provide the strategic policy guidance and program structure for daily AICPA educational related activities. The academic honorary for accounting students, Beta Alpha Psi, is also housed at the AICPA Manhattan offices. The goal of the Division and its committees is to support academic members of the AICPA in achieving excellence at institutions offering accounting programs. The Institute also makes available an associate, non-voting, class of membership to academics who are not CPAs in order to further establish communication among academics.

CPAs in Corporate Practice: Cultural and Career Dimensions

Writing over forty years ago in a volume edited by John L. Carey, chief staff officers of the American Institute, one of the section authors observed: "Accounting is the principal means of measuring economic relationships. Since accounting is the language of business, it is the best means of conveying public understanding of the economic facts of life."[102] Awareness of this essential information preparation and control responsibility of "in-house" CPAs traces to the beginning years of the organized profession. Writing in October, 1930, just a few years after the movement to achieve CPA legislation in all states had successfully concluded, Durand Springer a key figure in the early profession wrote the following on the subject.

> *The more certified public accountants representing qualified accountants, are engaged by private business enterprises, the better it will be for the profession of accountancy as a whole. ... The CPA engaged in private work should feel a responsibility for the maintenance of the ideals of the profession of accountancy just as strongly as the CPA who may be actually practicing as a public accountants.*

To Springer, a "CPA was a CPA" regardless of the environment of practice.

> *In this respect," he noted, " the practical workings of accountancy do not differ much from those of other professions. Many a lawyer forsakes the public practice of law for the purpose of...employment with a business organization.... Many a doctor finds that the public practice of medicine is not as alluring as a professorship in a medical school.... In fact one can not conceive of any profession in which, for the advancement of the profession itself ...it is not necessary for individual members to withdraw themselves from its public practice in order that the private demands may be properly met.*[103]

Sustaining this viewpoint, an influential textbook writer of the mid-century, Professor Bill Vatter included the following in his introductory comments to *Managerial Accounting*, published in 1950.

> *One of the basic functions of accounting is to report independently on the activities of others, so that information concerning what has happened may be relevant and unbiased. the major function served by both public and managerial accountants is to use their independent judgment with complete freedom; thus they may observe and evaluate objectively, the fortunes and results of enterprise operations. ... This is a highly important aspect of accounting , and it is one of the reasons for the separation of the accounting function from the rest of the management process. The detached and independent viewpoint of the accountant must be keep in mind....*[104]

In 1977, in the midst of a new wave of public scrutiny, a the third generation of CPAs weighed in on the issue of the role and responsibility of corporate CPAs and professionals, with the following observations:

> *Corporate internal professionals have had professional training in school and many of them have had outside professional experience. They consider themselves to be professionals. Do their professional responsibilities suddenly disappear when they become employees of corporations?* [105]

The question here relates to goal conflicts as between expectations of the CPA profession and expectations of the non-CPA organization employing the individual CPA.[106] In 1987 the AICPA membership overwhelmingly approved as a set of six proposals identified as the "Excellence Vote" which is among other items established CPE as a requirement for members in corporate practice. Now, as the fourth generation of corporate CPAs establishes itself, these issues have come to be more compelling because within the demographic structure of the organized profession corporate practitioners constitute the largest single segment, nearly 45%. A signal event which confirms this development is the nomination of Olivia Kirtley, a financial officer of Vermont-America Corporation, as the first Corporate CPA to serve as chair of the AICPA Board of Directors. Until now, all the principal leaders of this organization, since its inception in 1887, have been CPAs in public practice .

Financial Measurement and Management. The context of what a CPA in corporate practice "does" and what new activities CPAs are likely to be "doing, " especially with outsourcing being common, is relevant. How CPAs arrive at a corporate career path and where that leads is also of interest.

Accounting for thousands to millions of transaction events in financial and detail terms certainly is one view of what accountants do inside corporations. Such detail work of course is required to track the events which reflect the economic activity of the organization. This is the "mass production transaction information" function which has been greatly transformed by events of the 1980s. "The most significant shift in the role of management accountants began in the 1980s, triggered largely by the introduction of the personal computer (PC). Top management recognized that the PC could do more than just warehouse data: It could be an analysis tool, generating what-if scenarios..., data searches..., and real-time reporting....[107] These new value opportunities have caused some to identify this as an era of "New Accounting!" The focus now is not just to cut costs as to transaction accounting or report preparation but to add valuable information useful in achieving competitive advantage. Such value added services include investment analysis, managing financial instruments and developing sophisticated projection and performance measurement models. Corporate CPAs are leading a movement to make money, not just count it.

In such a setting it is easier to understand why corporate management may be less ready to outsource. Further, while an airline might, after consideration be persuaded to outsource even aircraft maintenance, would any business be willing to loose control of its vital and highly proprietary internal information processes? If so, to what extent? Payroll, 401(k) administration, internal auditing, tax filing?[108] Perhaps. Inventory, transactional data bases and archives? Perhaps not. What does seem vital to evaluating such measures is the ability to have readily available and fully committed individuals with the knowledge to provide critical strategic and decision making information. Routine tasks and tasks viewed as compliance driven seem likely subjects for outsourcing. Specialized and proprietary ones would be outsourced at some risk of control and availability—options which may not be desirable in a fast paced, competitive global environment.

Public CPAs who are keen to provide services which would permit businesses to outsource transactional and compliance functions have concluded from a study that few companies. "have yet outsourced or established shared service centers for key elements of their finance functions."[109]

The variety of career paths in corporate practice provide multiple opportunities for successful employment of skills and advancement. Considering one of these positions, that of a Chief Financial Officer (CFO), a greater appreciation for the relevant general responsibilities, and their relationship to career preparatory experience can be assessed. A CFO's duties are also affected by the ownership profile (public vs. private) as well as the market share/revenue profile. A global company publicly held, for instance would be expected to present an ultimate career objective, with the realization that many of the positions equivalent or near that position are equally rewarding and challenging and likely to fit the career path for a Corporate CPA. These include that of the Controller, the Treasurer, the Chief Information Officer (CIO), or Staff Directorship of Tax, or Internal Audit, or Pension or Compensation. The financial operating positions and paths in manufacturing, transportation, and financial service companies have counterparts in insurance and financial intermediary concerns such as mutual and pension fund activities as well.

Chief Financial Officers (CFOs), according to recent study of 300 chief financial officers around the world, spend nearly 1/4 of their time on financial operations issues. This is where their technical background and knowledge and experience is directly called upon. This is the largest single category identified in the survey. Cost planning and budgeting (19%) and performance management (16%) are the next two major areas, followed closely by treasury /tax management and by performance management. Currently financial strategy/shareholders initiatives was the lowest time user, rating at just over ten percent among the categories. The study revealed that this is very likely to change over the next few years. "Chief financial officers are taking ever more strategic responsibilities in their companies and...it is clear that managing and meeting shareholders expectations is becoming the primary role of top financial executives around the world."[110]

The Communication Function. Preparing mandated financial statements and reports, especially for publicly held companies under the jurisdiction of the SEC and other regulators, is one of the higher profile roles of CPAs in corporations. Managing the transformation of business reporting in companies from a package of single **statements**, including the balance sheet and income statement, to the broader set of annual financial **reports** has occupied most of the last quarter century. The interest of popular and business journalists is easily drawn to controversy about measurement and disclosure issues, especially at times when financial instruments, be they derivative investments or stock options, are involved. These somewhat mystical objects of accounting and financial construction are often features in stories of spectacular losses, as in the case of Barings Bank, or in eye-opening compensation packages as with Michael Eisner at Disney. To repeat the earlier quote: *"Accounting is the principal means of measuring economic relationships. Since accounting is the language of business, it is the best means of conveying public understanding of the economic facts of life."* Communicating economic relationships in the language of business of course sounds easier than it is. The need to preserve the right amount of protection for truly proprietary reasons, and yet to disclose to analysts, stakeholders, and owners in the spirit of full disclosure, while maintaining composure regarding the multiple business risks and uncertainties which are factored into every published statement, certainly takes someone more capable than would be provided for in a stereo-typical images of a senior accounting official. To be an artist with both words and numbers seems to be what is called for here. Someone who can paint the language of business in block letters which can be easily read and understood by a multitude of audiences.

CPAs as Financial and Operating Analysts. Analysts, working to review strategic internal investments and operations or externally in the investment community, acquire and evaluate substantial amounts of information provided by accounting and other internal activities. Market analysts, both as buy side (representing institutional investors) and sell side (representing brokers who typically sell shares to the public) are also involved in the dissemination of the corporate communication about the "economic facts of life ... of a business." CPAs by virtue of their technical training and due to contemporary market conditions also are capable of serving in analytic positions which constitute this link in the long chain of capital market communication. Little empirical evidence has come to light about the involvement of corporate CPAs in these roles, particularly the latter. Given however that there are now more mutual fund entities traded on major exchanges than operating companies, it can be expected that more opportunities for CPAs in the measurement and reporting of investment performance will be forthcoming.

> *Getting there "Cheshire Puss ... would you please tell me which way I ought to go from here?" asked Alice. "That depends a good deal on where you want to get to," said the Cat."* [111]

We do know something about how Corporate CPAs begin their careers and why. A large number of them, over eighty percent, begin in public accounting. Men experience a higher rate, and women a lower one. The reasons for this initial choice relate to perceptions about careers, counseling received in school and the desire to achieve the CPA certificate.[112] When one considers that overall less than fifty percent of CPAs are in public accounting, the understanding begins to develop that one's career plans are likely to be fulfilled in a corporation setting. The CFO position noted above might be the long-term prospect, but the likelihood of being an OFO (Only Financial Officer) in a substantial privately held corporate entity may also need to be considered. Let's conclude by reviewing a financial press item (detail removed) reporting such a career change. This is one considered typical of a higher level direct CFO placement, in contrast to a career path promotion from within the company. It involves the shift from public to corporate practice.

> *The "BB Co." a retailer [listed on the New York Stock Exchange] yesterday named "aa" age 36, chief financial officer effective July 1. "aa" has been in training at "BB Co" since last January and ... is a good selection for ...[the] post. "bb is not only a CPA but ... has spent the last 13 years with the public accounting firm of "CC" managing engagements for " DD Co." and "EE Co." [other retailers.]*[113]

Identifying Peers.   In addition to the AICPA, there are several professional associations which seek to serve and support the career needs of CPAs in corporate practice.   Although these organizations are not the size of the AICPA, they offer specialty attention to individuals who are identified with their corporate roles. Three examples of such organizations include:

- The Institute of Management Accountants (IMA).   The IMA is the largest (over 50,000 members).   It was founded shortly after World War I, and then named the National Association of Cost Accountants.   Its headquarters is in Montvale, New Jersey.   This organization sponsors programs awarding the Certified Management Accountant (CMA) and Certificate in Financial Management (CFM) credentials.

- The Financial Executives Institute (FEI), currently numbers 15,000 members in the United States and Canada.   It was founded in 1931 as the Controllers Institute of America. Its offices are in Morristown, New Jersey.

-   The Institute of Internal Auditors (IIA), with about 13,000 members was formed during the time of World War II (December 9, 1941).   Its headquarters location is Altamonte Springs, Florida.   This organization sponsors programs leading to the Certified Internal Auditor (CIA) designation.

The first two of these   national organizations are broader in scope of membership interest than the last. However it is quite common for an individual to belong to several if not all of these organizations as well as the AICPA.   The value which each organization, and its particular chapter or national entity, provides in terms of meeting location, program content, and peer contact often are important factors in deciding to select such organizations.   In January, 1997 the AICPA announced the establishment of a Center for Financial Management Excellence which would focus on the needs of CPAs in corporate practice.   The service competition afforded by these organizations and their programs of activities should improve the quality and cost of service to all CPAs and those working with them in financial management roles.

Collectively, these professional organizations have the potential to collaborate and form multidisciplinary groups when matters of public policy cut across the interests of their members. Such broad issues as environmentalism, professional educational and accreditation, SEC and FASB measurement and disclosure of stock options, or taxation of dividends are all examples of matters likely to bring about short-term differences often counterbalanced by needs to put in place short-term alliances occurring simultaneously, depending upon the issue. The "politics" of the CPA profession therefore extends to the need for diplomacy among peer organizations in order to determine what constitutes the public interest in complex accounting, and reporting matters affecting the capital markets.

The women and men who are the CPAs in corporate practice, serving as financial managers, controllers, and preparers and analysts of financial and business information serve in the "front lines" of the premier information profession. To a large extent it will be their record of integrity, objectivity, and competence which they fashion as representatives of the largest segment of practicing CPAs which will shape the future of the profession.

Summary

The services that CPAs provide to society through their occupations in public and corporate practice, government, and nonprofit positions and in education, are shaped by the needs of society, practitioner competence and capacity, and the expectations of peers. Yes, CPAs are what they do, both in traditional services, attest, taxation, and advisory services, as well as in emerging, albeit also long-standing services, such as financial planning and analysis, and business valuation services in public practice. The span of CPA services continues to expand over time, and now clearly includes the spectrum of information activities needed to construct and maintain the information system for the free enterprise and capital market system. From consultation services, to report preparation, to assurance through analysis, CPAs are involved.

Government regulators, peers, and users of financial and business information alike require the high level of service quality needed to protect the value and utility of the information which rightfully belongs to property owners and thus affects the public interest. CPAs in corporate and public practice have and will continue to face the challenge of preparing and providing assurance about information while withstanding the pressures which would compromise or diminish the need for full and fair disclosure in the marketplace. In this dynamic competitive environment the concern is to address the pressures of price competitiveness while maintaining the ability to produce the level of service revenue to permit proper compensation of professional personnel. This allows for increased capital intensive investments and profitability of the firm. At the same time services must meet the expectations of technical standards which are exacting, and government and peer oversight processes to protect society. All of this and working at the same time to continue to build the institution of the profession as a whole, as well as the character and ability of individual practitioners with differing personal goals, certainly presents a challenge for the profession's managers and leaders.

As public practice firms establish new services in global, diverse, highly competitive, outsourcing induced markets, in which audit service growth is no longer assured, the need to retain a commitment to serve the fundamental ideals of CPA professionalism, will challenge the firm's top managers. Changes which affect the range of services continue to occur at a pace which causes some to be concerned about the ability of the profession to retain a coherent image because of the variety of services being offered. Yet in terms of the fundamental ideals and competencies upon which the CPA profession has been built, skills and abilities fundamental to accounting, auditing, advising and analyzing, a continuity does exist--and from this the CPA profession of the future may be expected to draw its identity from "what it does."

It is also important for service professionals to remember that when a corporation or client engages them as CPAs there are certain expectations as a matter of **business**: *timely response: a minimum of "surprises" and the expectation that the CPA will be available or "on call" for advice and consultation.* While such expectations exist for all service business providers the expectations for CPAs as professionals are furthered by the explicit social contract regarding attest services, and by an implicit set of societal beliefs that a CPA should maintain a personal commitment to service, and to integrity, objectivity, and competence. It is upon these ideals that society overall will assess our profession's fitness. These expectations provide for what R. K. Elliott refers to as "permissions" given by society to a profession. These "permissions" assist in developing a pattern for decisions about the domain of the profession's scope of services.

Discussion Questions

1. How does outsourcing and the reduction of the growth in demand for audit services affect the scope of CPA services in public practice? Do these factors affect demand for services of corporate CPAs?

2. What is meant by test of review? Does it relate to all of the services offered by CPAs in public practice?

3. What issues are raised about CPA auditor independence when the auditor provides NAS services to an audit client.

4. Distinguish between Independence in "fact" and Independence in "appearance."

5. Consultative services may create positions of "advocacy." How does that affect the expectations about quality and professional behavior by a CPA in public practice.

6. What is functions are served by CPAs in corporate practice? How is value created in these roles?

7. Identify some legislation which has affected government practice at the federal level since the 1980s .

8. In what areas of practice to CPAs compete with attorneys? With accountants who are not CPAs?

Endnotes

[1] Barry Melancon, President, AICPA, in correspondence to G. J. Previts, June 1997.

[2] Calabro, Lori, "All Eyes on Internal Controls," *CFO (August 1993).*

[3] Hall, William D. "An Acceptable Scope of Practice," *CPA Journal* (February 1988):24,26-28,32-33.

[4] Briloff, Abraham J., "The Effectiveness of Accounting Communication," (Ph.D. diss., New York University, 1965), 227: "Scope of Service by CPA Firms," (Public Oversight Board Report, SEC Practice Section, Division for CPA Firms, AICPA, New York, 1979): "Perceptions of Management Advisory Services Performed by CPA Firms for Audit Clients," (Public Oversight Board Report, SEC Practice Section, Division for CPA Firms, AICPA, New York, 1986): Previts, Gary John, *The Scope of CPA Services: A Study of the Development of the Concept of Independence and the Profession's Role in Society* (New York: John Wiley & Sons, 1985): Parker, R. H., "The Development of the Accountancy Profession in Britain to the Early Twentieth Century," Monograph Five (The Academy of Accounting Historians, 1986, School of Accountancy, James Madison University): 46: Edwards, James B., "A Final Report to The National Commission on Fraudulent Financial Reporting; Subject: Expansion of Non-Audit Services and Audit Independence" (A special study sponsored by The National Association of Accountants, University of South Carolina, Sept. 1986): Mednick, R., and Previts, G. J., "The Scope of CPA Services: A View of the Future, *Journal of Accountancy* (May, 1987): 220- 238: Mednick, R., "Our Profession in the Year 2000: A Blueprint of the Future," *Journal of Accountancy* (August 1988): 54-58: Mednick, R., "Reinventing the Audit," *Journal of Accountancy* (August 1991): 71-78: Wallace, Wanda, "The Scope of Services Issue: Food for Thought," *Kent Accounting News,* Boston: Kent-Wadsworth, Vol. VIII, (February 1990):4-5: Chapter II of the monograph is titled, "The Benefits of a Broad Scope of Services," published jointly by Arthur Andersen & Co.; Coopers & Lybrand; Deloitte & Touche; Ernst & Young; KPMG Peat Marwick and Price Waterhouse, January 1991, 30pp.

[5] In the 1990s this same issue continues with regard to practice as the state level.

[6] Securities and Exchange Commission, "Disclosure of Relationships with Independent Public Accountants," Accounting Series Release 250, June 29, 1978, and "Scope of Services by Independent Accountants," Accounting Series Release 264, June 14, 1979.

[7]Burton, John C., "A Critical Look at Professionalism and Scope of Services," *The Journal of Accountancy* (April, 1980): 56.

[8]*Code of Professional Conduct*, American Institute of CPAs, New York, 1988.

[9]"US Spending on Outsourcing," Source: The Outsourcing Industry, *Annual Report 1996,* Snyder Communication, Inc., supplement to *US News & World Report* (June 23, 1997).

[10]Barr, Stephen. "Farming Out Internal Audits," *CFO* (June 1995):69,71,72.

[11]Corzine, Robert, "BP/Mobile to contract out finance operations," *Financial Times* (October 21, 1996):19.

[12]Martin, Peter, "In, out, shake it all about," *Financial Times* (May 16, 1996):10.

[13]Jones, Del, "Supreme Court ruling may stem outsourcing," *USA TODAY* (May 13, 1997):5B.

[14] See the unpublished doctoral research of Keith McMillan, S. J., London School of Economics, 1997.

[15]Miranti, Paul J., *Accountancy Comes of Age: The Development of an American Profession* (Chapel Hill, N.C.: University of North Carolina Press, 1990).

[16] In 1994 the Ohio Board of Accountancy, by way of example, defined public accounting as follows: "Practice of (or practicing) public accountancy means the performance or the offering to perform by a person or firm holding itself out to the public as a licensee, for a client or potential client, of one or more kinds of services involving the use of accounting or auditing skills, including the issuance of reports on financial statements, or of one or more kinds of management advisory, financial advisory or consulting services, or the preparation of tax returns or the furnishing of advice on tax matters. *Ohio CPA Newsletter* (November 1994):5. The recent move toward revising the Uniform Accountancy Act in order to obtain "substantial equivalency" can be expected to change definitions such as this one. The definition forthcoming may focus entirely on those audit, attest and financial assurance functions, leaving other activities less directly subject to Board control, so that CPAs may compete freely with other non-CPA providers, while employing self-regulatory processes to insure meeting the concerns of the public as consistent with professional responsibility.

[17] Michael Sutton, as quoted in: *Journal of Accountancy,* "News Report: Washington Update," (November 1966):13.

[18] "Accountants cautioned not to compromise when adding services," *Wall Street Journal* (December 11, 1996).

[19]Levitt, Arthur, "The Accountant's Critical Eye," Address to 24th Annual National Conference on Current SEC Developments, Washington, D.C., (December 10, 1996): 6pp.

[20] *Improving Business Reporting, A Customer Focus,* Comprehensive Report of the Special Committee on Financial Reporting, AICPA (1994).

[21] *Strengthening the Professionalism of the Independent Auditor,* Report to the Public Oversight Board of the SEC Practice Section, AICPA (September 1994).

[22] "Special Committee on Assurance Services Releases Recommendations to Improve, Expand CPA's Offerings," *The CPA Letter.*

[23] Griffith, Victoria "Who cares for the careers," *Financial Times* (April 7, 1997):16. "UK Securities Board Proposes Certified Web Sites," *Financial Times* (June 20, 1997).

[24] *The Meaning of "Presents Fairly In Conformity With Generally Accepted Accounting Principles,"* Statement on Auditing Standards, No. 69, AICPA (1992).

[25] "Auditing the auditors," *Economist* (November 1992).

[26] White, Lawrence, "Another Financial Regulation Disaster," *The Wall Street Journal* (February 22, 1991):A10.

[27] "Court upholds insider trading law," Associated Press-*electronic mail,* (June 25, 1997) posted 11:55 am EDT (details of O'Hagen decision of the US Supreme Court supporting misappropriation theory).

[28] "$400 Million Bargain for Ernst," (Business Day) *The New York Times* (November 25, 1992): C1.

[29] Elliott, Robert K. and Jacobson, Peter D. "The Treadway Report--Its Potential Impact," *CPA Journal* (November 1987): 20ff.

[30] Hynd, Alan, "The Man who Doped the Drug House," *TRUE: The Man's Magazine* (November 1957): 64-67 and various.

[31] Singleton, T. W., *EDP Auditing in North America: How its development brings insights to contemporary issues* (Ph.D. diss., University of Mississippi , 1995): 227.

[32] "2 ESM officials plead guilty in will forged after death," *The Plain Dealer* (Cleveland) (February 5, 1986): 10-A.

[33] Miller, John, "KPMG Free of Blame In Orange County Case," (Letters to the Editor), *The Wall Street Journal* (March 5, 1996): A15.

[34] "Rogue trader leaves bank with $20m headache," *Financial Times* (August 30, 1996):6.

[35] "Bre-X's Former Chief Geologist Takes Refuge at His Cayman Islands Estate," *The Wall Street Journal* (May 12 1997):A10.

[36] Sternberg, William, "Cooked Books," *Atlantic Monthly* (January 1992).

[37] Gilder, George, "The Victim of His Virtues," *The Wall Street Journal* (April 18, 1989):A26.

[38] O'Shea, James, *The Daisy Chain,* New York: Pocket Books, 1991.

[39] Harlan, Christi, "Jury Awards $550 Million in Damages to Ex-Bondholders of Miniscribe Case," (February 5, 1992):A3 and "Coopers & Lybrand Agrees to Payment of $95 Million in the MiniScribe Case," (October 10, 1992):A2, *The Wall Street Journal.*

[40] "The World's Sleaziest Bank," *Time* (July 29, 1991).

[41] Willinger, Stephen D. [Manager's Journal] "Phar-Mor--A Lesson in Fraud," *The Wall Street Journal* (March 28, 1994):A12.

[42]Ip, George, "Industrials Rumble Past 7500 on Blistering Pace," *The Wall Street Journal* (June 11, 1997):C1.

[43]*Strengthening the Professionalism of the Independent Auditor,* Advisory Panel on Auditor Independence, Public Oversight Board of the SEC Practice Section, Stamford CT (September 16, 1994): 46pp.

[44]"Directors, Management and Auditors: Allies in Protecting Shareholders Interests," Public Oversight Board of the SEC Practice Section, Stamford CT, 1995: 8 pp.

[45] "CALPERS to Back Corporate-Governance Standards," *The Wall Street Journal* (June 16, 1997): A2.

[46] Maremont, Mark, "Bean Counters get an Early Warning System," *Business Week* (December 9, 1996):68-69.

[47] "Consideration of Fraud in a Financial Statement Audit," Auditing Standards Board, AICPA, *Statement on Auditing Standards, No. 82* (February 1997): 45pp.

[48]Mancino, Jane M. "New Fraud Standard About to Be Issued," *In Our Opinion...,* AICPA, Vol. 13, No. 1 (January 1997).

[49]Lord, Alan T. and Zeune, Gary D. "The Impact of the New Fraud Standard on the Audit Practices of Local CPA Firms," unpublished research paper, Bowling Green State University (May 1997) 22pp.

[50]Montgomery, Robert H., *Auditing Theory and Practice*, (Chapter XXIII INVESTIGATIONS) (New York: Ronald Press, 1912).

[51]Costa, Shu Shu, "The Thief and the Accountant," *Business Philadelphia* (November 1993): 34-38.

[52]MacDonald, Elizabeth, "Accounting Sleuths Ferrett Hidden Assets," *The Wall Street Journal* (December 18, 1996): B1.

[53]*Report of the National Commission on Fraudulent Financial Reporting,* Washington, D.C. (1987): 187pp.

[54]MacDonald, Elizabeth, "More Accounting Firms Are Dumping Risky Clients," *The Wall Street Journal* (April 25, 1997):A2.

[55]Trueblood, Robert M., "The Management Service Function in Public Accounting," *Journal of Accountancy* (July 1961):37-44.

[56] Spindel, Fred S. "Independence and Non-Audit Services," (SEC Practice), *The CPA Journal* (January, 1989): 48,50-2, and US Securities and Exchange Commission Financial Reporting Release (FRR) #1, Section 600, Matters Relating to Independent Accountants, Washington, D.C. (May 21,1982).

[57] An AICPA Special Committee chaired by Vincent O'Reilly of Coopers & Lybrand operated from 1995 up through the announcement of the formation of the Independence Standards Board. Its search for principles regarding the management of independence issues in an NAS environment are reflected in some these of items. However no official position exists regarding the authoritativeness of these.

[58]See for example: Raby, William L., "Advocacy vs. Independence in Tax Liability Accrual," *Journal of Accountancy* (March 1972): 40-47; Jackson, Betty R. and Milliron, Valerie C., "Tax Preparers: Government Agents or Client Advocates?" *Journal of Accountancy,* (May 1989):76-82.

[59] "Tax Notes,--It's No Secret," *The Wall Street Journal* (May 26, 1993): A1.

[60]. Friedman, R. E., and Mendelson, D. L., "The Need for CPA-Client Privilege in Federal Tax Matters, *"The Tax Adviser* (March 1996):154-156.

[61]*Ohio CPA Newsletter* (July 1997):1.

[62]Herman, Tom, "Tax Notes," *The Wall Street Journal* (June 4, 1997):A1

[63] *Consultants News* (October 1983): Arthur Andersen & Co., 1988 Annual Report.

[64] "Timmins, Nicholas, "Outsourcing," *Financial Times* (June 19, 1997):IV.

[65] White, Joseph, "Andersen Draws New Nominee for CEO Post," *The Wall Street Journal* (June 2, 1997):A4.

[66] White, Joseph, and MacDonald, Elizabeth, "At Arthur Andersen, The Accountants Face an Unlikely Adversary," *The Wall Street Journal,* (April 23, 1997):A1,13.

[67]Santoli, M., "KPMG Dissolves Investment Venture with BayMark," *The Wall Street Journal* (January 13, 1997): B3.

[68]U.S. Securities and Exchange Commission, Accounting Series Releases No. 250 (1978) and 264 (1979).

[69]Shank, John K. "Independence: Accusations in Search of an Issue," *The Accounting Establishment in Perspective* (Chicago: 1978: Arthur Young & Co): 64.

[70]Cowen, Scott S., "Nonaudit Services: How Much is Too Much?" *Journal of Accountancy* (December 1980):51-56.

[71]Previts, Gary John, *The Scope of CPA Services* (New York: John Wiley & Sons, (1985):133.

[72]White, Joseph B., "Consulting Firms Post Revenue Records Due to Technology, Foreign Projects," *The Wall Street Journal* (March 3, 1997):A12.

[73]DeBenedictis, Don J., "Experts Held Accountable," *National Law Review* (June 20, 1994).

[74] "Client Negligence Argued before Ohio Supreme," *Ohio CPA Newsletter* (November 1995):1,4.

[75]Ansbery, Clare and Berton, Lee., "Price Waterhouse Is Found Liable in Hospital Case," *The Wall Street Journal* (July 21, 1988).

[76] *Scioto Mem. Hosp. Assn., Inc.* v. *Price Waterhouse* (1996), Ohio St. 3d, Supreme Court of Ohio.

[77] "Supreme Court Rules for Profession," *Ohio CPA Newsletter* (March 1996):1,3.

[78]Baliga, Wayne, "MAS and the Standard of Care," *Journal of Accountancy* (August 1989):96

[79]Mautz, R.K., Tiessen, P., and Colson, R.H., *Internal Auditing: Directions and Opportunities* (Altamonte Springs, Florida: The Institute of Internal Auditors, 1985).

[80]Opinion No. 17: Specialization, *Code of Professional Ethics*, New York: AICPA (1967).

[81]"Should the Profession Recognize Specialization," *LIGNIAPPE* (Louisiana Society of CPAs, November 1993):3.

[82]"Council Approves Accrediting Member Providing Specific CPA Services...." *The CPA Letter* (June 1994).

[83] Tuttle, M. and Opiela, N., "The Financial Planning Profession and the Institute: An Interview with Judith W. Lau," *Journal of Financial Planning* (February 1997):60-65.

[84] "Senate Bill Extends Effective Date of Investment Adviser Supervision Coordination Act," *Planner* (April-May 1997): 8.

[85]*Statements on Responsibilities in Personal Financial Planning Practice* (Statements No. 1-5) New York: AICPA, 1996.

[86] Trugman, Gary R. "A Threat to Business Valuation Practices," *Journal of Accountancy* (December 1991): 46.

[87]Hepp, Gerald., "Litigation Services Standards and Ethics," *Journal of Accountancy* (April 1997):57ff, and see a clarification *Journal of Accountancy* (June 1997):24.

[88]Cohen, Martin, Crain, Michael, and Sanders, Arthur, "Skills Used in Litigation Services," *Journal of Accountancy* (September 1996):101ff.

[89]*Alternative Dispute Resolution A Guide for State Societies*, AICPA, December 1993.

[90]*Application of AICPA Professional Standards in the Performance of Litigation Services*, MCS Special Report 93-1, AICPA, 1993.

[91]Elkin, Michael P., "Confidentiality and Privilege," *Florida CPA Today* (July 1994):22-25.

[92]Jaroslovsky, Rich., "Minor Memos" *The Wall Street Journal* (April 5, 1985): A1.

[93] Previts, Gary John and Brown, Richard, "The Development of Government Accounting: A Content Analysis of *The Journal of Accountancy* 1905 to 1989," *The Accounting Historians Journal* (December 1993): 119-138.

[94]Giles, Thomas S. "'Double-Your-Money' Scam Burns Christian Groups," *Christianity Today* (June 19, 1995): 40-41.

[95] "President Signs Single Audit Act of 1996," *Journal of Accountancy* (September 1996):15

[96] "Executing the CFO Act: CPAs will be Involved," *Journal of Accountancy* (March 1996):58.

[97]'Federal Financial Management Improvement Act of 1996 Is Now Law," *The CPA Letter* (November 1996): 7.

[98]"Board Releases Reporting Model Proposal," *Governmental Accounting Standard Series*, GASB (February 1997): 1.

[99] Frame, Randy., "The 'Post-New Era' Era," *Christianity Today* (July 17, 1995): 61.

[100] Bricker, R. J., and Previts, G. J., "The Sociology of Accountancy: A Study of Academic and Practice Community Schisms," *Accounting Horizons* (March 1990): 1-14.

[101]Williams, Doyle A., *Accounting Education: A Statistical Survey 1992-1993*, AICPA, 1994:18.

[102] Stans, Maurice, "The Profession of Accounting," *The CPA and His Profession* New York: AI[CP]A (1954):10.

[103] Springer, Durand. W. "The C.P.A. in Private Practice," *The Certified Public Accountant* (October 1930):218-219.

[104] Vatter, William J., *Managerial Accounting*, New York: Prentice-Hall (1950): 8.

[105] Kapnick, Harvey, "Corporate internal professionals also have public responsibilities," Before the 16th Annual Institute of the Northwestern University School of Law, October 13, 1977. (Two Volumes: Selected Addresses and Articles by Harvey Kapnick: *Accounting and Financial Reporting in the Public Interest,* Chicago: Arthur Andersen & Co, . 1979) Vol. II:67-71.

[106] Campfield, William, "When the CPA Works for a Non-CPA Organizations: Reconciling Role Conflicts," (Working Paper 88-1, School of Accounting, Florida International University).

[107] Zarowin, Stanley, "Finance's Future: Challenge or Threat?" *Journal of Accountancy* (April 1997): 38.

[108] "Outsourcing is now Common," *The Financial Executives Briefing* (Vanderwicken's *Financial Digest*) Volume VI, Number A 1997: 8.

[109] Kelly, Jim, "Make money instead of just counting it," *Financial Times* (January 24, 1997): 12.

[110] Summers, Diane, "Finance role change," *Financial Times* (June 23 1997).

[111] Carroll, Lewis, *Alice's Adventures in Wonderland.*

[112] Families and Work Institute, *Experience and Views of CPAs in Industry* (New York: AICPA, 1995): 6-7.

[113] Sabath, Donald, "OfficeMax hires ex-Revco execs," *The Plain* Dealer (Cleveland) (June 18, 1997): C1.

The Next Horizons

CHAPTER 9

Becoming the Premier
Global Information Profession[1]

"You cannot hope to build a better world without
improving individuals. We all must work for our
own improvement and at the same time share a
general responsibility for all humanity."
Marie Curie[2]

Introduction

"It is hard to leave something which has been so good to you for so long" commented Dominic Tarantino, AICPA Board Chair to a 1994 meeting of the AICPA Council with regard the shift away from an audit services. By then the change had gone so far that CPAs services would not ever again be driven by auditing as its growth engine. Then, one might ask, where do we find our engine of growth. In what economic order or arrangement can CPAs be most valued as information professionals?

Repositioning the services which CPAs provide so as to be adaptive to market directed not only mandated needs has been one of the principal developments of the last decade.   Swift and continuing change in supply demographics and delivery technology have reconfigured the economics of practice in a "mature" market for auditing. Global focusing by corporations as to their "core" businesses has placed many support functions into a service and commodity status. Together these factors have produced such lasting shifts in the delivery of professional services by CPAs that any time before the recent past may provide only limited guidance for the future.

Thus watchwords for the future include being adaptive and resourceful in assessing opportunities, contingencies, and trends.

The value of historical perspective to assist in developing a value added understanding of future political and economic developments should not be dismissed, however. On a broad scale, historians and economists help us understand how trade, armed conflict, and political consolidation are all ingredients of past stages of achieving globalism. Between 1801 and 1871, for example, the modern state of Germany was carved from the Holy Roman Empire. In 1801 Germany was a language and not a nation. The armed conflicts incited by Napoleon would reduce the baronies of Germania from several hundred to several dozen, but not until 1871 would it become a unified nation. Not until after 1918 would it begin to face the full economic consequences of its nationhood, in the post war depression and ruinous inflation.[3]

With regard to accountants and particular knowledge of the past in the United States, Charles Bowsher, Comptroller General of the GAO, commented in 1991:

> *I served on the Bedford Committee some years back, and one of the things I emphasized was the importance of history in the business. Our accounting majors and business schools don't have enough of a grounding in the history of our business world. History tells us that a lot of the accounting shenanigans that went on in the 1980s with leveraged buy outs and mergers and acquisitions really are not too much different from what went on in the later 1920s;[4]*

One of the questions related to this is the process by which globalism will be achieved. Will it occur in unpatterned, dynamic, and spontaneous fashion, or will it occur in a country trade partner manner, by armed conflict or by trading blocks?[5] In fact all forms of these options are being employed, whether through most favored trade treaties, the Gulf War, the North American Free Trade Agreement (NAFTA), or by competition between NAFTA and the European Community as a trade bloc. Appreciating these developments, and their potential importance in each case of business service are among the types of strategic skills and knowledge which will be needed to make CPAs premier information professionals providing high level skills in consultation, information preparation, assurance, and analysis.

The Sixth Stage of Economic Order: The Knowledge Growth Engine

Writing in the *Atlantic Monthly* Peter Drucker observed:

> *A survey of the epoch that began early in this century, and an analysis of its latest manifestations... [indicate] an economic order in which knowledge, not labor or raw material or capital, is the key resource;[6]*

Drucker and other writers observe that the inequality brought about by lack of knowledge (ignorance) is not merely an economic issue, but a political one as well, for without education, as the root function of an advanced social order, there can be no hope for responsible voter action and only short term popularity (polling) serves as the basis of democracy.[7]   Such a threat to the value of democratic process, challenges the claim that since the Berlin Wall collapsed (and Francis Fukuyama proclaimed that history was at an end), western democracy and capitalism have triumphed as the models for mankind.

The importance of education as the sixth stage of economic order may be better understood if the five previous are identified. "Originally, there were three basic industries" observed Frederick C. Crawford, a founder and former chairman of TRW Corporation, "food, clothing and shelter. When I was a boy, no one could see transportation getting as big as it has, but today it's fourth. We think the next great industry will be communications...."[the fifth].[8]

What follows next in development envisioned by Drucker and others is the sixth stage, that of knowledge, and education. Drucker sees "The School as Society's Center."[9]   The CPA profession in order to participate, direct and draw from this knowledge engine of global growth, must become even more recognized as being knowledge-based. One measure of this, in traditional terms, means that the CPA Profession will become a "learned" profession, as in the case of medicine and law. Advanced formal educational programs, and the schools to provide them, will become even more important when "lifelong learning" applications become the content of continuing professional education requirements.

Given a CPA profession of this caliber and background, the sixth stage, a knowledge age, will be the setting for identifying the needs of users in the marketplace for decision services and information.   The year 2000 signals an important step in that direction since beginning with this year the AICPA will require new members to have achieved the equivalent of graduate degree level education to be eligible for admission. An advanced postgraduate educational requirement, one sign of a learned profession, may readily become the sought for standard in the first quarter of the next century.[10]

Belonging. There is something fundamental in humanity requiring "belonging" — to a group, a family, a cause, a nation, a religious perspective.   CPAs of course belong to a profession and from peer activity draw guidance and an identity which is commercially and socially valuable. One of implications of belonging is observing the values, obligations, and requirements as such of the group. In turn such groups or entities have increased abilities to solve and serve the needs of other groups and individuals.   The role of professional associations in this sixth economic order, which values knowledge and depends on information in achieving it, will be even more vital.   If as some contend, old organizational structures of corporate entities will give way to a work model where members of teams are organized as needed around finite projects, then professional" associations will fulfill the role of being where individuals "belong" for the longer term.[11] You will be known most, not by "what you do," but by the peer group with which you become identified.

Leadership. As the sixth order dawns repositioning the CPA service market will require continuous assessment. For while the service market provides the economic substance for a CPAs income, the repositioning implies that CPAs will not be only delivering the services, but planning them, and developing them strategically not just commercially. In short the CPA member of any "commercial team" will have to be the *information leader* for the project, joint venture or entity. The role of information leadership in an organization is more complex and demands a higher order of knowledge and skills than preparing and disseminating information alone. Expectations, therefore, as to the knowledge, skill, ability, and attitude of a future professional are likely to be substantially increased in the sixth economic order's global service market.

Competence. Of course all CPAs will not be expected to "practice" in the capacity of diplomats in behalf of their profession. The fundamental role of being an informational professional will dominate most working lifetimes. This will mean serving as an accredited specialty practitioner, maintaining general information and accountancy based skills as needed to relate to or execute significant information preparation, assurance, and analysis assignments. If incompetence is the worst form of corruption, then maintaining the credibility of the profession will require attention to lifelong learning in order to maintain such competence. The ability to measure and direct continuing education into a value added experience is an immediate goal which faces CPA leaders. Continuing education will evolve toward measures which add value and are less compliance driven.

What the Future Holds

In the global electronic knowledge order in which all accounting professionals practice, there will be greater emphasis on continuing to acquire knowledge for competency's sake. CPAs in public practice and in corporate practice will conduct their practice in an environment where change is a way of life.

Visions and Goals. Envisioning scenarios about the world in years to come, for example, the development of a sixth economic order, consistent with coexisting previous economic stages, is one aspect of a process which must be a part of any profession in order to remain viable. In 1997, for instance, the AICPA initiated an extensive vision project. But achieving more immediate goals is also important. Achieving them, in fact, lends the validity of accomplishment to the process of visioning. Executing major programs to achieve several goals proposed by the organized profession, as represented by the AICPA, are now among the centerpiece activities needed to secure the immediate future of the profession's practice. These include:

1. Achieving a de facto *postgraduate* education and *substantial equivalency* practice environment in the United States. Each of these initiatives serves to support the competency and mobility of the CPA profession of the future. The former has been the subject of study and implementation action for nearly two decades. The latter is expected to be achieved more swiftly. Each enforces the other in its attempt to create value in the marketplace by identifying through experience, education, and examination the common qualifications of the profession.

2. Leading the development of a conceptual framework and related dissemination technology from which the *business reporting* model will be communicated. The century-long evolution from a balance sheet, to the income statement focus in accounting was advanced in the 1970s by the report of a special committee which emphasized the need for a reporting process which would provide information useful in predicting cash flows and, as well, emphasize that financial reports, not statements alone, were the focus of communication. The next development is to expand the information horizon of reporting to equitably serve the needs of all users, individual as well as institutional. The business reporting model provides the rationale, based on research, to improve the quality of disclosure in the interest of competitively reducing the cost of capital.

3. Leading both the expansion of *assurance services* and of the spirit of entrepreneurial activity to sustain a profession in a competitive market. The development of assurance services in public practice promises to provide new value from those skills and abilities long identified with public practice. And, according to persons directly involved in the development of assurance services, these "product lines" will not be limited only to public practice. "Corporate CPAs, like CPAs in public practice, must adopt a customer focus, identifying customers' decision making needs for information. They should take a broad view of their potential activities, at least as broad as what is given in the special committees definition of assurance services.[12] The message about assurance services seems clear, CPAs in public and corporate service must think beyond financial information only, and beyond making single step improvements only. Assurance services, those which improve the quality of information, or its context, for decision makers, represents one of the most potent product lines in the emerging knowledge era.

4. Representing the interests of the public in matters of *corporate governance* related to information rights of investors, owners, and third parties in a global capital market system increasingly directed by large institutional investors. The 1994 study of the Public Oversight Panel headed by former FASB Chairman Don Kirk emphasized, as noted in a previous chapter, that the CPA should not be

viewed as the only participant in the corporate disclosure and communication process.   The other members must accept and be identified with their responsibility to work for the best interests of third party users who rely on the data. The matter of effective corporate disclosure and investor communication becomes therefore,   not a matter for management alone but for the Board of Directors, its audit committee, and the key institutional investors who supply capital to the firm.

5. Developing the process and   standards for *auditor independence* which are consistent with the needs of capital providers and users of business reports.[13] The public, as well as preparers of corporate reports, auditors, and investors, have a stake in making the concept of independence meaningful. The social contract which originally awarded the audit franchise to the CPA profession is related to the notion that in the audit relationship individual auditors are to be guided by their best professional judgment without client pressure or influence. The preservation of an independent mental attitude or state of mind is a core value of the auditing function.

Most of these goal propositions trace directly to significant institutional studies and/or initiatives sponsored by the profession and reflect various visions about the future needs of society and the role of our profession within it.[14]   The success of the actions related to these studies, and initiatives will, of course, reflect the soundness of the studies themselves, the changes which occurred subsequent to their delivery, and the leadership and will of the individual members, who "belong" to the profession.

Values and Culture. Independence in mental attitude has and continues to be the recognized cornerstone of attest and financial assurance services. It is among several important positive goal oriented and aspirational values of the profession. *Further, all CPA services, whether provided by corporate CPAs or by members of CPAs firms, identified and managed as such, are expected to observe a culture of integrity, objectivity, and competence.*

As CPAs of the sixth order provide global services, in corporate and public practice, they will enter business environments and   partnerships with those not familiar, as are traditional CPAs, with these values. A variety of issues arise. How will those who have not been trained and tested in this culture become acquainted with these values? Should relationships with practitioners from other disciplines be resolved by a mind set rooted solely in a competitive philosophy and/or a profit motive? That is, do CPAs adopt a business culture (profit) model in lieu of a professional one?   How does one now respond to that age-old query? If not for yourself, who is? If only for yourself what are you? Which situations, management selection, or a firm's communication message will produce anomalous signals? How should these be resolved?[15]

Values vary and are acquired from one's heritage and religious beliefs, education and association and experiences in life. The tone at the top of a business organization, a service organization or a campus is as significant as any signal one is likely to obtain about an organization. If then the leadership of a professional firm is identified with the values ascribed to a profession, the organization is likely to follow such values in the eyes of the public.

Current major examples of this being attempted include efforts to establish a global "Code of Ethics for Professional Accountants," by the International Federation of Accountants (IFAC);[16] leadership succession issues facing consulting and accounting partners of a global firm;[17] the decision by a corporate CPA or a consulting CPA to resign a position or engagement. These all have one important element: they are about resolving common values. In the application of all CPA services, from consultation through preparation, attest, and analysis, an expectation of integrity, objectivity, and competence among members of the profession seems a reasonable one. Would anything less sustain the true meaning of being a professional?

Education Change

In the early 1990s the American Accounting Association (AAA) began a planned program to implement a series of changes detailed in the Association's Bedford Committee Report and several follow-up studies. [18]

The Bedford Committee made 28 specific recommendations and included the fundamental conclusion that the future structure of accounting education should span three distinct areas of university education:

1. General education 2 to 4 years

2. General professional education 2 years

3. Specialized professional education 1 year

In April 1989 the AAA established the Accounting Education Change Commission (AECC) to continue to focus the attention of the academic community on the need for reform. During its tenure the AECC was directed, in turn, by Professors Doyle Z. Williams, Gary Sundem, and Richard Flaherty. It has encouraged and financially supported innovation in curriculum and advanced the need to reward teaching excellence. The AECC has disseminated a single message: *Accounting education must be dynamic!* With funds provided by major practice units, it has supported program and instructional changes in all types of program environments. When AECC concluded its work, the AAA developed, as a part of its strategic plan, a full-time professional staff position for a Director of Faculty Development. The first director was hired in 1997 and is expected to address the ongoing needs of the membership rooted in the aspirations of the AECC and the Bedford Committee.

The marketplace for traditional CPA exam focused education, as in auditing, has matured to the point where intense competition and reformulation of programs and target populations is occurring. Non traditional and international students now represent substantial populations and are providing a new type of candidate to recruiters. The implementation of the de facto postgraduate entry-level education requirement for the CPA profession is also further segmenting the market, but it will not be clear for many years, until after the year 2000, what patterns will be in evidence as a result of adjusting to all of these changes.

The geo Politics of Professionalism. In the twenty-first century and the knowledge age, finding norms will be complicated by the lack of a single sovereign global government authority to influence the activities of professions in the transnational capital markets. The organized CPA profession will likely assert its own self-regulatory standard setting and disciplinary process to accommodate the need for public trust, the absence of which would cripple capital market operations by reducing the credibility of the information process. The notion of "world accounting" or attempting to get the world's leading stock market regulators to agree on a common financial reporting language for listed/public companies, would affect over 4,000 of the world leading companies listed in New York, London, Toronto, and Tokyo.   Organizations such as the Arab Society of Certified Accountants, representing twenty two countries, have recently supported the proposal by the International Accounting Standards Committee (IASC), which seeks to displace other national standard setting agencies with a single world body.[19] The outcome of various world accounting proposals, like many past attempts at harmonization, appears easier said than done. Nationalism, and sourcing of capital by nation, continue to represent a significant factor in determination of such decisions. If those who have the "gold" tend to make the rules, and if one major supplier of investment capital feels less than comfortable with the outcome of some such a process, how does the world standard setting agency achieve enforcement? While a League of Nations or United Nations model and corresponding arguments for world standards continue to hold promise for the future, they may be at best veiled transfers of national sovereignty over the golden rules of corporate disclosure. Formation of an International Strategy Special Committee by the AICPA in 1997 led by former Board chair Tom Rimerman and charged with "formulating an AICPA international vision...., strategy [and] strategic initiatives," indicates that the issue is being carefully considered by that group.[20] It seems for the near future at least, that despite appeals to efficiency and transparency, progress in this arena will be hastened but perhaps only slightly.

Technology. The palm top personal computer, linked by wireless technology to any site with global positioning technology access, will bring access to the internet, the world's number one information bureau.[21] Electronic deposit requirements for payroll and income taxes were mandated for 1997 and E-money activity shows sign of developing and along with fundamental forms of commerce appearing on the internet are generating market and regulatory demands for privacy and assurance services regarding information.[22] AICPA President Melancon, for instance, announced at a White House Conference in July 1997 that: "The CPA Profession will soon launch a new service to provide assurance to consumers using the Internet for on-line commercial transactions."[23]

Demographics. Academic study of the accounting and other professional communities reflects increased saturation (fewer individuals per practitioner) in most major professions in the United States. The impact of changes in technology and delivery organizations in a "graying" individual market is difficult to assess. While the United States represents a wealthy economy prone to invest for retirement purposes, the data suggests that there is no definitive profile as to what is the best ratio of population to practitioner. What is undeniable is that there appears to be downward trend in the numbers as between the AICPA, engineering, law and medicine. This alone suggests that at a certain point the capacity of the individual market to sustain a professional will be met. The data are not, however, fully comparable. Thus to better provide for comparability, a line which indicates "accountants," which is a census classification similar to that for the other professional groups, has been provided.

Table 9.1	Individuals per Service Professional

(No. of Individuals in the U.S. Population for Each Professional)

	1910	1930	1950	1970	1990
AICPA Member	61,280	17,595	6,771	1,885	644
(Accountant)	1,563	441	283	197	132
Engineer	792	390	204	116	102
Lawyer	530	526	601	541	261
Physician	401	540	552	549	328

Adapted from: Stephen J. Young, "The Changing Profile of the AICPA:
Demographics of a Maturing Profession," *Research in Accounting Regulation*, 1995.
U.S. Population Age 16 and older: Source: U.S. Dept. of Commerce, Bureau of Census

Other demographic evidence found in scholarly studies suggest that the rate of growth of the CPA profession, as evidenced by the pace of new members, has slowed, from a rate in the low teens and high single digits, to about three percent currently. The larger base of membership over time, of course can produce this type of reduction in growth statistics. And, even though extended time series data about the gender structure of the AICPA is not available, it is clear that women are an increasing proportion of every membership category as the age of the group or category becomes younger. This suggests that women have and will continue to play an increasingly larger role in the profession. This trend is entirely consistent with the apparent boom in businesses owned by women. [24]In the near term the AICPA's special data base project dubbed *Operation Access* is expected to have the capability of conducting and providing the type of demographic data development and analysis consistent with a census taking activity. This should assist not only in developing needed time series data, but also provide the basis for studying economic trends on a per capita CPA basis.

Consolidation of Service Professions.   One of the interesting speculations which abounds in a world which has developed during the period of service outsourcing is not whether, but when large law firms, engineering firms, and accounting firms will merge to provide "mega" service agencies. Engineer and Attorney staff members in CPA firms and individuals who are both CPAs and lawyers seem more common today than at any time in the past.   In the United Kingdom there are already examples of attorney accounting firm alliances being undertaken. Whether or not this is a sustainable development or merely another example of experimentation, as in the case of investment services, remains to be determined. It may prove to be one of the more interesting developments given the "learned" and distinctive status of each of the disciplines involved.   A few years ago, 1991, the American Bar Association's (ABA) House of Delegates voted by the slim margin of 197-186 in favor of amending their Model Rules of Conduct—which guide State High Courts who set practice bounds—to prohibit lawyers from providing nonlegal "ancillary" services.   A managing partner of a large law firm which operates consultative services, downplayed the vote, noting: "In most states, this proposal will not be adopted."[25]

Moving Ahead Together

Bringing about the reforms and reorientations in education, practice, and establishing a professional service community to support truly global electronic and business enterprise is a daunting challenge. Of course, skeptics doubt that the profession will adapt as rapidly as might be needed and critics doubt the need to change some aspect or at all. The chances for change though seem more so now that ever before given the disposition of the profession's leadership to encourage rapid adjustment to market opportunity.

How warranted is the aspiration for the CPA profession to become the premier global information profession? Are the efficiency and cost-saving programs and "rightsizing" justifications sufficient and the only reasons to support such a vision? Is there a recognition, beyond that of being merely self-serving, that our profession has the chance to assist in changing the way of life of many societies by providing and/or increasing quality business decision services?   Each generation must satisfy these inquiries for itself and will likely be held to both the market and regulatory standards for doing or not doing so.

Not providing new services consistent with our "permissions" is itself a response, of course. And when we do not provide such services, others, perhaps less able may try. But when there are insufficient and unsatisfactory responses, the capital markets system may be reduced to a "riskier casino," reflecting the inherent human frailties of self-interest and avarice without the assurance and value of impartial information. In such a state, markets are riskier, and are likely to charge more for providing sufficient amounts of investment capital to support a better standard of living worldwide.

Summary

The vision of new horizons related in this chapter is completed with a view from the past, mindful of this chapter's opening admonition by Marie Curie. Quoting from "The Duties and Responsibilities of The Public Accountant," a chapter in his 1913 book, Sir Arthur Lowes Dickinson's comments were written for members of the U.S. CPA profession which had evolved in the post-Civil War era. The chapter concludes with a portrait of the qualities desired in an individual practitioner:

> . . . it may not be out of place to call attention to the mental qualifications required by one who essays to attack and determine accounting problems.
>
> These are: ability, coupled with tact and honesty, to ascertain facts without friction and with impartiality; a mind unbiased by previous conceptions, and free to reach independent and reliable conclusions of fact; and a will strong enough to maintain such conclusions against arguments, opinions, or desires of opponents interested in some opposite or inconsistent conclusions, and yet to adapt such parts of their arguments as may throw new light on the questions at issue.[26]

Discussion Questions

1. What trends are foreseen for world economic activity and how will these affect practice in the future?

2. What issues are foremost in the minds of CPAs as to the future of their profession?

3. What role does the EEC and the international network of capital markets have in shaping future practice?

4. What demographic factors influence the possible composition of the profession in the year 2000? In the United States? In the world?

5. What changes will drive the education model of the future?

Endnotes

[1] An identifying term for the CPA Profession continues to evolve. A 1970 Report of the Council to the membership of the AICPA entitled *The Courage of Making Choices,* employed three full pages to describe the professional practice of CPAs. Mednick and Previts [*Journal of Accountancy,* May 1987:230] refer to the CPA as an Independent Information Professional. Writing in the same Journal in August 1988 Mednick envisioned CPAs in the year 2000 as "premier" information professionals. The addition of the world "global" in the chapter title reflects the true, world-scope of electronic information which supports today's capital markets.

[2] Meaden & Moore CPAs *Highlighter* (June 1997).

[3] Lyons, John F., *The Life and Times of Bishop Louis-Amadeus Rappe*, privately published, Cleveland, Ohio 1997:1.

[4] Bowsher, Charles A., "Financial and Accounting Issues of the 1990's" in *Work in Process for the Year 2000*, Proceedings of the Fifteenth Annual Meeting, Federation of Schools of Accountancy, G. Fred Streuling, ed., Brigham Young University (1992):88. The Bedford Committee was a special committee of the American Accounting Association which addressed needs of the future of Accounting Education. Its efforts led ultimately to the formation of the Accounting Education Change Commission.

[5] Thurow, Lester, "New Rules for Playing the Game," *Phi Kappa Phi Journal* (Fall 1992).

[6] Drucker, Peter, "The Age of Social Transformation," *Atlantic Monthly* (November 1994):53ff.

[7] Adonis, Andrew, "Lessons for the millennium," *Financial Times* (March 20, 1996):12. This is a review of Conor Cruise O'Brien's book, *On the Eve of the Millennium.*

[8] Yerak, Rebecca, "A chat with a local legend," *The Plain Dealer* (Cleveland) (February 4, 1990):E1.

[9] Drucker, Peter, ibid.

[10] Previts, Gary John, "Accounting Education: The Next Horizon," *Journal of Accountancy* (October 1991):35-36.

[11] Stewart, Thomas, *Intellectual Capital, The New Wealth of Organizations,* Nicholas Brealey: 1997.

[12] Elliott, Robert K., and Pallais, Don M., "First: Know Your Market," *Journal of Accountancy* (July 1997):57.

[13] Previts, Gary John, "Financial Reporting in an Investor Fund Economy: Regulation and Reports to Portfolio Investors," *Research in Accounting Regulation* (1992):201-210.

[14]Roy, Robert H., and MacNeill, James H., *Horizons for a Profession: The Common Body of Knowledge for Certified Public Accountants* (New York: AICPA:1967). The other studies or initiatives are noted in the endnotes to Chapter 8. The findings of the AICPA Special Committee on Regulation and Structure, chaired by J. Curt Mingle were consolidated into a joint committee with the National Association of State Boards of Accountancy in 1997. That group outlined the issues underlying the issue of "substantial equivalency" for interstate practice.

[15] "Those who live by the Golden Rule can be beaten out by more sophisticated players who clean out those 'too moral' for their own good ." Christopher Meyer, "Mother nature Nurtures Managers, too," Ernst & Young LLP, "Executive Upside" (June 1997):1. The passage continues: "The winners revert to the Golden Rule behavior among sophisticated opponents who understand the game." Such "survival of the fittest" warnings should not be innocently ignored, but whether they are appropriate moral guidance remains questionable.

[16] "IFAC Proposes Ethics Upgrade," *Journal of Accountancy* (June 1997):24.

[17]Kelly, Jim, "Andersen partners fail again to agree on new chief," *Financial Times* (June 26, 1997):1.

[18]Arthur Andersen & Co., et al., *Perspectives on Education: Capabilities for Success in the Accounting Profession* (New York, April, 1989): 8; "Future Accounting Education: Preparing for the Expanding Profession" (Report of the Committee on the Future Structure, Content and Scope of Accounting Education), *Issues in Accounting Education*, Vol. 1, No. 1, 1986; Bedford, N. M., and Shenkir, W. G., "Reorienting Accounting Education," *Journal of Accountancy* (August 1987): 84/6/8/90-1; Schultz, J. J. ed., "Reorienting Accounting Education: Reports on the Curriculum, Professorate and Environment of Accounting," *Education Series Monograph No. 10* (Sarasota: American Accounting Association, 1989).

[19]Kelly, Jim, "World accounting wins more converts," *Financial Times* (June 9 1997).

[20] AICPA Board of Directors Agenda Materials, Item No. 14, February 13-14, 1997.

[21]Rigdon, Joan E., "Internet's No. 1 Use: Information Bureau," *The Wall Street Journal* (March 13, 1996):B1.

[22]Weber, Thomas E., "Privacy Concerns Force Public To Confront Thorny Issues," *The Wall Street Journal* (June 19, 1997):B6; Graham, George, "Financial Watchdog calls for certified web sites," *Financial Times* (June 20, 1997):9.

[23] *News Release*: "AICPA President Barry Melancon participates in White House Event on Global Electronic Commerce, " AICPA: New York, July 1, 1997, 2 pp.

[24] "Managing" *The Globe and Mail* (Toronto), (August 12, 1996):B5. The story reports that the *Economist* states that women own eight million U.S. Companies-- one-third of all firms -- and their number is growing at double the rate of those owned by men.

[25] Law: "Delegates Back prohibition on ancillary businesses for law firms," *The Wall Street Journal* (August 14, 1991).

[26]Dickinson, A.L., *Accounting Practice and Procedure* (New York: The Ronald Press Co., 1914): 249.

APPENDIX A

AICPA Code of
Professional Conduct

Code of Professional Conduct
The American Institute of CPAs

as amended January 14, 1992

The Code of Professional Conduct of the American Institute of Certified Public Accountants was adopted by its membership to provide guidance and rules to all members. It was last amended January 1992.

CONTENTS

- Rule 503 Commissions and Referral Fees
- Rule 505 Form of Organization and Name

Appendix A Council Resolution Designating Bodies to Promulgate Technical Standards
Appendix B Council Resolution Concerning Form of Organization and Name

Composition, Applicability, and Compliance

The Code of Professional Conduct of the American Institute of Certified Public Accountants consists of two sections -- (1) the Principles and (2) the Rules. The Principles provide the framework for the Rules, which govern the performance of professional services by members. The Council of the American Institute of Certified Public Accountants is authorized to designate bodies to promulgate technical standards under the Rules, and the bylaws require adherence to those Rules and standards.

The Code of Professional Conduct was adopted by the membership to provide guidance and rules to all members -- those in public practice, in industry, in government, and in education -- in the performance of their professional responsibilities.

Compliance with the Code of Professional Conduct, as with all standards in an open society, depends primarily on members' understanding and voluntary actions, secondarily on reinforcement by peers and public opinion, and ultimately on disciplinary proceedings, when necessary, against members who fail to comply with the Rules.

Other Guidance

The Principles and Rules as set forth herein are further amplified by interpretations and rulings contained in AICPA Professional Standards (volume 2).

Interpretations of Rules of Conduct consist of interpretations which have been adopted, after exposure to state societies, state boards, practice units and other interested parties, by the professional ethics division's executive committee to provide guidelines as to the scope and application of the Rules but are not intended to limit such scope or application. A member who departs from such guidelines shall have the burden of justifying such departure in any disciplinary hearing.

Ethics Rulings consist of formal rulings made by the professional ethics division's executive committee after exposure to state societies, state boards, practice units and other interested parties. These rulings summarize the application of Rules of Conduct and interpretations to a particular set of factual circumstances. Members who depart from such rulings in similar circumstances will be requested to justify such departures.

Publication of an interpretation or ethics ruling in the *Journal of Accountancy* constitutes notice to members. Hence, the effective date of the pronouncement is the last day of the month in which the pronouncement is published in the *Journal of Accountancy*. The professional ethics division will take into consideration the time that would have been reasonable for the member to comply with the pronouncement.

A member should also consult, if applicable, the ethical standards of his state CPA society, state board of accountancy, the Securities and Exchange Commission, and any other governmental agency which may regulate his client's business or use his report to evaluate the client's compliance with applicable laws and related regulations.

Section I -- Principles

Preamble

Membership in the American Institute of Certified Public Accountants is voluntary. By accepting membership, a certified public accountant assumes an obligation of self-discipline above and beyond the requirements of laws and regulations.

These Principles of the Code of Professional Conduct of the American Institute of Certified Public Accountants express the profession's recognition of its responsibilities to the public, to clients, and to colleagues. They guide members in the performance of their professional responsibilities and express the basic tenets of ethical and professional conduct. The Principles call for an unswerving commitment to honorable behavior, even at the sacrifice of personal advantage.

Article I-Responsibilities

In carrying out their responsibilities as professionals, members should exercise sensitive professional and moral judgments in all their activities.

As professionals, certified public accountants perform an essential role in society. Consistent with that role, members of the American Institute of Certified Public Accountants have responsibilities to all those who use their professional services. Members also have a continuing responsibility to cooperate with each other to improve the art of accounting, maintain the public's confidence, and carry out the profession's special responsibilities for self-governance. The collective efforts of all members are required to maintain and enhance the traditions of the profession.

Article II-The Public Interest

Members should accept the obligation to act in a way that will serve the public interest, honor the public trust, and demonstrate commitment to professionalism.

A distinguishing mark of a profession is acceptance of its responsibility to the public. The accounting profession's public consists of clients, credit grantors, governments, employers, investors, the business and financial community, and others who rely on the objectivity and integrity of certified public accountants to maintain the orderly functioning of commerce. This reliance imposes a public interest responsibility on certified public accountants. The public interest is defined as the collective well-being of the community of people and institutions the profession serves.

In discharging their professional responsibilities, members may encounter conflicting pressures from among each of those groups. In resolving those conflicts, members should act with integrity, guided by the precept that when members fulfill their responsibility to the public, clients' and employers' interests are best served.

Those who rely on certified public accountants expect them to discharge their responsibilities with integrity, objectivity, due professional care, and a genuine interest in serving the public. They are expected to provide quality services, enter into fee arrangements, and offer a range of services -- all in a manner that demonstrates a level of professionalism consistent with these Principles of the Code of Professional Conduct.

All who accept membership in the American Institute of Certified Public Accountants commit themselves to honor the public trust. In return for the faith that the public reposes in them, members should seek continually to demonstrate their dedication to professional excellence.

Article III-Integrity

To maintain and broaden public confidence, members should perform all professional responsibilities with the highest sense of integrity.

Integrity is an element of character fundamental to professional recognition. It is the quality from which the public trust derives and the benchmark against which a member must ultimately test all decisions.

Integrity requires a member to be, among other things, honest and candid within the constraints of client confidentiality. Service and the public trust should not be subordinated to personal gain and advantage. Integrity can accommodate the inadvertent error and the honest difference of opinion; it cannot accommodate deceit or subordination of principle.

Integrity is measured in terms of what is right and just. In the absence of specific rules, standards, or guidance, or in the face of conflicting opinions, a member should test decisions and deeds by asking: "Am I doing what a person of integrity would do? Have I retained my integrity?" Integrity requires a member to observe both the form and the spirit of technical and ethical standards; circumvention of those standards constitutes subordination of judgment.

Integrity also requires a member to observe the principles of objectivity and independence and of due care.

Article IV-Objectivity and Independence

A member should maintain objectivity and be free of conflicts of interest in discharging professional responsibilities. A member in public practice should be independent in fact and appearance when providing auditing and other attestation services.

Objectivity is a state of mind, a quality that lends value to a member's services. It is a distinguishing feature of the profession. The principle of objectivity imposes the obligation to be impartial, intellectually honest, and free of conflicts of interest. Independence precludes relationships that may appear to impair a member's objectivity in rendering attestation services.

Members often serve multiple interests in many different capacities and must demonstrate their objectivity in varying circumstances. Members in public practice render attest, tax, and management advisory services. Other members prepare financial statements in the employment of others, perform internal auditing services, and serve in financial and management capacities in industry, education, and government. They also educate and train those who aspire to admission into the profession. Regardless of service or capacity, members should protect the integrity of their work, maintain objectivity, and avoid any subordination of their judgment.

For a member in public practice, the maintenance of objectivity and independence requires a continuing assessment of client relationships and public responsibility. Such a member who provides auditing and other attestation services should be independent in fact and appearance. In providing all other services, a member should maintain objectivity and avoid conflicts of interest.

Although members not in public practice cannot maintain the appearance of independence, they nevertheless have the responsibility to maintain objectivity in rendering professional services. Members employed by others to prepare financial statements or to perform auditing, tax, or consulting services are charged with the same responsibility for objectivity as members in public practice and must be scrupulous in their application of generally accepted accounting principles and candid in all their dealings with members in public practice.

Article V-Due Care

A member should observe the profession's technical and ethical standards, strive continually to improve competence and the quality of services, and discharge professional responsibility to the best of the member's ability.

The quest for excellence is the essence of due care. Due care requires a member to discharge professional responsibilities with competence and diligence. It imposes the obligation to perform professional services to the best of a member's ability with concern for the best interest of those for whom the services are performed and consistent with the profession's responsibility to the public.

Competence is derived from a synthesis of education and experience. It begins with a mastery of the common body of knowledge required for designation as a certified public accountant. The maintenance of competence requires a commitment to learning and professional improvement that must continue throughout a member's professional life. It is a member's individual responsibility. In all engagements and in all responsibilities, each member should undertake to achieve a level of competence that will assure that the quality of the member's services meets the high level of professionalism required by these Principles.

Competence represents the attainment and maintenance of a level of understanding and knowledge that enables a member to render services with facility and acumen. It also establishes the limitations of a member's capabilities by dictating that consultation or referral may be required when a professional engagement exceeds the personal competence of a member or a member's firm. Each member is responsible for assessing his or her own competence -- of evaluating whether education, experience, and judgment are adequate for the responsibility to be assumed.

Members should be diligent in discharging responsibilities to clients, employers, and the public. Diligence imposes the responsibility to render services promptly and carefully, to be thorough, and to observe applicable technical and ethical standards.

Due care requires a member to plan and supervise adequately any professional activity for which he or she is responsible.

Article VI-Scope and Nature of Services

A member in public practice should observe the Principles of the Code of Professional Conduct in determining the scope and nature of services to be provided.

The public interest aspect of certified public accountants' services requires that such services be consistent with acceptable professional behavior for certified public accountants. Integrity requires that service and the public trust not be subordinated to personal gain and advantage. Objectivity and independence require that members be free from conflicts of interest in discharging professional responsibilities. Due care requires that services be provided with competence and diligence.

Each of these Principles should be considered by members in determining whether or not to provide specific services in individual circumstances. In some instances, they may represent an overall constraint on the nonaudit services that might be offered to a specific client. No hard-and-fast rules can be developed to help members reach these judgments, but they must be satisfied that they are meeting the spirit of the Principles in this regard.

In order to accomplish this, members should:

- Practice in firms that have in place internal quality-control procedures to ensure that services are competently delivered and adequately supervised.

- Determine, in their individual judgments, whether the scope and nature of other services provided to an audit client would create a conflict of interest in the performance of the audit function for that client.

- Assess, in their individual judgments, whether an activity is consistent with their role as professionals (for example, is such activity a reasonable extension or variation of existing services offered by the member or others in the profession?).

Section II -- Rules

Applicability

The bylaws of the American Institute of Certified Public Accountants require that members adhere to the Rules of the Code of Professional Conduct. Members must be prepared to justify departures from these Rules.

INTERPRETATION OF APPLICABILITY SECTION

[The professional ethics executive committee has issued the following interpretation of the applicability section of the Code, effective November 30, 1989.]

For purposes of the applicability section of the Code, a "member" is a member or international associate of the American Institute of CPAs.

1. The Rules of Conduct that follow apply to all professional services performed except (a) where the wording of the rule indicates otherwise and (b) that a member who is practicing outside the United States will not be subject to discipline for departing from any of the rules stated herein as long as the member's conduct is in accord with the rules of the organized accounting profession in the country in which he or she is practicing. However, where a member's name is associated with financial statements under circumstances that would entitle the reader to assume that U.S. practices were followed, the member must comply with the requirements of rules 202 and 203.

2. A member may be held responsible for compliance with the rules by all persons associated with him or her in the practice of public accounting who are either under the member's supervision or are the member's partners or shareholders in the practice.

3. A member shall not permit others to carry out on his or her behalf, either with or without compensation, acts which, if carried out by the member, would place the member in violation of the rules.

Definitions*

*Pursuant to its authority under the bylaws (section 3.6.2.2) to interpret the Code of Professional Conduct, the professional ethics executive committee has issued these definitions of terms appearing in the Code effective November 30, 1989 (revised April 1992 and May 1996).

Client. A client is any person or entity, other than the member's employer, that engages a member or a member's firm to perform professional services or a person or entity with respect to which professional services are performed. The term "employer" for these purposes does not include those entities engaged in the practice of public accounting.

Council. The Council of the American Institute of Certified Public Accountants.

Enterprise. For purposes of the Code, the term "enterprise" is synonymous with the term "client."

Financial statements. A presentation of financial data, including accompanying notes, if any, intended to communicate an entity's economic resources and/or obligations at a point in time or the changes therein for a period of time, in accordance with generally accepted accounting principles or a comprehensive basis of accounting other than generally accepted accounting principles.

Incidental financial data to support recommendations to a client or in documents for which the reporting is governed by Statements on Standards for Attestation Engagements and tax returns and supporting schedules do not, for this purpose, constitute financial statements. The statement, affidavit, or signature of preparers required on tax returns neither constitutes an opinion on financial statements nor requires a disclaimer of such opinion.

Firm. A form of organization permitted by state law or regulation whose characteristics conform to resolutions of Council that is engaged in the practice of public accounting, including the individual owners thereof.

Holding out. In general, any action initiated by a member that informs others of his or her status as a CPA or AICPA-accredited specialist constitutes holding out as a CPA. This would include, for example, any oral or written representation to another regarding CPA status, use of the CPA designation on business cards or letterhead, the display of a certificate evidencing a member's CPA designation, or listing as a CPA in local telephone directories.

Institute. The American Institute of Certified Public Accountants.

Interpretations of Rules of Conduct. Pronouncements issued by the division of professional ethics to provide guidelines concerning the scope and application of the Rules of Conduct.

Member. A member, associate member, or international associate of the American Institute of Certified Public Accountants.

Practice of public accounting. The practice of public accounting consists of the performance for a client, by a member or a member's firm, while holding out as CPA(s), of the professional services of accounting, tax, personal financial planning, litigation support services, and those professional services for which standards are promulgated by bodies designated by Council, such as Statements of Financial Accounting Standards, Statements on Auditing Standards, Statements on Standards for Accounting and Review Services, Statement on Standards for Consulting Services, Statements of Governmental Accounting Standards, Statements on Standards for Attestation Engagements, and Statement on Standards for Accountants' Services on Prospective Financial Information.

However, a member or a member's firm, while holding out as CPA(s), is not considered to be in the practice of public accounting if the member or the member's firm does not perform, for any client, any of the professional services described in the preceding paragraph.

Professional services. Professional services include all services performed by a member while holding out as a CPA.

Rules

Rule 101 Independence

A member in public practice shall be independent in the performance of professional services as required by standards promulgated by bodies designated by Council.

INTERPRETATION OF RULE 101

[The professional ethics executive committee issued interpretation 101-1 January 12, 1988, and revised it effective June 30, 1990, and January 1, 1992.]

Interpretation 101-1. Independence shall be considered to be impaired if, for example, a member had any of the following transactions, interests, or relationships:

A. During the period of a professional engagement or at the time of expressing an opinion, a member or a member's firm

  1. Had or was committed to acquire any direct or material indirect financial interest in the enterprise.

  2. Was a trustee of any trust or executor or administrator of any estate if such trust or estate had or was committed to acquire any direct or material indirect financial interest in the enterprise.

  3. Had any joint, closely held business investment with the enterprise or with any officer, director, or principal stockholders thereof that was material in relation to the member's net worth or to the net worth of the member's firm.

  4. Had any loan to or from the enterprise or any officer, director, or principal stockholder of the enterprise except as specifically permitted in interpretation 101-5.

B. During the period covered by the financial statements, during the period of the professional engagement, or at the time of expressing an opinion, a member or a member's firm

  1. Was connected with the enterprise as a promoter, underwriter or voting trustee, as a director or officer, or in any capacity equivalent to that of a member of management or of an employee.

  2. Was a trustee for any pension or profit-sharing trust of the enterprise.

The above examples are not intended to be all-inclusive.

[The professional ethics executive committee revised interpretation 101-5 effective January 1, 1992.]

Interpretation 101-5, Loans From Financial Institution Clients and Related Terminology.
Interpretation 101-1.A.4 provides that, except as permitted in this interpretation, a member's independence shall be considered to be impaired if the member has any loan to or from the enterprise or any officer, director, or principal stockholder of the enterprise. This interpretation does not consider independence to be impaired for certain grandfathered loans and other permitted loans from financial institution clients for whom services are performed requiring independence as set forth below under "Grandfathered Loans" and "Other Permitted Loans," respectively.

Grandfathered Loans

This interpretation grandfathers the following types of loans obtained from a financial institution under that institution's normal lending procedures, terms, and requirements, and that meet the other specified conditions stated herein, and (a) that exist as of January 1,1992; (b) that were obtained from a financial institution prior to its becoming a client requiring independence; (c) that were obtained from a financial institution for which independence was not required and that were later sold to a client for which independence is required; or (d) that were obtained from a firm's financial institution client requiring independence, by a borrower prior to his or her becoming a member* with respect to such client. However, independence will be considered to be impaired if, after January 1, 1992, a member obtains a loan of the type described in this paragraph from an entity that, at the time of obtaining the loan, is a client requiring independence. Grandfathered loans must, at all times, be current as to all terms and such terms shall not be renegotiated after the latest of the dates in (a) through (d) above.

1. Home mortgages.

2. Other secured loans. The collateral on such loans must equal or exceed the remaining balance of the loan at January 1, 1992 and at all times thereafter.

3. Loans not material to the member's net worth.

Other Permitted Loans

This interpretation permits the following types of personal loans obtained from a financial institution client for which independence is required under that institution's normal lending procedures, terms, and requirements. Such loans must, at all times, be kept current as to all terms.

1. Automobile loans and leases collateralized by the automobile.

2. Loans of the surrender value under terms of an insurance policy.

3. Borrowings fully collateralized by cash deposits at the same financial institution (e.g., "passbook loans").

4. Credit cards and cash advances on checking accounts with an aggregate balance not paid currently of $5,000 or less.

Terminology

For purposes of interpretations 101-1.A.4 and 101-5, the following terms are defined:

Loan. A loan is considered to be a financial transaction, the characteristics of which generally include, but are not limited to, an agreement that provides for repayment terms and a rate of interest. A loan includes a guarantee of a loan, a letter of credit and a line of credit. A loan to a limited partnership in which members have a combined investment exceeding 50 percent of the total limited partnership interest is considered a loan to those members.

Financial institution. A financial institution is considered to be an entity that, as part of its normal business operations, makes loans to the general public.

Normal lending procedures, terms, and requirements. "Normal lending procedures, terms and requirements" relating to a member's loan from a financial institution are defined as lending procedures, terms, and requirements that are reasonably comparable with those relating to loans of a similar character committed to other borrowers during the period in which the loan to the member is committed. Accordingly, in making such comparison and in evaluating whether a loan was made under "normal lending procedures, terms, and requirements," the member should consider all the circumstances under which the loan was granted, including --

1. The amount of the loan in relation to the value of the collateral pledged as security and the credit standing of the member or the member's firm.

2. Repayment terms.

3. Interest rates including "points."

4. Closing costs.

5. General availability of such loans to the public.

Related prohibitions that may be more restrictive are prescribed by certain state and federal agencies having regulatory authority over such financial institutions. Broker-dealers, for example, are subject to regulation by the Securities and Exchange Commission.

Rule 102 Integrity and Objectivity

In the performance of any professional service, a member shall maintain objectivity and integrity, shall be free of conflicts of interest, and shall not knowingly misrepresent facts or subordinate his or her judgment to others.

Rule 201 General Standards

A member shall comply with the following standards and with any interpretations thereof by bodies designated by Council.

    A. *Professional Competence.* Undertake only those professional services that the member or the member's firm can reasonably expect to be completed with professional competence.

    B. *Due Professional Care.* Exercise due professional care in the performance of professional services.

    C. *Planning and Supervision.* Adequately plan and supervise the performance of professional services.

    D. *Sufficient Relevant Data.* Obtain sufficient relevant data to afford a reasonable basis for conclusions or recommendations in relation to any professional services performed.

        (See appendix A)

Rule 202 Compliance With Standards

A member who performs auditing, review, compilation, management consulting, tax, or other professional services shall comply with standards promulgated by bodies designated by Council.

        (See appendix A)

Rule 203 Accounting Principles

A member shall not (1) express an opinion or state affirmatively that the financial statements or other financial data of any entity are presented in conformity with generally accepted accounting principles or (2) state that he or she is not aware of any material modifications that should be made to such statements or data in order for them to be in conformity with generally accepted accounting principles, if such statements or data contain any departure from an accounting principle promulgated by bodies designated by Council to establish such principles that has a material effect on the statements or data taken as a whole. If, however, the statements or data contain such a departure and the member can demonstrate that due to unusual circumstances the financial statements or data would otherwise have been misleading, the member can comply with the rule by describing the departure, its approximate effects, if practicable, and the reasons why compliance with the principle would result in a misleading statement.

Rule 301 Confidential Client Information

A member in public practice shall not disclose any confidential client information without the specific consent of the client.

This rule shall not be construed (1) to relieve a member of his or her professional obligations under rules 202 and 203, (2) to affect in any way the member's obligation to comply with a validly issued and enforceable subpoena or summons, or to prohibit a member's compliance with applicable laws and government regulations, (3) to prohibit review of a member's professional practice under AICPA or state CPA society or Board of Accountancy authorization, or (4) to preclude a member from initiating a complaint with, or responding to any inquiry made by, the professional ethics division or trial board of the Institute or a duly constituted investigative or disciplinary body of a state CPA society or Board of Accountancy.

Members of any of the bodies identified in (4) above and members involved with professional practice reviews identified in (3) above shall not use to their own advantage or disclose any member's confidential client information that comes to their attention in carrying out those activities. This prohibition shall not restrict members' exchange of information in connection with the investigative or disciplinary proceedings described in (4) above or the professional practice reviews described in (3) above.

Rule 302 Contingent Fees

A member in public practice shall not

(1) Perform for a contingent fee any professional services for, or receive such a fee from, a client for whom the member or the member's firm performs

    a)   an audit or review of a financial statement; or

    b)   a compilation of a financial statement when the member expects, or reasonably might expect, that a third party will use the financial statement and the member's compilation report does not disclose a lack of independence; or

    c)   an examination of prospective financial information;

or

(2) Prepare an original or amended tax return or claim for a tax refund for a contingent fee for any client.

The prohibition in (1) above applies during the period in which the member or the member's firm is engaged to perform any of the services listed above and the period covered by any historical financial statements involved in any such listed services.

Except as stated in the next sentence, a contingent fee is a fee established for the performance of any service pursuant to an arrangement in which no fee will be charged unless a specified finding or result is attained, or in which the amount of the fee is otherwise dependent upon the finding or result of such service. Solely for purposes of this rule, fees are not regarded as being contingent if fixed by courts or other public authorities, or, in tax matters, if determined based on the results of judicial proceedings or the findings of governmental agencies.

A member's fees may vary depending, for example, on the complexity of services rendered.

INTERPRETATION OF RULE 302

*[The professional ethics executive committee issued
interpretation 302-1, effective May 20, 1991.]*

Interpretation 302-1, Contingent Fees in Tax Matters. This interpretation defines certain terms in rule 302 and provides examples of the application of the rule.

Definitions of Terms

a) Preparation of an original or amended tax return or claim for tax refund includes giving advice on events which have occurred at the time the advice is given if such advice is directly relevant to determining the existence, character, or amount of a schedule, entry, or other portion of a return or claim for refund.

b) A fee is considered determined based on the findings of governmental agencies if the member can demonstrate a reasonable expectation, at the time of a fee arrangement, of substantive consideration by an agency with respect to the member's client. Such an expectation is deemed not reasonable in the case of preparation of original tax returns.

Examples

The following are examples, not all-inclusive, of circumstances where a contingent fee would be permitted:

1. Representing a client in an examination by a revenue agent of the client's federal or state income tax return.

2. Filing an amended federal or state income tax return claiming a tax refund based on a tax issue that is either the subject of a test case (involving a different taxpayer) or with respect to which the taxing authority is developing a position.

3. Filing an amended federal or state income tax return (or refund claim) claiming a tax refund in an amount greater than the threshold for review by the Joint Committee on Internal Revenue Taxation ($1 million at March 1991) or state taxing authority.

4. Requesting a refund of either overpayments of interest or penalties charged to a client's account or deposits of taxes improperly accounted for by the federal or state taxing authority in circumstances where the taxing authority has established procedures for the substantive review of such refund requests.

5. Requesting, by means of "protest" or similar document, consideration by the state or local taxing authority of a reduction in the "assessed value" of property under an established taxing authority review process for hearing all taxpayer arguments relating to assessed value.

6. Representing a client in connection with obtaining a private letter ruling or influencing the drafting of a regulation or statute.

The following is an example of a circumstance where a contingent fee would not be permitted:

1. Preparing an amended federal or state income tax return for a client claiming a refund of taxes because a deduction was inadvertently omitted from the return originally filed. There is no question as to the propriety of the deduction; rather the claim is filed to correct an omission.

Rule 401

[There are currently no rules in the 400 series.]

Rule 501 Acts Discreditable

A member shall not commit an act discreditable to the profession.

Rule 502 Advertising and Other Forms of Solicitation

A member in public practice shall not seek to obtain clients by advertising or other forms of solicitation in a manner that is false, misleading, or deceptive. Solicitation by the use of coercion, over-reaching, or harassing conduct is prohibited.

Rule 503 Commissions and Referral Fees

A. Prohibited Commissions

A member in public practice shall not for a commission recommend or refer to a client any product or service, or for a commission recommend or refer any product or service to be supplied by a client, or receive a commission, when the member or the member's firm also performs for that client

a) an audit or review of a financial statement; or

b) a compilation of a financial statement when the member expects, or reasonably might expect, that a third party will use the financial statement and the member's compilation report does not disclose a lack of independence; or

c) an examination of prospective financial information.

This prohibition applies during the period in which the member is engaged to perform any of the services listed above and the period covered by any historical financial statements involved in such listed services.

B. Disclosure of Permitted Commissions

A member in public practice who is not prohibited by this rule from performing services for or receiving a commission and who is paid or expects to be paid a commission shall disclose that fact to any person or entity to whom the member recommends or refers a product or service to which the commission relates.

C. Referral Fees

Any member who accepts a referral fee for recommending or referring any service of a CPA to any person or entity or who pays a referral fee to obtain a client shall disclose such acceptance or payment to the client.

Rule 504

[There is currently no rule 504.]

Rule 505 Form of Organization and Name

A member may practice public accounting only in a form of organization permitted by state law or regulation whose characteristics conform to resolutions of Council.

A member shall not practice public accounting under a firm name that is misleading. Names of one or more past owners may be included in the firm name of a successor organization. Also, an owner surviving the death or withdrawal of all other owners may continue to practice under a name which includes the name of past owners for up to two years after becoming a sole practitioner.

A firm may not designate itself as "Members of the American Institute of Certified Public Accountants" unless all of its owners are members of the Institute.
(See Appendix B)

APPENDIX A

Council Resolution Designating Bodies to Promulgate Technical Standards

Financial Accounting Standards Board

WHEREAS: In 1959 the Council designated the Accounting Principles Board to establish accounting principles, and

WHEREAS: The Council is advised that the Financial Accounting Standards Board (FASB) has become operational, it is

RESOLVED: That as of the date hereof the FASB, in respect of statements of financial accounting standards finally adopted by such board in accordance with its rules of procedure and the bylaws of the Financial Accounting Foundation, be, and hereby is, designated by this Council as the body to establish accounting principles pursuant to rule 203 and standards on disclosure of financial information for such entities outside financial statements in published financial reports containing financial statements under rule 202 of the Rules of the Code of Professional Conduct of the American Institute of Certified Public Accountants provided, however, any accounting research bulletins, or opinions of the accounting principles board issued or approved for exposure by the accounting principles board prior to April 1, 1973, and finally adopted by such board on or before June 30, 1973, shall constitute statements of accounting principles promulgated by a body designated by Council as contemplated in rule 203 of the Rules of the Code of Professional Conduct unless and until such time as they are expressly superseded by action of the FASB.

Governmental Accounting Standards Board

WHEREAS: The Governmental Accounting Standards Board (GASB) has been established by the board of trustees of the Financial Accounting Foundation (FAF) to issue standards of financial accounting and reporting with respect to activities and transactions of state and local governmental entities, and

WHEREAS: The American Institute of Certified Public Accountants is a signatory to the agreement creating the GASB as an arm of the FAF and has supported the GASB professionally and financially, it is

RESOLVED: That as of the date hereof, the GASB, with respect to statements of governmental accounting standards adopted and issued in July 1984 and subsequently in accordance with its rules of procedure and the bylaws of the FAF, be, and hereby is, designated by the Council of the American Institute of Certified Public Accountants as the body to establish financial accounting principles for state and local governmental entities pursuant to rule 203, and standards on disclosure of financial information for such entities outside financial statements in published financial reports containing financial statements under rule 202.

AICPA COMMITTEES AND BOARDS

WHEREAS: The membership of the Institute has adopted rules 201 and 202 of the Rules of the Code of Professional Conduct, which authorizes the Council to designate bodies to promulgate technical standards with which members must comply, and therefore it is

Accounting and Review Services Committee

RESOLVED: That the AICPA accounting and review services committee is hereby designated to promulgate standards under rules 201 and 202 with respect to unaudited financial statements or other unaudited financial information of an entity that is not required to file financial statements with a regulatory agency in connection with the sale or trading of its securities in a public market.

Auditing Standards Board

RESOLVED: That the AICPA auditing standards board is hereby designated as the body authorized under rules 201 and 202 to promulgate auditing and attest standards and procedures.

RESOLVED: That the auditing standards board shall establish under statements on auditing standards the responsibilities of members with respect to standards for disclosure of financial information outside financial statements in published financial reports containing financial statements.

Management Consulting Services Executive Committee

RESOLVED: That the AICPA management consulting services executive committee is hereby designated to promulgate standards under rules 201 and 202 with respect to the offering of management consulting services, provided, however, that such standards do not deal with the broad question of what, if any, services should be proscribed.

AND FURTHER RESOLVED: That any Institute committee or board now or in the future authorized by the Council to issue enforceable standards under rules 201 and 202 must observe an exposure process seeking comment from other affected committees and boards, as well as the general membership.

Attestation Standards

RESOLVED: That the AICPA accounting and review services committee, auditing standards board, and management consulting services executive committee are hereby designated as bodies authorized under rules 201 and 202 to promulgate attestation standards in their respective areas of responsibility.

APPENDIX B

Council Resolution Concerning Form of Organization and Name

A. RESOLVED: That the characteristics of an organization permitted by state law or regulation under rule 505 are as follows:

1. A super majority (66 2/3 percent) of the ownership of the firm in terms of financial interests and voting rights must belong to CPAs. The non-CPA owner would have to be actively engaged as a firm member in providing services to the firm's clients as his or her principal occupation. Ownership by investors or commercial enterprises not actively engaged as firm members in providing services to the firm's clients as their principal occupation is against the public interest and continues to be prohibited.[1]

2. There must be a CPA who has ultimate responsibility for all the services provided by the firm and by each business unit[2] performing financial statement attest and compilation services and other

engagements governed by Statements on Auditing Standards or Statements on Standards for Accounting and Review Services.

3. Non-CPA owners could not assume ultimate responsibility for any financial statement attest or compilation engagement.

4. Non-CPAs becoming owners after adoption of Council's resolution would have to possess a baccalaureate degree and, beginning in the year 2010, have obtained 150 semester hours of education at an accredited college or university.

5. Non-CPA owners would be permitted to use the title "principal," "owner," "officer," "member" or "shareholder," or any other title permitted by state law, but not hold themselves out to be CPAs.

6. Non-CPA owners would have to abide by the AICPA Code of Professional Conduct. AICPA members may be held responsible under the Code for acts of co-owners.

7. Non-CPA owners would have to complete the same work-related CPE requirements as set forth under AICPA bylaw section 2.3 for AICPA members.

8. Owners shall at all times own their equity in their own right and shall be the beneficial owners of the equity capital ascribed to them. Provision would have to be made for the ownership to be transferred to the firm or to other qualified owners if the non-CPA ceases to be actively engaged in the firm.

9. Non-CPA owners would not be eligible for membership in the AICPA.

Footnotes

[1] Existing firms not in compliance when these standards are adopted would have three years in which to bring themselves into compliance.

[2] "Business unit" is meant to indicate geographic (such as offices) and functional arrangements (such as tax and management consulting services).

Source: American Institute of Certified Public Accountants
Reprinted with permission

State CPA Regulations

All CPA candidates must pass the Uniform CPA Examination to quality for the CPA certificate and permit to practice. A majority of states have enacted laws that require CPA candidates to meet the 150-hour education requirement by the year 2000. For information about the requirement in a particular state, please contact the state board of accountancy.

Jurisdiction	Age	Citizen	Required in State: Residency R, Employment, E or Office O
ALABAMA	19	Yes	Not required
ALASKA	19	No	Not required
ARIZONA	18	No	Not required
ARKANSAS	N/A	No	R/E/O
CALIFORNIA	18 (c)	No	Not required (waiver of exam applicants only)
COLORADO	N/A	No	Not required
CONNECTICUT	N/A	No	Not required
DELAWARE	18	No	Not required
DIST. OF COLUMBIA	18	No	R/E (6 months)
FLORIDA	N/A	No	Not Required
GEORGIA	18	No	Not required
GUAM	N/A	N/A	R (3 mos.)/E/O
HAWAII	18	No	Not required
IDAHO	18	No	R (d)
ILLINOIS	18	No	Not required
INDIANA	18	No	R (60 days actual or 6 mos. Legal residency)
IOWA	N/A	No	R/E/O
KANSAS	N/A	No	Not required
KENTUCKY	18	No	Not required
LOUISIANA	18	No	R (1 year legal residency)
MAINE	18	No	R/E/O
MARYLAND	18	No	Not required
MASSACHUSETTS	18	No	Not required
MICHIGAN	18	No	R/E/O
MINNESOTA	18	No	R/E/O
MISSISSIPPI	N/A	N/A	R
MISSOURI	21	No	R/E/O
MONTANA	N/A	No	Not required
NEBRASKA	N/A	No	R/E/O
NEVADA	N/A	No	Not required
NEW HAMPSHIRE	21	No	Not required
NEW JERSEY	18	No	Not required
NEW MEXICO	18	No	R/O
NEW YORK	21	No	Not required

Jurisdiction	Age	Citizen	Required in State: Residency R, Employment, E or Office O
NORTH CAROLINA	18	Yes	Not required
NORTH DAKOTA	N/A	No	R
OHIO	18	No	R/E/O
OKLAHOMA	N/A	No	R
OREGON	N/A	No	Not required
PENNSYLVANIA	18	No	R/E or O
PUERTO RICO	21	Yes	R/E/O
RHODE ISLAND	N/A	No	R/E/O
SOUTH CAROLINA	18	No	Not required
SOUTH DAKOTA	N/A	No	Not required
TENNESSEE	N/A	No	R/E/O
TEXAS	N/A	No	Not required
UTAH	N/A	No	Not required
VERMONT	18	No	E or O
VIRGINIA	N/A	No	Not required
VIRGIN ISLANDS	21	Yes	R/E or O
WASHINGTON	N/A	No	Not required
WEST VIRGINIA	18	No	R/E or O
WISCONSIN	18	No	Not required
WYOMING	19	No	R/E or O

Jurisdiction	EDUCATION College Education: Years/ Baccalaureate/ Graduate Study	EXPERIENCE Years	EXPERIENCE License/ Permit to Certificate	EXPERIENCE THAT QUALIFIES Public Accounting Experience Required to Practice	EXPERIENCE THAT QUALIFIES Acceptable Nonpublic Accounting Experience as Deemed Acceptable by the Board
ALABAMA	Baccalaureate 150-Hours graduate	0	2	2	5
ALASKA	Baccalaureate	2-3	2-3 (a)	2-3	4-6 (b)
ARIZONA	Baccalaureate	2	2 (a)	2	2
ARKANSAS	Baccalaureate Graduate	0 0	2 1	2 1	2 1
CALIFORNIA	2 year Baccalaureate	2-4 2-3	2-4 2-3 (a)	2-4 2	2-4 2-4
COLORADO	Baccalaureate Graduate	1 0	1 (a) 0 (a)	1 0	1 0
CONNECTICUT	Baccalaureate	2-3	2-3	3	3
DELAWARE	2 Baccalaureate Graduate	0 0 0	2-4 2 1	4 2 1	4 4 2
DIST. OF COLUMBIA	Baccalaureate	0	2	2	2
FLORIDA	Baccalaureate Graduate	0 0	0 (a) 0 (a)	0 0	Non acceptable 0
GEORGIA	Baccalaureate	0	2	2	5
GUAM	Baccalaureate Graduate	0 0	2 1	2 1	2 1
HAWAII	Baccalaureate Graduate	4.5 2	4.5 (a) 2 (a)	4.5 2	Not acceptable Not acceptable
IDAHO	Baccalaureate	1	1 (a)	2	2 (e)
ILLINOIS	Baccalaureate	0	1	1	1
INDIANA	Baccalaureate Graduate	3 2	3 (a) 1	3 3	3-6 3-6
IOWA	Baccalaureate	0	2	2	Not acceptable
KANSAS	Baccalaureate	0	1-2 (l)	1-2 (l)	
KENTUCKY	Baccalaureate	1-2	2 (a)	(m)	2 (m)
LOUISIANA	Baccalaureate Graduate	0 0	2 1	2 1	Allowed (h) Allowed (h)
MAINE	Baccalaureate Graduate	2 1	2 1 (a)	2 1	Allowed Allowed
MARYLAND	Baccalaureate	0	0	0	0
MASSACHUSETTS	Baccalaureate Graduate	3 2	3 (a) 2 (a)	3 2	6-9 4-6
MICHIGAN	Baccalaureate	2 1	2 (a) 1 (a)	2	2
MINNESOTA	0 2	5 3	1 2	6 5	Not acceptable Not acceptable
MISSISSIPPI	Baccalaureate + 150 hour rule	0	1	1	1
MISSOURI	Baccalaureate	0	2-4	2	2-4
MONTANA	Baccalaureate	0	1-2	1	2
NEBRASKA	Baccalaureate	0	2	2	3-3.5

Jurisdiction	EDUCATION — College Education: Years/ Baccalaureate/ Graduate Study	EXPERIENCE — Years	License/ Permit to Certificate	EXPERIENCE THAT QUALIFIES — Public Accounting Experience Required to Practice	Acceptable Nonpublic Accounting Experience as Deemed Acceptable by the Board
NEVADA	Baccalaureate	2	2 (a)	2	Allowed
NEW HAMPSHIRE	Baccalaureate	0	2 (i)	2	2 (j)
	Graduate	0	1	1	11
NEW JERSEY	Baccalaureate	1	1	2	2-4
NEW MEXICO	Baccalaureate	1	1	1	3
NEW YORK	0	15	15 (a)	15	Not acceptable
	Baccalaureate	2	2 (a)	2	2
	Graduate	1	1 (a)	1	1
NORTH CAROLINA	2	4	4 (a)	4	Not acceptable
	Baccalaureate	2	2 (a)	2	5
	Graduate	1	1 (a)	1	4
NORTH DAKOTA	0	4	4	4	4 (k)
	Baccalaureate	0	0	0	0
OHIO	Baccalaureate	2	2	2	6
	Graduate	1	1	1	4
OKLAHOMA	Baccalaureate	0	0	0	0
OREGON	Baccalaureate	2	2	1	1
	Graduate	1	1	1	1
PENNSYLVANIA	Baccalaureate	2	2 (a)	2	2
	Graduate	1	1 (a)	1	1
PUERTO RICO	Non-Accounting	8	8 (a)	8	16
	Baccalaureate	0	0 (a)	0	0
RHODE ISLAND	Baccalaureate	2	2 (a)	2	Not acceptable
	Graduate	1	1 (a)	1	Not acceptable
SOUTH CAROLINA	Baccalaureate	2	2 (a)	2	2
SOUTH DAKOTA	Associate	0	2	2	Not acceptable
	Baccalaureate	0	1	1	Not acceptable
TENNESSEE	Baccalaureate	0	1	1	Not acceptable
	150 hours	2	2 (a)	2	2-3
	Graduate	1	1 (a)	1	2
TEXAS	Baccalaureate	2	2 (a)	2	2
	150 Hours	1	1 (a)	1	1
	Graduate	1	1 (a)	1	1
UTAH	Baccalaureate	1	1	1	3
VERMONT	60 semester hours	2	2	2	Acceptable
VIRGINIA	Baccalaureate	1	1	1	3
VIRGIN ISLANDS	0	6	6	6	Not acceptable
	Baccalaureate	3	3	3	3
	Graduate	2	2	2	2
WASHINGTON	Baccalaureate	0	1	1	1
WEST VIRGINIA	Baccalaureate	0	2	2	2
WISCONSIN	Baccalaureate	3	3 (a)	3	3
WYOMING	Baccalaureate	0	2	2	Not acceptable

(a) There is no distinction between a license and a certificate.

(b) Based on the point system in which different kinds of experience carry with them different point values, one must accumulate 4 to 8 experience points according to the level of education attained.

(c) No minimum age to sit for the Uniform CPA Examination. However, one must be over 18 to be issued a certificate.

(d) Residency required for examination applicants only.

(e) Equivalent experience may be longer than 2 calendar years.

(f) Must have 6 months auditing experience.

(g) Only in certain agencies of state government, or 4 years experience and successful completion of the IRS examination.

(h) Acceptable equivalent experience may be 4 calendar years.

(i) In New Hampshire the license is referred to as a certificate.

(j) Governmental only.

(k) Governmental accounting or auditing can qualify.

(l) 1 year accounting experience under direct supervision of licensed CPA for permit to do tax and compilation work. 2 years accounting experience; one year with CPA firm, full-time, including 1,000 hours auditing, all under direct supervision of licensed CPA for permit to do all accounting, including audits and reviews.

(m) Must be supervised by a CPA with an active permit to practice.

Source: Digest of State Accountancy Laws and State Board Regulations, American Institute of CPAs and National Association of State Boards of Accountancy, 1996, pp. 119-121. Reprinted with permission.

State Boards of Accountancy

Alabama State Board of Accountancy
RSA Plaza
770 Washington Avenue
Montgomery, Alabama 36130
Att: Boyd E. Nicholson, Jr., CPA
    Executive Director
Telephone: (334) 242-5700
Facsimile: (334) 242-2711

Alaska State Board of Public Accountancy
Department of Commerce and
  Economic Development
Division of Occupational Licensing
P.O. Box 110806
Juneau, Alaska 99811-0806
Att: Steven B. Snyde
    Licensing Examiner
Telephone: (907) 465-2580
Facsimile: (907) 465-2974
Web Site: http://www.state.ak.us
  /local/adpages/
  commerce/occ/ic.htm

Arizona State Board of Accountancy
3110 N. Nineteenth Avenue
Suite 140
Phoenix, Arizona 85015-6038
Att: Ruth R. Lee
    Executive Director
Telephone: (602) 255-3648
Facsimile: (602) 255-1283

Arkansas State Board of Accountancy
101 East Capitol, Suite 430
Little Rock, Arkansas 72201
Att: Rollie L. Friess, CPA
    Executive Director
Telephone: (501) 682-1520
Facsimile: (501) 682-5538

California State Board of Accountancy
2000 Evergreen Street, Suite 250
Sacramento, California 95815-3832
Att: Carol B. Sigmann
    Executive Director
Telephone: (916) 263-3680
Facsimile: (916) 263-3674
E-mail: casboa@casboa.ca.gov

Colorado State Board of Accountancy
1560 Broadway, Suite 1370
Denver, Colorado 80202
Att: Mary Lou Burgess
    Administrator
Telephone: (303) 894-7800
Facsimile: (303) 894-7790
Web site: http://www.state.co.us

Connecticut State Board of Accountancy
Secretary of the State
30 Trinity Street, P.O. Box 150470
Hartford, Connecticut 06115-0470
Att: David L. Guay
    Executive Director
Telephone: (860) 566-7835
Facsimile: (860) 566-5757

Delaware State Board of Accountancy
Cannon Building, Suite 203
P.O. Box 1401
Dover, Delaware 19903
Att: Sheila H. Wolfe
    Administrative Assistant
Telephone: (302) 739-4522
Facsimile: (302) 739-2711
E-mail: @board@prof#reg

District of Columbia Board of Accountancy
Department of Consumer and
Regulatory Affairs
614 H Street, N.W., Room 923
c/o P.O. Box 37200
Washington, D.C. 20013-7200
Att: Harriette E. Andrews
Administrator
Telephone: (202) 727-7468
Facsimile: (202) 727-8030

Florida Board of Accountancy
2610 N.W. 43rd Street, Suite 1A
Gainesville, Florida 32606-4599
Att: Martha P. Willis
Division Director
Telephone: (352) 955-2165
Facsimile: (352) 955-2164

Georgia State Board of Accountancy
166 Pryor Street, S.W.
Atlanta, Georgia 30303
Att: Barbara W. Kitchens
Executive Director
Telephone: (404) 656-2281
Facsimile: (404) 651-9532

Guam Territorial Board of Public Accountancy
P.O. Box 5753
Agana, Guam 96910
Att: Todd S. Smith, CPA
Chairman
Telephone: (671) 646-3884
Facsimile: (671) 649-4932

Hawaii Board of Public Accountancy
Department of Commerce and
Consumer Affairs
P.O. Box 3469
Honolulu, Hawaii 96801-3469
Att: Verna Oda
Executive Officer
Telephone: (808) 586-2694
Facsimile: (808) 586-2689

Idaho State Board of Accountancy
P.O. Box 83720
Boise, Idaho 83720-0002
Att: Patricia L. Johnson
Executive Director
Telephone: (208) 334-2490
Facsimile: (208) 334-2615

Illinois Board of Examiners
10 Henry Administration Building
506 S. Wright Street
Urbana, Illinois 61801-3260
Att: Joanne Vician
Executive Director
Telephone: (217) 333-4213
Facsimile: (217) 333-3126

Illinois Department of Professional Regulation
Public Accountancy Section
320 West Washington Street, 3rd Floor
Springfield, Illinois 62786-0001
Att: Judy Vargas
Manager
Telephone: (217) 785-0800
Facsimile: (217) 782-7645

Indiana Board of Accountancy
Indiana Professional Licensing Agency
Indiana Government Center South
302 West Washington Street, Room E034
Indianapolis, Indiana 46204-2246
Att: Nancy Smith
Exam Coordinator
Telephone: (317) 232-5987
Facsimile: (317) 232-2312

Iowa Accountancy Examining Board
1918 S.E. Hulsizer Avenue
Ankeny, Iowa 50021-3941
Att: William M. Schroeder
Executive Secretary
Telephone: (515) 281-4126
Facsimile: (515) 281-7411
E-mail: bschroe@max.state.ia.us
Web site:
http://www/state.ia.us/governmentacct/
com/prof/acct.htm

Kansas Board of Accountancy
Landon State Office Building
900 S.W. Jackson, Suite 556
Topeka, Kansas 66612-1239
Att: Glenda S. Moore
Executive Director
Telephone: (913) 296-2162

Kentucky State Board of Accountancy
332 West Broadway, Suite 310
Louisville, Kentucky 40202-2115
Att: Susan G. Stopher
Executive Director
Telephone: (502) 595-3037
Facsimile: (502) 595-4281

State Board of CPAs of Louisiana
1515 World Trade Center
2 Canal Street
New Orleans, Louisiana 70130
Att: Mildred M. McGaha, CPA
Executive Director
Telephone: (504) 566-1244
Facsimile: (504) 566-1252

Maine Board of Accountancy
Dept. of Professional & Financial
Regulation
State House Station 35
Augusta, Maine 04333
Att: Sandra Leach
Board Clerk
Telephone: (207) 624-8603
Facsimile: (207) 624-8637

Maryland State Board of Public Accountancy
501 St. Paul Place, 9th Floor
Baltimore, Maryland 21202-2272
Att: Sue Mays
Executive Director
Telephone: (410) 333-6322
Facsimile: (410) 333-6314
Web site:
http://www.dllr.state.md.us/dllr

Massachusetts Board of Public Accountancy
Saltonstall Building, Government
Center
100 Cambridge Street, Room 1315
Boston, Massachusetts 02202
Att: Leo H. Bonarrigo, CPA
Executive Secretary
Telephone: (617) 727-1806
Facsimile: (617) 727-0139

Michigan Board of Accountancy
Department Of Commerce-BOPR
P.O. Box 30018
Lansing, Michigan 48909-7518
Att: Suzanne U. Jolicoeur
Licensing Administrator
Telephone: (517) 373-0682
Facsimile: (517) 373-2795

Minnesota State Board of Accountancy
85 East 7th Place. Suite 125
St. Paul, Minnesota 55101
Att: Dennis J. Poppenhagen
Executive Director
Telephone: (612) 296-7937
Facsimile: (612) 282-2644

Mississippi State Board of Public Accountancy
653 North State Street
Jackson, Mississippi 39202
Att: Susan M. Harris, CPA
Executive Director
Telephone: (601) 354-7320
Facsimile: (601) 354-7290

Missouri State Board of Accountancy
P.O. Box 613
Jefferson City, Missouri 65102-0613
Att: William E. Boston III
Executive Director
Telephone: (573) 751-0012
Facsimile: (573) 751-0890
E-mail: bboston@mail.state.mo.us

Montana State Board of Public Accountants
Arcade Building, Lower Level
111 North Jackson
P.O. Box 200513
Helena, Montana 59620-0513
Att: Susanne M. Criswell
Administrator
Telephone: (406) 444-3739
Facsimile: (406) 444-1667

Nebraska State Board of Public Accountancy
P.O. Box 94725
Lincoln, Nebraska 68509-4725
Att: Annette L. Harmon
Executive Director
Telephone: (402) 471-3595
Facsimile: (402) 471-4484

Nevada State Board of Accountancy
200 S. Virginia Street, Suite 670
Reno, Nevada 89501-2408
Att: N. Johanna Brand
Executive Director
Telephone: (702) 786-0231
Facsimile: (702) 786-0234

New Hampshire Board of Accountancy
57 Regional Drive
Concord, New Hampshire 03301
Att: Louise O. MacMillan
Executive Assistant to the Board
Telephone: (603) 271-3286
Facsimile: (603) 271-2856

New Jersey State Board of Accountancy
P.O. Box 45000
Newark, New Jersey 07101
Att: Jay J. Church
Executive Director
Telephone: (201) 504-6380
Facsimile: (201) 648-3355

New Mexico State Board of Public Accountancy
1650 University N.E., Suite 400-A
Albuquerque, New Mexico 87102
Att: g. Trudy Beverley
Executive Director
Telephone: (505) 841-9108
Facsimile: (505) 841-9113

New York State Board for Public Accountancy
State Education Department
Cultural Education Center, Room 3013
Albany, New York 12230
Att: C. Daniel Stubbs, Jr., CPA
Executive Secretary
Telephone: (518) 474-3836
Facsimile: (518) 473-6995

North Carolina State Board of CPA Examiners
　　1101 Oberlin Road, Suite 104
　　P.O. Box 12827
　　Raleigh, North Carolina 27605-2827
　　Att: Robert N. Brooks
　　　　Executive Director
　　Telephone: (919) 733-4222
　　Toll Free: 1-800-211-7930
　　　　　　Licensing & Exam
Applications Only
　　Facsimile: (919) 733-4209
　　E-mail: 75361.3404@compuserve.com

North Dakota State Board of Accountancy
　　2701 South Columbia Road
　　Grand Forks, North Dakota 58201
　　Att: Jim Abbott
　　　　Executive Director
　　Telephone: (701) 775-7100
　　Facsimile: (701) 775-7430
　　E-mail:
　　103132.2525@compuserve.com

Accountancy Board of Ohio
　　77 South High Street, 18th Floor
　　Columbus, Ohio 43266-0301
　　Att: Timothy D. Haas
　　　　Executive Director
　　Telephone: (614) 466-4135
　　Facsimile: (614) 466-2628

Oklahoma Accountancy Board
　　4545 Lincoln Boulevard, Suite 165
　　Oklahoma City, Oklahoma 73105
　　Att: Diana Collinsworth
　　　　Executive Director
　　Telephone: (405) 521-2397
　　Facsimile: (405) 521-3118

Oregon Board of Accountancy
　　3218 Pringle Road SE, Suite 110
　　Salem, Oregon 97302-6307
　　Att: Karen DeLorenzo
　　　　Administrator
　　Telephone: (503) 378-4181
　　Facsimile: (503) 378-3575
　　E-mail: www.boa@teleport.com

Pennsylvania State Board of Accountancy
　　613 Transportation & Safety Building
　　P.O. Box 2649
　　Harrisburg, Pennsylvania 17105-2649
　　Att: Dorna J. Thorpe
　　　　Board Administrator
　　Telephone: (717) 783-1404
　　Facsimile: (717) 787-7769

Puerto Rico Board of Accountancy
　　Box 3271, Old San Juan Station
　　San Juan, Puerto Rico 00902-3271
　　Att: Antonio Cruz Murphy
　　　　Director
　　Telephone: (787) 722-2122
　　Facsimile: (787) 721-8399

Rhode Island Board of Accountancy
　　Department of Business Regulation
　　233 Richmond Street, Suite 236
　　Providence, Rhode Island 02903-4236
　　Att: Norma A. MacLeod
　　　　Executive Secretary
　　Telephone: (401) 277-3185
　　Facsimile: (401) 277-6654

South Carolina Board of Accountancy
　　Board of Accountancy
　　Suite 101
　　P.O. Box 11329
　　Columbia, South Carolina 29211-1329
　　Att: Robert W. Wilkes, Jr.. CPA
　　　　Administrator
　　Telephone: (803) 734-4228
　　Facsimile: (803) 734-9571

South Dakota Board of Accountancy
301 East 14th Street, Suite 200
Sioux Falls, South Dakota 57104
Att: Lynn J. Bethke
    Executive Director
Telephone: (605) 367-5770
Facsimile: (605) 367-5773

Tennessee State Board of Accountancy
500 James Robertson Parkway, 2nd
Floor
Nashville, Tennessee 37243-1141
Att: Darrel Tongate, CPA
    Executive Director
    Don Hummel
    Director of Administration
Telephone: (615) 741-2550
Facsimile: (615) 532-8800

Texas State Board of Public Accountancy
333 Guadalupe Tower III, Suite 900
Austin, Texas 78701-3900
Att: William Treacy
    Executive Director
Telephone: (512) 505-5500
Facsimile: (512) 505-5575

Utah Board of Accountancy
160 East 300 South
P.O. Box 45805
Salt Lake City, Utah 84145
Att: Dan S. Jones, Esq.
    Administrator
Telephone: (801) 530-6720
Facsimile: (801) 530-6511

Vermont Board of Public Accountancy
Pavilion Office Building
Montpelier, Vermont 05609-1106
Att: Loris Rollins
    Staff Assistant
Telephone: (802) 828-2837
Facsimile: (802) 828-2496

Virginia Board for Accountancy
3600 West Broad Street
Richmond, Virginia 23230-4917
Att: Nancy T. Feldman
    Assistant Director
Telephone: (804) 367-8590
Facsimile: (804) 367-2474

Virgin Islands Board of Public Accountancy
P.0, Box 3016, No 1 A Gallows Bay
Mkt, Plaza Christiansted
St. Croix, Virgin Islands 00822
Att: Pablo O'Neil, CPA
Telephone: (809) 773-4305
Facsimile: (809) 773-9850

Washington State Board of Accountancy
P.O. Box 9131
210 East Union, Suite A
Olympia, Washington 98507
Att: Carey L. Rader. CPA
    Executive Director
Telephone: (360) 753-2585
Facsimile: (360) 664-9190
E-mail:
103124.2013@compuserve.com

West Virginia Board of Accountancy
200 L&S Building
812 Quarrier Street
Charleston, West Virginia 25301-2695
Aft: JoAnn Walker
    Executive Director
Telephone: (304) 558-3557
Facsimile: (304) 558-1325

Wisconsin Accounting Examining Board
1400 East Washington Avenue
P.O. Box 8935
Madison, Wisconsin 53708-8935
Att: Patricia H. Reuter
    Bureau Director
Telephone: (608) 266-1397
Facsimile: (608) 267-0644

Wyoming Board of Certified Public Accountants
>
> First Bank Building
> 2020 Carey, Suite 100
> Cheyenne, Wyoming 82002
> Att: Peggy Morgando
>   Executive Director
> Telephone: (307) 777-7551
> Facsimile: (307) 777-3796
> E-mail: pmorga@missc.state.wy.us

Source: Digest of State Accountancy Laws and State Board Regulations, American Institute of CPAs and National Association of State Boards of Accountancy, 1996, pp. 159-162. Reprinted with permission.

State/Jurisdiction CPA Societies

Alabama Society of CPAs
1103 South Perry Street
Montgomery, AL 36103
Phone: (334) 834-7650
E-mail: webmaster@ascpa.org
http://www.ascpa.org

Alaska Society of CPAs
341 West Tudor, Suite 105
Anchorage, AK 99503
Phone: (907) 562-4334
         (800) 292-1754
Fax: (907) 562-4025
E-mail: akcpa@alaska.net
http://www.accountingnet.com/society/ak/

Arizona Society of CPAs
432 N. 44th Street, Suite 300
Phoenix, AZ 85008-7602
Phone: (602) 273-0100
         (888) 237-0700 In State Only
Fax: (602) 275-2752
http://www.ascpa.com

Arkansas Society of CPAs
415 North McKinley, Suite 970
Little Rock, AR 72205-3022
Phone: (501) 664-8739
         (800) 482-8739 In State Only
Fax: (501) 664-8320
E-mail: ascpa@arcpa.org
http://www.arcpa.org

California Society of CPAs
E-mail: wiremail@calcpa.org
http://www.calcpa.org
Main Office
275 Shoreline Drive
Redwood City, CA 94065-1412
Phone: (415) 802-2600
Fax: (415) 802-2225
Glendale Office
330 North Brand Boulevard, Suite 710
Glendale, CA 91203-2308
Phone: (818) 246-6000
Fax: (818) 246-4017
Sacramento Office
1201 "K" Street, Suite 1000
Sacramento, CA 95814-3922
Phone: (916) 441-5351
Fax: (916) 441-5354

Colorado Society of CPAs
7979 East Tufts Avenue, Suite 500
Denver, CO 80237-2843
Phone: (303) 773-2877
         (800) 523-9082
Fax: (303) 773-6344
E-mail: cpa-staff@cscpa.denver.co.us
http://www.cocpa.org

Connecticut Society of CPAs
179 Allyn Street, Suite 201
Hartford, CT 06103
Phone: (860) 525-1153
         (800) 232-2232 In State Only
Fax: (860) 549-3596
E-mail: cscpa@cs-cpa.org
http://www.cs-cpa.org

Delaware Society of CPAs
28 The Commons
3520 Silverside Road
Wilmington, DE 19810
Phone: (302) 478-7442
Fax: (302) 478-7412
http://www.accountingnet.com/society/de

Florida Institute of CPAs
325 West College Avenue
Tallahassee, FL 32301
Phone: (904) 224-2727
Fax: (904) 222-8190
E-mail: webmaster@ficpa.org
http://www.ficpa.org

Georgia Society of CPAs
3340 Peachtree Road NE, Suite 2700
Atlanta, GA 30326-1026
Phone: (404) 231-8676
            (800) 330-8889 In State Only
Fax: (404) 237-1291
E-mail: gscpaweb@gscpa.org
http://www.gscpa.org

Greater Washington Society of CPAs
1023 15th Street N.W. 8th Floor
Washington, D.C. 20005-2602
Phone: (202) 789-1844
Fax: (202) 789-1847
E-mail: info@gwscpa.org
http://www.gwscpa.org

Guam Society of CPAs
361 South Marine Drive
Tamuning, GU 96911
Phone: (671) 646-3884
Fax: (671) 649-4265

Hawaii Society of CPAs
P.O. Box 1754
Honolulu, HI 96806
Phone: (808) 537-9475
Fax: (808) 537-3520
http://www.accountingnet.com/society/hi

Idaho Society of CPAs, Inc.
250 Bobwhite Court, Suite 240
Boise, ID 83706
Phone: (208) 344-6261
Fax: (208) 344-8984
http://www.idcpa.org

Illinois CPA Society
http://www.icpas.org
Chicago Office
222 S. Riverside Plaza, 16th Floor
Chicago, IL 60606
Phone: (312) 993-0393
            (800) 993-0393 In State Only
Fax: (312) 993-9432
Springfield Office
511 W. Capitol, Suite 101
Springfield, IL 62704
Phone: (217) 789-7914
            (800) 572-9870 In State Only
Fax: (217) 789-7924

Indiana CPA Society
8250 Woodfield Crossing Blvd. , #305
Indianapolis, IN 46240-2054
Phone: (317) 726-5000
Fax: (317) 726-5005
E-mail: info@incpas.org
http://www.incpas.org

Iowa Society of CPAs
950 Office Park Road, Suite 300
West Des Moines, IA 50265-2548
Phone: (515) 223-8161
Fax: (515) 223-7347

Kansas Society of CPAs
400 Croix P.O. Box 5654
Topeka, KS 66605-0654
Phone: (913) 267-6460
Fax: (913) 267-9278
http://www.copilot.greensoft.com/kscpa

Kentucky Society of CPAs
1735 Alliant Avenue
Lousville, KY 40299-6326
Phone: (502) 266-5272
              (800) 292-1754 In State Only
Fax: (502) 261-9512
E-mail: kycpa@kycpa.org
http://www.kycpa.org

Society of Louisiana CPAs
2400 Veterans Blvd., Suite 500
Kenner, LA 70062
Phone: (504) 464-1040
Fax: (504) 469-7930

Maine Society of CPAs
153 US Rt. 1, Suite 8
Scarborough, ME 04074-9053
Phone: (207) 883-6090
              (800) 660-2721 In State Only
Fax: (207) 883-6211
http://www.mecpa.org

Maryland Association of CPAs
1300 York Road, Building C
P.O. Box 4417
Lutherville, MD 21094
Phone: (410) 296-6250
Fax: (410) 296-8713
E-mail: Info@macpa.org
http://www.macpa.org

Massachusetts Society of CPAs, Inc.
105 Chauncy St.
Boston, MA 02111
Phone: (617) 556-4000
Fax: (617) 556-4126
E-mail: mscpa@mscpaonline@org
http://www.mscpaonline.org

Michigan Association of CPAs
28116 Orchard Lake Road
Farmington Hills, MI 48333-9054
Phone: (248) 855-2288
Fax: (248) 855-9122
E-mail: macpa@michcpa.org
http://www.michcpa.org

Minnesota Society of CPAs
7900 Xerxes Ave. So. STE 1230
Bloomington, MN 55431
Phone: (612) 831-2707
              (800) 331-4288 In State Only
Fax: (612) 831-7875
http://www.accountingnet.com/society/mn

Mississippi Society of CPAs
Highland Village, Suite 246
Jackson, MS 39236
Phone: (601) 366-3473
              (800) 772-1099 In State Only
Fax: (601) 981-6079
E-mail: mscpa@compuserve.com
http://www.accountingnet.com/society/ms

Missouri Society of CPAs
275 N. Lindbergh Blvd., Suite 10
P.O. Box 419042
St. Louis, MO 63141-9042
Phone: (314) 997-7966
              (800) 264-7966
http://www.accountingnet.com/society/mo

Montana Society of CPAs
P.O. Box 138
Helena, MT 59624-0138
Diamond Block, 3rd Floor, 44 West 6th Ave.
Helena, MT 59601
Phone: (406) 442-7301
Fax: (406) 443-7278
http://www.accountingnet.com/society/mt

Nebraska Society of CPAs
635 South 14th Street, Suite 330
Lincoln, NE 68508
Phone: (402) 476-8482
Fax: (402) 476-8731

Nevada Society of CPAs
5250 Neil Road, Suite 205
Reno, NV 89502
Phone: (702) 478-7442
              (800) 554-8254
Fax: (702) 826-7942
http://www.accountingnet.com/society/nv

New Hampshire Society of CPAs
Three Executive Park Drive
Bedford, NH 03110
Phone: (603) 622-1999
Fax: (603) 626-0204
E-mail: info@nhscpa.org
http://www.nhscpa.org

New Jersey Society of CPAs
425 Eagle Rock Avenue
Roseland, NJ 07068
Phone: (201) 226-4494
Fax: (201) 226-7425

New Mexico Society of CPAs
1650 University NE, Suite 450
Albuquerque, NM 87102-1733
Phone: (505) 246-1699
        (800) 926-2522 In State Only
Fax: (505) 246-1686
E-mail: nmcpa@nmcpa.org
http://www.nmcpa.org

New York State Society of CPAs
530 Fifth Avenue, Fifth Floor
New York, NY 10036-5101
Phone: (212) 719-8300
Fax: (212) 719-3364
http://www.nysscpa.org

North Carolina Society of CPAs
P.O. Box 80188
Raleigh, NC 27623
3100 Gateway Center Blvd.
Morrisville, NC 27560
Phone: (919) 469-1040
Fax: (919) 469-3959
E-mail: ncacpa@interpath.com
http://www.ncacpa.org

North Dakota Society of CPAs
2701 South Columbia Road
Grand Forks, ND 58201
Phone: (701) 775-7100
Fax: (701) 775-7430
http://www.ndscpa.org

Ohio Society of CPAs
535 Metro Place South
P.O. Box 1810
Dublin, OH 43017-7810
Phone: (614) 764-2727
        (800) 686-2727
Fax: (614) 764-5880
E-mail: oscpa@ohio-cpa.com
http://www.ohioscpa.com

Oklahoma Society of CPAs
1900 NW Expressway St., Suite 910
Oklahoma City, OK 73118-1804
Phone: (405) 841-3800
        (800) 522-8261 In State Only
Fax: (405) 841-3801
http://www.oscpa.com

Oregon Society of CPAs
P.O. Box 4555
Beaverton, OR 97076-4555
10206 SW Laurel Street
Beaverton, OR 97005-3209
Phone: (503) 641-7200
        (800) 255-1470 In State Only
Fax: (503) 626-2942
Email: oscpa@orcpa.org
http://www.orcpa.org

Pennsylvania Institute of CPAs
1608 Walnut Street, 3rd Floor
Philadelphia, PA 19103-5457
Phone: (215) 735-2635
        (888) 272-2001 In State Only
Fax: (215) 735-3694
http://www.picpa.com

Colegio de Contadores Publicos
Autorizados de Puerto Rico
Call Box 71352
San Juan, PR 00936-1352
Edif. Capital Center Ave.
Arterial Hostos #3
Buzon 1401
Hato Rey, PR 00918
Phone: (809) 754-1950
Fax: (809) 753-0212
http://www.prccpa.org

Rhode Island Society of CPAs
One Franklin Square
Providence, RI 02903
Phone: (401) 331-5720
Fax: (401) 454-5780
http://www.accountingnet.com/society/ri

South Carolina Association of CPAs
570 Chris Drive
West Columbia, SC 29169
Phone: (803) 791-4181
Fax: (803) 791-4196
E-mail: info@scacpa.org
http://www.scacpa.org

South Dakota CPA Society
P.O. Box 1798
Sioux Falls, SD 57101-1798
1000 West Ave. North #1000
Sioux Falls, SD 57104
Phone: (605) 334-3848
Fax: (605) 334-8595

Tennessee Society of CPAs
201 Powell Place
P.O. Box 187
Brentwood, TN 37024-0187
Phone: (615) 377-3825
              (800) 762-0272 In State Only
Fax: (615) 377-3904
E-mail: tncpa@tncpa.org
http://www.tncpa.org

Texas Society of CPAs
14860 Montfort, Suite 150
Dallas, TX 75240
Phone: (972) 687-8500
              (800) 428-0272
Fax: (972) 687-8646
http://www.tscpa.org

Utah Association of CPAs
455 East 400 South, Suite 202
Salt Lake City, UT 84111-3011
Phone: (801) 359-3533
              (800) 676-2776
Fax: (801) 359-3534
http://www.uacpa.org

Vermont Society of CPAs
100 State Street
Montpelier, VT 05602
Phone: (802) 229-4939
Fax: (802) 223-0360
E-mail: vscpa@sover.net
http://www.accountingnet.com/society/vt

Virginia Society of CPAs
P.O. Box 4620
Glen Allen, VA 23058-4620
4309 Cox Road
Glen Allen, VA 23060
Phone: (804) 270-5344
Fax: (804) 273-1741
http://www.vscpa.com

Virgin Islands Society of CPAs
P.O. Box 1734
Kings Hill
St. Croix, VI 00851
Phone: (809) 776-1852
Fax: (809) 776-1845

Washington Society of CPAs
902 140th Avenue NE
Bellevue, WA 98005-3480
Phone: (425) 644-4800
Fax: (425) 562-8853
E-mail: memberservices@wscpa.org
http://www.wscpa.org

West Virgiana Society of CPAs
P.O. Box 1142
Charleston, WV 25324
Phone: (304) 342-5461
         (800) 352-3855
Fax: (304) 344-4636
http://www.wvscpa.org

Wisconsin Society of CPAs
P.O. Box 1010
Brookfield, WI 53008-1010
235 N. Executive Drive, #200
Brookfield, WI 53005
Phone: (414) 785-0445
Fax: (414) 785-0838

Wyoming Society of CPAs
1721 Warren Avenue
Cheyenne, WY 82001
Phone: (307) 634-7039
Fax: (307) 634-5110

Source: Compiled by Gokhan Alanya, Graduate
Assistant, University of Miami, 1997.

World Wide Web Sites

This is a sampling of World Wide Web Internet sites containing information relevant for current and prospective CPAs. Many of the sites, particularly those under General Accounting Sites, have extensive links to other accounting sites such as CPA firms, corporate employers and universities. Internet sites for State Boards of Accountancy and State CPA Societies are provided in Appendices C and D, when available.

Professional Accounting Associations and Related Sites

AMERICAN INSTITUTE OF CERTIFIED PUBLIC ACCOUNTANTS
http://www.aicpa.org

BRITISH ACCOUNTING ASSOCIATION
http://www.bham.ac.uk/BAA

CERTIFIED GENERAL ACCOUNTANTS ASSOCIATION OF CANADA
http://www.cga-canada.org

CANADIAN INSTITUTE OF CHARTERED ACCOUNTANTS
http://www.cica.ca/new/index.htm

EUROPEAN ACCOUNTING ASSOCIATION
http://www.bham.ac.uk/EAA/homepage.htm

THE INSTITUTE OF CHARTERED ACCOUNTANTS IN IRELAND
http://www.icai.ie

NATIONAL ASSOCIATION OF STATE BOARDS OF ACCOUNTANCY
http://www.nasba.org

THE ACADEMY OF ACCOUNTING HISTORIANS
http://weatherhead.cwru.edu/Accounting

Standard Setting Groups

FINANCIAL ACCOUNTING STANDARDS BOARD
http://www.fasb.org

GOVERNMENTAL ACCOUNTING STANDARDS BOARD
http://www.financenet.gov/gasb.htm

INTERNATIONAL ACCOUNTING STANDARDS COMMITTEE
http://www.iasc.org.uk

Governmental Agencies

SECURITIES AND EXCHANGE COMMISSION
http://www.sec.gov

INTERNAL REVENUE SERVICE
http://www.irs.ustreas.gov

General Accounting Sites Including Employment Information

RUTGERS ACCOUNTING WEB
http://www.rutgers.edu/Accounting

ACCOUNTINGNET
http://accountingnet.com

TAX AND ACCOUNTING SITES DIRECTORY
http://www.uni.edu/schmidt/sites.html

ANET
http://anet.scu.edu.au/anet

ROBERT HALF INTERNATIONAL AND ACCOUNTEMPS
http://www.rhii.com
http://www.accountemps.com

Academic Related Sites

BETA ALPHA PSI
http://www.bap.org

AMERICAN ACCOUNTING ASSOCIATION
http://www.rutgers.edu/Accounting/raw/aaa

Journals

ACCOUNTING TODAY/FAULKNER AND GRAY
http://www.electronicaccountant.com

JOURNAL OF ACCOUNTANCY
THE CPA LETTER
THE PRACTICING CPA
   http://www.aicpa.org

RESEARCH IN ACCOUNTING REGULATION
   http://weatherhead.cwru.edu/dept/rar

Related Professional Associations and Designations

ASSOCIATION FOR INVESTMENT MANAGEMENT AND RESEARCH (CFA)
   http://www.aimr.org

CFP BOARD
   http://www.cfp-board.org

ASSOCIATION OF CERTIFIED FRAUD EXAMINERS
   http://www.acfe.org

THE INSTITUTE OF INTERNAL AUDITORS
   http://www.theiia.org

INSTITUTE OF MANAGEMENT ACCOUNTANTS (CMA)
   http://www.rutgers.edu/Accounting/raw/ima